Remembering War

Helene Keyssar   Vladimir Pozner

REMEMBERING

WAR

A U.S.—Soviet Dialogue

New York   Oxford
OXFORD UNIVERSITY PRESS
1990

Oxford University Press

Oxford   New York   Toronto
Delhi   Bombay   Calcutta   Madras   Karachi
Petaling Jaya   Singapore   Hong Kong   Tokyo
Nairobi   Dar es Salaam   Cape Town
Melbourne   Auckland

and associated companies in
Berlin   Ibadan

Copyright © 1990 by Helene Keyssar and Vladimir Pozner

Published by Oxford University Press, Inc.,
200 Madison Avenue, New York, New York 10016

Oxford is a registered trademark of Oxford University Press

Library of Congress Cataloging-in-Publication Data
Remembering war : a U.S.-Soviet dialogue
[compiled by] Helene Keyssar and Vladimir Pozner.
p.   cm.
Based on the May 7, 1985, television broadcast,
Remembering war.
ISBN 0-19-505126-2
1. World War, 1939–1945—United States.
2. World War, 1939–1945—Soviet Union.
3. World War, 1939–1945—Personal narratives, American.
4. World War, 1939–1945—Personal narratives, Soviet.
I. Keyssar, Helene.   II. Pozner, Vladimir.
D769.R42   1990   940.53′73—dc20   89-36911   CIP

Frontispiece: US Elbe Vet William Robertson and USSR Elbe Vet Alexander Silvashko
embrace in image from Moscow watched by US audience in San Diego
during May 1985 Space Bridge, *Remembering War.*
(*Elizabeth Sisco*)

9 8 7 6 5 4 3 2 1

Printed in the United States of America
on acid-free paper

For the Children
In Order That They Remember

Preface

Not so long ago, a book such as this—a book about World War II that is a cooperative effort by Soviets and Americans—would have been impossible. For the last forty years, Soviet and American memories of World War II have remained isolated, each from the other. Since 1945, neither Soviets nor Americans have had much opportunity to acknowledge publicly their perceptions of each other as allies and the relation of those recollections to their subsequent confusions and fears about each other. This book thus presents an unusual occasion for citizens of both countries to enrich each of our histories and to remember collectively why and how we fought, and fought as allies, in World War II.

To remember war is to encounter our images of war in the present and future as well as in the past. Remembering together, Soviets and Americans each animate the other's recollections. As a record of these memories, this book is an attempt to acknowledge both those who were present at the events of World War II and those who can and will only know this war as history. To confront the unprecedented horrors of this particular war and to reemphasize the importance of the U.S.–Soviet alliance to the eventual defeat of the Axis is, we hope, to contribute to the avoidance of a future nuclear war.

Survey research, examination of school texts from both the Soviet Union and the United States, and evidence from numerous recent studies suggest that there are many areas of misunderstanding and ignorance about World War II in each culture. Few Americans know the extent of loss of life and destruction of cities, farmlands, and industry suffered by the Soviets in the war; many Americans do not even know on which side the Soviets fought in what the United States called the "Good War." While Soviets are keenly aware of the toll World War II took on their own lives and society, they have limited knowledge of the U.S. lend-lease program, of the U.S. engagement in the war in the Pacific, and of the effects of the conflict on American society.

Despite this mutual ignorance, many Soviets and Americans suspect that the values and practices of our current societies have been shaped by each of our experiences of World War II. Profound differences in our experiences of modern war have contributed to differing fears and aspirations in each country. The memories of invasion in the Soviet Union and the absence of that experience in the United States loom large in each of our social consciousnesses. The extraordinary feats of production in the United States during the 1940s renewed Americans' faith in their ability to overcome material obstacles to success. The phoenix-like resurrection of manufacturing facilities repeatedly destroyed by the Nazi invasion of the Soviet Union and the heroic efforts of women and children to maintain necessary production of war materials provided heartening models of strength and endurance for a Soviet citizenry faced with the task of rebuilding whole cities and towns once the defeat of the Axis was complete. The waters of the River Lethe induce forgetfulness of the past. Remembering, we may arm ourselves against the lethal weapons of the present.

The subtitle of this book, "A U.S.–Soviet Dialogue," refers to not one but many interactions that inform these pages. In addition to the dialogue between past and present, there is, at the core of this work, the dialogue between two cultures; it is in the juxtaposition of Soviet and American voices and in the montage of Soviet and American photographs, posters, drawings, and cartoons that this book comes to life. Our cooperation as authors is one obvious manifestation of this intercultural dialogue. From the beginning, however, the recollections and reflections of Soviets and Americans who participated in World War II have been the true center of this endeavor. Some of the names of the men and women who tell their stories here—names like Roosevelt and Arbatov—will be familiar to readers in both countries, but most of those who have contributed to this book are not public figures; they are ordinary men and women whose experiences of World War II were both remarkable and representative of the experiences of hundreds of thousands of people in each country. As these veterans of the battlefronts and home fronts of World War II tell their stories, events that have been forgotten or seemingly emptied of meaning take on new significance because they are being recalled in a public forum by Soviets *and* Americans. The "Grand Alliance" of World War II is not only momentarily renewed, but reencountered with a critical edge that allows both participants and readers a distinctive terrain on which to examine their understandings of themselves and each other.

This book and the U.S.–Soviet dialogue it presents have their origins in a live, interactive television program or "spacebridge" entitled *Remembering War* that was jointly produced by Soviets and Americans on May 7,

1985. Intended to commemorate the fortieth anniversary of the end of World War II in Europe, *Remembering War*, the television event, was an early instance of the emergent spacebridge medium. Superficially similar to teleconferences, spacebridges exploit new television technologies to link people who are geographically and culturally separated; during a one- to two-hour period, a group of citizens in the Soviet Union and a comparable group in the United States see and hear each other simultaneously on video monitors or on large video screens and through speakers. The communication is accomplished electronically, using satellites; interaction occurs in "real" time. Some spacebridges have been aired live in both the Soviet Union and the United States, but, in most instances, including that of *Remembering War*, the live interaction has been recorded on video tape, edited in each country, and then aired on television.

The *Remembering War* spacebridge was designed by Soviet and American producers to allow for spontaneity and to ensure focus on the topic at hand—World War II. To implement that design, producers brought together Soviet and American veterans of home fronts and battlefronts, historians, writers, and students of the wartime period. As agreed, each country selected approximately a dozen key participants, each of whom could address different aspects of the war experience. We decided that it was particularly important to include four "types" of men and women: soldiers of various ranks who had been on active duty during World War II; "production-line" soldiers who could personally speak on the home-front experience in each country; citizens of each country who had specific experiences working with each other as allies; and veterans of the U.S.– Soviet meeting at the Elbe.

In addition to these eyewitnesses of the war experience, several contemporary prominent historians, teachers, and students were among the group gathered for the spacebridge. Among them was Robert Dallek, a specialist in the policies of Franklin Roosevelt. He concluded his remarks by noting that it was his greatest hope "that young people in both countries would see this program and be informed about the extraordinary effort that was made on both sides, and understand the terrible suffering that was brought on by war to all people in all societies." Dallek added that he hoped that this program would help others to understand "how impermissible such a struggle would be again in this modern world."

We have not included these voices of contemporary historians of the war because their work is otherwise available in print, and to treat their research with any justice would be impossible in a book intended to highlight the recollections of war veterans and home-front workers from the war period. This book has, however, profited from the insights of many historians and has come into being, in large part, because all of us who participated in the television event share Professor Dallek's conviction and hope that if men and women in both countries—young people especially—

are better informed about the sufferings and the alliance of Soviets and Americans in the past, they will be better prepared to avoid war in the future.

We have tried to maintain the integrity of comments made by participants during the television program and have thus transcribed the stories and remarks of participants exactly as they occurred. Since, however, a book does not have the time restriction of a television program, we took the opportunity in creating this book to include stories and details told before and after the two-hour production and retold to project staff in later interviews.

The visual elements of *Remembering War* presented a different opportunity and challenge when we came to transforming the television program into this book. The inclusion of still photographs, segments of archival documentary and narrative film footage, music and dramatic performances, in the television special was not a matter of ornamentation but central to the program concept. In the months before the production, both sides made considerable efforts to research appropriate representational materials; the selected materials were collaboratively edited into a series of video roll-ins intended both to mediate discussion among the participants and to present an alternative dialogue between the two cultures. In the end, we had far more visual material than we could use in the two-hour period. This book provides a welcome opportunity to present a broader array of visual materials than we could accommodate in the live production.

It was also obvious when we began working on this book that the emphasis on film footage in the television program would be impossible in printed text; nor could we recapture the dramatic readings of Robert Frost's "The Bonfire" and Archibald MacLeish's "The Young Dead Soldiers" performed by actors Robyn Hunt, Dick Anthony Williams, and Gloria Edward Williams. On the other hand, certain kinds of visual representations that were central to the war culture in each country and that show significant differences as well as commonalities between the two countries are more amenable to book form. These materials include posters, cartoons, advertisements, and still photographs. Some of these images were used in the television program, either in video roll-ins or in set decoration, but many new visual representations have been added to *Remembering War* for this book. In selecting these visual materials, we have kept in mind the basic goals of *Remembering War:* to create a dialogue between the two societies that will enable citizens of both countries to recollect their own war experience, to share in the experience of the other, and to better comprehend their past history as allies.

No one articulated these goals better than S. Frederick Starr, the U.S. moderator of the spacebridge:

> Dear friends, the United States and the Soviet Union have perhaps more than we realize a common history. Today, we come together to remember

an important moment in that common history, namely, when we fought together as allies during the Second World War, the Great Patriotic War. We want to remember today that wartime experience, and in a way that it may guide us toward a more peaceful future. To this end, we have brought together Americans and Soviets with a wide range of experiences and memories. They have in common that they were all allies, allies who fought on the battlefront, the home front, with guns, with words, with plows, to make a better world for their children.

Of the men and women who came together on May 7, 1985, in San Diego and Moscow, few had ever told their stories in a public context. For many, the invitation to participate in the spacebridge was welcome but disconcerting. Ed Ruff, a veteran of the 1945 U.S.–Soviet meetings at the Elbe River in Germany, was living in his hometown of Riverside, New Jersey, at the time of the spacebridge. His response to our invitation to participate in the program reflected the sentiments of many:

○ I couldn't believe it when I first got the call from San Diego. I thought, Geez, what is this—some left-wing group that I would get involved in? But the more I talked to them, I thought, No, this sounds legitimate. I thought, Geez, this sounds great. I'll probably hyperventilate and have tension and pass out and everything else with this thing, but I'm going to do it! I was ready to foot the bill and go out and everything else. Then they said what they were trying to do and I thought, Geez, this would be great. If Joe [deceased U.S. Elbe veteran Joe Polowski] were here, it would fit right in with what he was trying to do. ○

What Joe Polowski was trying to do was to keep others remembering the meeting of Soviet and American soldiers along the Elbe River on April 25, 1945. Year after year, until his death on October 18, 1983, Joe Polowski appeared on the Michigan Avenue bridge in Chicago on April 25 with a sign that read: "Halt the spread of nuclear weapons." For Polowski, these vigils, the reunions of Elbe veterans he organized, the letters he wrote to political leaders, and the conversations he initiated with men and women all over the world were necessary implementations of the oath he had taken with his fellow American and Soviet soldiers at the Elbe. In that oath, Joe Polowski had sworn never to forget, and he took that promise to mean that he must try to prevent others from forgetting as well. He believed that if we remembered the joint celebration at the Elbe of U.S.–Soviet alliance, if we remembered that brief moment of mutual acknowledgment, we would also remember that World War II was the context for the creation of nuclear weapons. Remembering, we would be less willing to take up arms against each other.

The television program, *Remembering War,* provided the occasion for the beginnings of conversations that have continued in and around this book. Not long after the airing of the special, Novosti, the Soviet state publishing house, asked both of us—as Soviet moderator and American producer—about the possibility of a book that would use the program as a point of departure. We both responded favorably, as did Oxford University Press in New York. Our experience with the television program had made it clear that Soviets and Americans were eager to understand better each other's World War II experiences; we also were aware that because of the limited time allocated to each participant in the spacebridge, many important details, as well as entire stories, were yet to be told. A book that included vignettes and remarks from the television program but then exploited the unique abilities of the print medium to clarify historical situations provided the appropriate context for continuation of the dialogue we had begun.

With this in mind, we invited the men and women who had participated in the television program to contribute to this book by elaborating on the stories they had told and the reflections they had shared. With the exception of a few participants who were incapacitated by serious illnesses, everyone we approached generously accepted this invitation; in most instances, this meant that one of us or our associates (Carol Axel and Jillaine Smith) met with the participant in his or her home and tape-recorded several hours of oral history. For two of the American participants, Anne Smith and Bernard Koten, who had both traveled from New York City to San Diego for the television event but had had no opportunity to speak during the spacebridge, these recorded interviews provided the first occasion to tell their stories publicly.

These interviews also created an opportunity for all of the participants to respond to comments made during the spacebridge. General Elliott Roosevelt, the son of President Franklin Delano Roosevelt, was, for example, somewhat frustrated during the spacebridge because there was insufficient time for him to respond to Soviet criticisms of the timing of the Second Front; in these pages, General Roosevelt presents his perspective concerning the Second Front in some detail; similarly, Soviet Admiral Nikolai Ivliyev further reflects on the Second Front and adds a revealing anecdote to the comments on this topic made by other Soviets during the program.

This book has also given us the opportunity to apply understandings gained in the joint U.S.–Soviet process of producing the television spacebridge and to bring research and historical revelations that have occurred since 1985 to our dialogue about the U.S.–Soviet experience of World War II. In preliminary discussions of interactive television program topics, the U.S. group had initially dismissed a World War II theme on grounds that there remained too many areas of controversy, too many potential minefields for the discussion to be fruitful. For Soviets and Americans, the dilemma was how to remember war while avoiding certain aspects of this particular war that would almost certainly lead to disputes that could not be substantively addressed in a television program for a general audience. In addition, each country wished to avoid discussion of certain aspects of World War II, but we differed on which aspects were problematic. These concerns had led to the decision to emphasize the stories and reflections of veterans and home-front workers—how did ordinary people from each country experience and recall the war? We thus avoided the tendency to fall into chronological patterns of organization for historical events, which, in turn, would have necessitated choices of "major" events and would have called attention to any exclusions of political or military decisions.

In preparing this book, we decided to establish a similar framework, although we agreed that our written account of the American and Soviet experiences of World War II could and should include far more detailed descriptions of the relevant historical situations than were appropriate for the television program. Our joint avoidance of inflammatory topics in the special was not intended to obscure differences between the United States and the Soviet Union but was aimed at subordinating individual and cultural recriminations to questions and reflections that could be discussed without venom. The television program had been deliberately designed to encourage new understandings and to disseminate information by explicitly emphasizing and fostering mediation as an essential element of intercultural communication. This meant that we did not simply ask veterans, home-front workers, and historians to talk to each other; instead, we articulated key themes relevant to the experiences of men and women in both countries—What the Soldiers Saw, the Home Front, the Alliance—and we began each thematic section of the program with presentations of specifically relevant film clips, photographs, music, and theater that served as catalysts for discussion as well as discrete elements of nonverbal dialogue.

The fruits of this design were most evident about halfway through the program when Charlie Miller, an American ex-POW, rose from the U.S. audience to recall his experiences of World War II. Obviously abashed at finding himself "on stage," Miller began hesitantly to describe his experiences as a soldier in Europe. With self-deprecating humor, he noted that he had escaped seven times from German POW camps, adding that we would probably find him "pretty stupid" since his seven escapes meant that he had been captured seven times. Yes, he went on, he and his buddies had suffered, but no one had suffered as much as "those Russians" in German forced-labor camps. Miller's tears prevented him from finishing his next sentence. Moved, but uncertain how to respond, the U.S. studio audience was initially quiet and then broke into applause. Charlie Miller gestured to the audience to cease their clapping. "I'm not going to apologize," he declared. "I'm not going to apologize for my tears. Maybe if there were more of them, like we've seen here today, maybe we wouldn't need all these summits and such. . . ."

Shortly after the live event, a political scientist who had been in the American audience remarked that Charlie Miller had given him a new understanding of the import of the Cold War. In the United States, the postwar flood of anti-Soviet propaganda and the public exposures of men and women deemed by some to be "un-American" had obviously assaulted progressives and "fellow travelers"; what had not been so obvious was that the Cold War had silenced the voices of America's Charlie Millers. For forty years, men and women like Charlie Miller had repressed their memories of World War II, because to speak as Miller did during the spacebridge, with empathy and admiration for the Soviets, was to risk being labeled a traitor. Miller's testimony in *Remembering War* revealed that for some Americans the price of the Cold War was not just confusion; the Cold War had made a significant past inaccessible to many Americans. Stalin was not alone in understanding that he who controls the past controls the future.

While the spontaneity of Charlie Miller's account during the spacebridge cannot be reenacted in a book, we can and do take advantage here of understandings gained during or in the aftermath of the television event. Several provocative exchanges and perplexing remarks made during the spacebridge are clarified and made accessible to anyone who opens this volume. During the spacebridge, for example, the most confrontational moment occurred in a barbed exchange between the Soviets Vladimir Mikhailov and Stanislav Menshikov and the American political scientist William Taubman. The dispute emerged from comments about the Second Front and focused on each country's approach to history, turning the discussion of the U.S.–Soviet alliance from a tone of nostalgia to an admonitory reminder of the limitations of that alliance during and after World War II. When Menshikov called for "realism," Taubman retorted that the Soviets could use more of this attribute in their own interpretations of history. Menshikov subsequently reaffirmed his argument for realism but augmented his previous comments with a remarkable plea for more constructive use of the positive lessons of the past and less hostile rhetoric from both sides. This plea was directed at his Soviet colleagues as much as at Americans. He reminded both audiences that we had avoided war for the last forty years, and that during these years, we had negotiated important treaties that should not be forgotten. In writing this book, we have not only confronted the specific issue of the Second Front, but we have kept in mind these basic reminders from both sides.

Much that occurred in behind-the-scenes discussions for the television program is also now brought forward into our introductions to each chapter. One central concern articulated by U.S. consultants was the susceptibility of the topic to an imbalanced presentation of each nation's role in World War II; since there was nothing comparable in the U.S. experience to the losses of lives and the hardships suffered by the Soviets, it might be difficult to maintain the desired parity of exchange of information and creation of new understandings. The unspoken premise in many joint U.S.–Soviet projects is that success is measured in terms of each side's ability to believe that it "looks better" than the other. Given the ambiguity of what this means in terms of representations of World War II as well as the great differences in the two nations' experiences, *Remembering War* is vulnerable to a partial success that ultimately signals failure.

In jointly addressing World War II, the different beginnings and ends of the war have emerged as perhaps the most controversial areas for both countries. As the following Soviet and American "introductions" testify, not only did each country officially enter World War II on different dates but the circumstances before and at the time of each's entry into the war were also complex and susceptible to mutual recriminations. To take December 7, 1941, as a starting point for discussion of World War II would not only imply erroneously that the war only began once the United States was fully involved but would also belittle the months of desperate struggle for survival that followed the Nazi assault on the Soviet Union that had begun on June 22, 1941. Yet, naming June 22, 1941, as a starting point of the war would be equally biased and inaccurate, not because the United States was not yet officially at war, but because this would evade discussion of the Nazi invasions of Czechoslovakia and Poland, of the Soviet-Nazi Non-Aggression Pact of 1939, and of the Soviet's incorporation by force of Latvia, Lithuania, Estonia, and parts of Poland into the Soviet Union. Many Westerners date the beginning of World War II from the German invasion of Poland in 1939, but others, including Soviets, might well ask, Why not begin with 1938 then? Why should the invasion of Poland count in a different way than the *Anschluss*, the union of Germany and Austria unabashedly imposed by Hitler?

The end of the war is equally problematic, not only because of territorial issues that continue to be debated to this day but also because even the symbolic end of the war is divided between VE (Victory in Europe) Day and VJ (Victory in Japan) Day. In addition, discussion of the end of World War II inevitably culminates in judgments concerning the U.S. development and use of the first atomic bombs. For many people around the world, the emergence of nuclear weapons is the most significant legacy of the war, but this topic also can distract attention from the complexities of the war experience and transform the intricate process of joint remembering into a ritual admission of U.S. guilt for the dangers of the atomic age.

This book does not pretend to provide definitive, mutually satisfactory answers to unsettling questions; nor does it attempt to resolve disputes about the past or future. Changes in U.S.–Soviet relations in the last few years and in the domestic policies of the Soviet Union, as well as the different constraints of the television and print media, have meant that topics that were once taboo, such as Stalin's policies in the late 1930s, can now be discussed. This book is a marker in time. The historical perspectives in these pages are different from what they might have been a few years ago and from what they are likely to be in the future.

Those who have participated in U.S.–Soviet negotiations on other matters (often, of course, matters of far greater import than a joint television event) will find a familiar pattern in this account. "The devil is in the details," as some would say. Yet, it is precisely the details recalled by the men and women who tell their stories in this book that teach us the difficulty of recognizing cultural bias and differences in points of view. The details shield us from distortions of cultural history and prevent us from blurring the contrast between Soviet and U.S. experiences of the war. The first Russian words suggested as an equivalent for the proposed English title literally meant "The Remembrance of War," but one Soviet contributor perspicaciously noted that there was a significant if subtle difference between the active notion of "remembering" war and the more enclosed, set connotation of "remembrance."

For those of us who have participated in creating this book, there has been a strong sense that by joining together in a common project, however modest in its aims, we could achieve something of value that could not be accomplished by either side alone. This is true not only of the cooperation on this project between Soviets and Americans, between Novosti and Oxford University Press, but also of the collaborative efforts among Soviets and among Americans. The credit roll for the spacebridge *Remembering War* may have been the longest in either Soviet or American television history; while it would be excessive to rerecord all of those credits here, we do wish to note that without the generosity and wisdom of all those who created the television program, this book would not exist. U.S. co-executive producer Christopher Makins played a central role in shaping the content and structure of the spacebridge, and his judicious voice continues to echo in these pages. Tracy Gray not only coordinated the production project for the Roosevelt Center for American Policy Studies, but her research and writing of the *Companion Guide to* Remembering War inform many pages of this book. Roger Molander, then president of the Roosevelt Center, supported and guided *Remembering War* from its inception. Without the technical guidance and commitment to *Remembering War* of Sherman George, director of Audio Visual Services at the University of California, San Diego, neither this book nor the television event would have occurred.

The television program, *Remembering War,* could also not have occurred without the generous financial support of the Carnegie Corporation of New York, the Benton Foundation, the Roosevelt Center for American Policy Studies, the Institute for Global Conflict and Cooperation of the University of California, the Chancellor's Associates Fund of the University of California at San Diego, the Richard Lounsbery Foundation, the W. Alton Jones Foundation, the Armand Hammer Foundation, and an anonymous donor. We are grateful for their help.

Many of those who contributed to the television program were also key contributors to this book. First among these are the men and women who tell their stories on these pages. In an authentic sense, they share with us authorship of this book, although any errors or omissions are, of course, not their responsibility but ours.

It is not uncommon for an author to claim the indispensibility of one or another friend or assistant. The contributions of Jillaine Smith and Carol Axel to the making of this book were, however, authentically out of the ordinary. Between them, they conducted and transcribed the post-spacebridge interviews with the American participants. Their wisdom, skill, and empathy in this endeavor made possible the American portion of this book.

Helene Keyssar's son, David D. Franke, was responsible for much of the visual research and organization of photographs and other visual materials for this book; we are grateful for his assistance, as well as for the knowledge that mother and son could work well together toward a common goal. For translation from Russian to English of the testimonies of the Soviet participants, we are indebted as well to Boris Kayser, who teaches Russian language and literature at the University of California, Santa Cruz. James Wertsch also helped considerably with translations from the Russian, not only of language but also of culture. Elizabeth Vaughn, the management services officer of the Department of Communication at the University of California, San Diego, was a wonderful godmother to the numerous stages of word processing and printing that went into the preparation of the manuscript; Patricia Wells took on cheerfully the cumbersome task of making one consistently typed manuscript out of many parts.

Were it not for the remarkable patience and support of our Oxford University Press editor, Sheldon Meyer, and comparable support on the Soviet side from our Novosti editor, Sergei Ivanko, there would be only a fleeting idea for this book.

Vladimir Pozner would like to reassert that this book could not have been written without a coming together of certain people and events: the Soviet and American veterans of World War II, whose passion and dedication brought their experience of forty years ago to life in a unique television spacebridge; his co-author, Helene Keyssar, whose determination was equaled only by her patience in putting up with someone as unpredictable and undisciplined as he; his son, Peter, whose assistance as part-time interviewer/researcher taught both of them something; finally, and most important, his wife, Katherin, his "home front," without whom he could never have won a single battle.

Helene Keyssar wishes to acknowledge the personal support of Tracy B. Strong and Anise Strong, both of whom understood the importance of building bridges between the United States and the Soviet Union. She also wishes to note the value and pleasure of friendship built on joint endeavors with her co-author, Vladimir Pozner. Scott Lenz of Oxford University

Press also deserves many thanks for his extraordinary patience and good judgment in editing the English edition of *Remembering War*.

   This book thus stands as another instance in the fragile, but encouraging, history of common U.S.–Soviet endeavors. Hundreds of books and articles have been written by Americans and by Soviets about World War II. We make no claims to challenge or replace the arguments and evidence of these texts. Instead, we aim to look and listen to the retelling of this history from a perspective that has remained mostly hidden or inaccessible for the last forty years—the perspective of a common history that, for good or for ill, has given us a common future.

La Jolla, CA   H. K.
July 1989

Moscow   V. P.
July 1989

Contents

Remembering War

The Great Patriotic War and the Good War

A Soviet View

In the early dawn hours of June 22, 1941, fascist Germany attacked the Soviet Union along a front stretching from the Baltic sea in the north to the Black sea in the south. Thus began Operation Barbarossa: 190 divisions, 5,500,000 men supported by 5,000 aircraft, 4,000 tanks, and nearly 50,000 guns and mortars, were hurled eastward—the greatest attack force and invasion launched in history.

Predicting the outcome of this surprise attack in a conversation with General Jodl, Hitler had said: "We have only to kick in the door and the whole rotten structure will come crashing down." His confidence was not unjustified. The Wehrmacht enjoyed an overwhelming superiority over the Red Army: 1.8 times more men, 1.25 times more guns and mortars, 1.6 times more tanks, and a 3 to 1 advantage in modern aircraft.

By July 10, the German forces had advanced a staggering 450 to 600 kilometers, occupying Latvia, Lithuania, part of Estonia, Belorussia, a large part of the Ukraine, and Moldavia. The planned-for goal of victory in a maximum of five months seemed guaranteed. As Chief of Staff Halder noted in his diary, "The campaign against Russia has been won in 14 days."

How could this have happened? Why was the Soviet Union so clearly unprepared for war? Those are legitimate questions, but before answering them, let us note that this campaign began as anything but a walkover for the hitherto invincible Wehrmacht. The German steamroller was held up for two months at Smolensk, a fact that would play a major role in allowing the Soviet forces to regroup and bring in reserves from the east. By mid-July, the Germans had suffered over one hundred thousand casualties and had lost some two thousand tanks and nearly thirteen hundred aircraft.

Operation Typhoon, aimed at capturing Moscow, began on October 2. On the following day in an address to the German people, Hitler said, "I declare today, and I declare without reservation, that the enemy in the East has been struck down and will never rise again." But two months later, on December 1, the German forces launched what was their last all-out assault against the Soviet capital. It petered out on the following day on the outskirts of Moscow; the invader had been drained by the ferocious resistance of the Soviet forces; four days later these forces launched a powerful counter offensive that sent the foe reeling back from the walls of Moscow. By February 1942, the enemy had lost a million men. But he had lost even more, as testified to by the noted American historian William Shirer, one of the authorities on that period: "The blow was so sudden and so shattering that the German Army and the Third Reich never fully recovered from it. For the first time in more than two years of unbroken military victories, the armies of Hitler were retreating before a superior force." Chief of Staff Halder put it even more succinctly: "The myth of the invincibility of the German Army was broken."

Could this have happened had the Soviet Union been totally unprepared for war? Probably not. So was the U.S.S.R. prepared? As pleasing as an unequivocal "Yes" or "No" might be, neither would be correct, for, as is usually the case in history, the situation itself was anything but unequivocal.

On the one hand, the Soviet leaders were fully aware of the threat presented by fascism. As early as 1923 Georgi Chicherin, then the people's commissar for foreign affairs, noted: "A fascist triumph in Germany could be the first step in a crusade against us." The clairvoyance of that thought was corroborated ten years later, in May 1933, when Adolf Hitler addressed a public rally: "Some 14 to 15 years ago I stated to the German nation that I saw my historical duty in destroying Marxism. Since then I have consistently repeated those words. They are not empty words but a sacred oath which I will carry out until I give up the ghost." The handwriting on the wall could have been missed only by the blind—and the Soviet leadership's vision was not impaired.

Time and time again, Soviet representatives at various international conferences had proposed and called for agreements which, had they been accepted, would have nipped Hitler's plans in the bud and made World

War II impossible. Here are just some of those proposals: complete and total disarmament (1932); the creation of a system of regional collective security in the Pacific with the participation of the United States, China, and Japan (1933); the transformation of the World Disarmament Conference into a Permanent Peace Conference (1934); the organization of a system of collective security in Europe (1934); agreeing to an internationally ratified definition of aggression (1935); the creation of a system of collective security to eradicate the threat of a new World War (1938). Certainly, these proposals testify to both concern and awareness on the part of the Soviet Union. The rise of Hitler in Germany was reason enough for concern. But there was another—appeasement on the part of the West.

In March 1935, Nazi Germany introduced general conscription and announced the creation of the Luftwaffe, both measures being flagrant violations of the Treaty of Versailles. The West did not raise an eyebrow. That same year Great Britain signed a sea treaty with Germany, allowing the Germans to build a navy—yet another violation of the Versailles Treaty. In October 1936, Mussolini invaded Abyssinia; in 1936 Hitler occupied the Rhineland; and on June 18, 1936, a fascist military putsch occurred in Spain. Fascism was on the march. But the West did nothing. Why? The answer may be found in this most amazingly candid statement made by Lord Halifax after meeting with Hitler at Obersalzberg on November 19, 1937: "I and other members of the British government fully realize that the Führer has achieved much not only in Germany itself but, as the result of having destroyed communism in his country, he has barred the latter from Western Europe. And Germany may therefore rightfully be considered the West's bastion against Bolshevism."

What civil war and foreign intervention, followed by economic boycott, the *cordon sanitaire*, and diplomatic nonrecognition had failed to accomplish in bringing about the downfall of the Soviet Union, Hitler would now do. That was what the West was banking on. The policy of appeasement was based on the hope that Nazi Germany would strike eastward and destroy the first and only socialist state. That explains why Hitler was allowed to march into Austria on March 12, 1938. That is why, on September 29 and 30, in Munich, Prime Ministers Chamberlain of Great Britain and Daladier of France sold out Czechoslovakia on the Sudetenland question. That is why, when Germany invaded and occupied Czechoslovakia on March 15, 1939, the only Western response was words, not action. Finally, even though France and Great Britain did declare war on Germany on September 3, two days after it invaded Poland, neither country actually engaged the enemy for nine months. The Germans called it *Sitzkrieg;* the British, the Phony War; the French, *La Drôle de guerre,* for not even a single soldier was wounded on either side until May 10, 1940. Notwithstanding, the military confirmed the fact that Hitler could have been destroyed. Here are just two testimonies:

> The success against Poland was only possible by almost completely baring our western border. If the French had used the engagement of the German forces in Poland, they would have been able to cross the Rhine without our having been able to prevent it and would have threatened the Ruhr area, which was the most decisive factor of the German conduct of war. (Chief of Staff Halder)

▪ ▪ ▪ ▪

> If we didn't collapse in 1939, that was due only to the fact that during the Polish campaign the approximately 110 French and British divisions in the West were held completely inactive against 23 German divisions. (General Jodl)

The Western Powers turned a deaf ear to all Soviet proposals, refusing to sign any agreements, while simultaneously giving Hitler a green light to attack and destroy the Soviet Union. In light of that situation, when the German government proposed to the Soviet Union a nonaggression pact, there were several reasons for accepting it: 1) to count on Western support was suicidal; 2) it would furnish the Soviet Union with some extra time to make ready for the inevitable; 3) a refusal would almost certainly be used by the Nazis as a pretext to react to the Soviet Union's "aggressive intentions"—which is exactly what they desired. The pact was, in Mafia terms, an offer the Soviet side could not refuse. It had, on the one hand, been forced on the U.S.S.R. by the Western policy of appeasement. But on the other hand. . .

The purges of the 1930s in the Soviet Union had not spared the military. Joseph Stalin's lust for absolute power, his infinite suspicion bordering on paranoia, had led him to strike at the flower of his high command. As a result, the armed forces were literally beheaded: forty thousand officers were executed, no less than 80 percent of those who had been trained to command the Soviet armed forces. This was more than the number lost during the war itself. In addition to that, Stalin trusted no one, including those who at mortal risk furnished him with the exact date of the Nazi onslaught—June 22. More than anything else, Stalin was fearful of provoking Hitler, of furnishing him a pretext to begin hostilities. Could not that information be part of a diabolical Nazi plot to draw Soviet fire? Fighting for time, Stalin not only ignored information coming from unimpeachable sources, not only allowed a significant number of officers to take their annual vacations in June, but also issued an order forbidding under penalty of death any member of the Red Army to challenge border transgressions committed by the Germans on land, in the air, or on the sea—of which there were many. This explains why most of the losses the Soviet air force suffered on June 22 were on land: The planes never took off and were sitting ducks for Luftwaffe fire.

People in Moscow listening to the first radio announcement of the war *(Y. Haldei)*

Women digging ditches around Moscow *(News Press Agency)*

Recruits line up at the conscription office on the first day of the war *(A. Ustinov)*

Clipped heads and long johns

And so, the answer to that fateful question about whether or not the Soviet Union was prepared is . . . yes . . . and no; there exists no unequivocal answer. But there do exist unequivocal facts: the blitzkrieg failed. Far from falling, Moscow became the first victory over a supposedly unbeatable war machine, and that both crushed the Wehrmacht's morale and bolstered that of Allied fighting men and of those in the resistance movements. In the final analysis, the decisive factor in those crucial months of the 1941–42 winter campaign was the high morale of the Soviet soldier who knew why he was fighting and what he was fighting for, who demonstrated not fanaticism but a conscientious will to resist and triumph—no matter what the odds. This war was about the very existence of the Soviet people, of the U.S.S.R. itself. The entire population rose up to defend their country. It was truly a great patriotic war.

An American View

When the United States entered World War II on December 7, 1941, much of the world was already at war. The thirty-eight nations that were officially in conflict had among them a sphere of operations that extended from Ethiopia to Papua, New Guinea, and from the Arctic Circle to the Tropic of Capricorn. In joining England and the Soviet Union in what Winston Churchill was to call the "Grand Alliance," the United States had become involved in a truly global conflagration. Millions of lives had already been lost, and many millions more were at stake. For those who had been fighting for months or years, the United States' entry into the war provided hope that, in Churchill's words, "the life of the world may move forward into broad, sunlit uplands." The alternative, for those armed against the Axis powers led by Germany, Italy, and Japan, was "to sink into the abyss of a new dark age, made more sinister, and perhaps more protracted, by the lights of perverted science."

Yet, before December of 1941, despite this specter on the horizon, many Americans opposed United States involvement in the war. The passage in 1924 of the national-origins quota law that restricted immigration to the United States emblematized the isolationist tendencies in American society that had been evident since well before World War I. This law appeared to assuage a strong undercurrent of anxiety among Americans about ethnic diversity. Then came the Depression. It called into question the long-held American dream of the promised land where hard work would bring riches to all, and it brought many Americans face-to-face with raw fears about their daily bread.

Americans in the 1930s were also deeply divided in their judgments of developments in other countries. Although it remains an almost-forgotten part of U.S. history, some Americans left the United States in the 1930s,

seeking new frontiers and alternative social structures in other lands.
These journeys were often the expression of a longing for what America
had once seemed to embody: the energy and sense of community that
could build the world anew in a spirit of freedom and justice for all. In the
name of the just and the possible, thousands of Americans went to the
Soviet Union, to Spain, to China. Most returned to the United States, but
their reasons for doing so were complex and often brought about by specific events, such as the purge trials in the Soviet Union, the frustrating end to
the civil war in Spain, the chaos and imperialist threat of Japan in China.

At the same time, memories of World War I cast a long shadow of
doubt about American involvement in Europe's conflicts. While some perceived clear threats to democracy in the rise to power of Hitler in Germany,
Mussolini in Italy, and Franco in Spain, others took positions of disengaged
tolerance toward these dictators and their aggressions; when Mussolini
took Ethiopia in 1935, the United States responded by declaring the Neutrality Acts, which prohibited the sale of arms to any belligerent nation and,
as amended in 1937, forbade the entry of American ships and citizens into
areas of sea or land designated as war zones.

As the name implies, the Neutrality Acts were intended to prevent
American involvement on either side of any conflict that arose outside the
United States. It soon became clear, however, that Americans were divided
in their identifications of "belligerent" nations. While some insisted that
the war in Spain was a local conflict, journalists reported on the German
and Italian intervention in this "civil" war. Men and women, poet Archibald MacLeish for one, warned their fellow citizens that Spain was not a
metaphor for war but was the beginning of the real war against fascism.
Some Americans were imbued by this belief and joined the loyalists in
Spain on the battlefields. Among those who saw the defeat of Communism
as a primary goal, there were strong sentiments of support for Germany,
Italy, and fascist Spain; in the late 1930s especially, others, including President Roosevelt, clearly identified the fascist countries, including Japan with
Germany, Italy, and Spain, as aggressors who should be treated differently
from victims of assault such as China, Czechoslovakia, Ethiopia, and, ultimately, the rest of Europe.

As the 1930s came to a close and evidence accumulated of racism,
armed aggression, and violation of treaties by Germany and Italy on one
side of the world and Japan on the other, most Americans turned their
verbal support to the Allies and condemned Germany, at least, for its
arrogant, nationalistic policies and violent practices. At the same time,
however, according to polls conducted in 1939, the vast majority of Americans were opposed to U.S. involvement in what was by then, undeniably,
war in Europe; opposition to participation in a Pacific war was even stronger. Both the 1938 Munich agreements among Germany, France, and
England and the 1939 Soviet-Nazi pact contributed to the ambivalence

and confusion of many Americans in the months directly preceding World War II. British Prime Minister Neville Chamberlain promised "peace in our time" on his return from Munich in 1938, but within a few months, Hitler demonstrated the hollowness of such assurances. Most Americans who had not turned against the Soviet Union during the mid-1930s purge trials did so with particularly intense rage when the Soviets signed a mutual nonaggression pact with Germany.

Uncertain about who were the "good guys" abroad and vulnerable to economic hardships and confusing cultural changes at home, few Americans were eager to enter a war that seemed remote and promised only new dangers and difficulties. In contrast, President Roosevelt, like Winston Churchill in England, while hardly eager for war, held clear convictions about the identity of the enemy and the danger ahead. Speaking in Chicago in 1937, Roosevelt called for a "moral quarantine" against Germany, Italy, and Japan, and shortly thereafter, he began to voice his unease with the constraints imposed by the Neutrality Acts. General Elliott Roosevelt, son of then-President Franklin D. Roosevelt, recalls vividly his father's relief in 1940 when the new law providing for a draft of American men into the armed services passed Congress.

These were only the first steps in what some would later call America's "undeclared war" on the Axis powers. After Great Britain's declaration of war on Germany on September 3, 1939, the U.S. Congress agreed to repeal some portions of the Neutrality Acts in order to defend U.S. merchant ships at sea and to make arms and supplies available to England. Equally important, President Roosevelt urged Americans to become "the great arsenal of democracy," and Congress, in turn, allocated twenty-six billion dollars to war production for American defense. This was followed in early 1941 by passage of the Lend-Lease Act which authorized the United States to "lend or lease" planes, tanks, munitions, other war materials, and food and clothing to Great Britain and her allies; seven billion American dollars were allocated to lend-lease production in early 1941, and another six billion were committed in aid to the Allies in October of that same year. Between war production for home defense and materials supplied to Great Britain and, eventually, to the Soviet Union, there was, indeed, a production "miracle" in the United States. Americans in factories across the country responded positively to the call to sacrifice themselves to this effort, and with each week that passed, more and more Americans risked their lives on the Atlantic in the effort to deliver the goods to their unofficial allies abroad.

Whatever hesitations about full engagement in the war that remained were dispelled by the shock of the Japanese attack on Pearl Harbor, the first assault on American land in the war. President Roosevelt had little difficulty declaring war after December 7, 1941, when the surprise attack caught American forces unprepared. It was, he declared, "a day that will

live in infamy," and Americans quickly responded with expressions of out-
rage, bewilderment, and patriotism. Men now lined up to enlist faster than
they could be accommodated by the armed services, and both men and
women joined the "front line" of production workers at home. Indeed,
throughout the war, "Remember Pearl Harbor" was the battle cry from
which few Americans could shrink.

Lauretta Beaty Foy, one of the participants in *Remembering War*, remembered well during a post-spacebridge interview the day Pearl Harbor
was bombed:

○ Sue and I had bought a Piper Cub that had been repossessed. We got it
real cheap. And so we had this airplane. It was a Sunday afternoon, and I
asked Jimmy [her son], who was six years old then, if he wanted to go
flying. He was crazy about flying. We flew for about forty-five minutes or
so. It was a beautiful day, big puffy clouds everywhere; we'd dive through a
few clouds, which you don't do now.

There was no control tower then, and if they wanted to stop somebody
or something, they would put some red flags out in the middle of the
runway. I was circling around [to land], and they had two guys standing out
there with red flags, and they were waving everybody down, and I said to
Jimmy, "I wonder what's wrong? I can't imagine what's going on down
there." Nobody had crashed because there wasn't any airplane that looked
bad down there. So finally, we got a chance to land and . . . this guy comes
up and says, "Taxi into your hangar right away!" And I said, "What's going
on?" And he said, "Pearl Harbor!"

And of course, Pearl Harbor didn't mean anything to me. We taxied
into the hangar where we kept the ship, and everybody was buzzing around,
excited, and I went in the office, and I said to Anne Colbert [she was the
wife of the operator], "Ann, what's going on?" And she said, "Pearl Harbor." And I said, "What's Pearl Harbor?" And she said, "The Japs have
attacked pearl Harbor." And I said, "How could they do that?" because
Hawaii was a long way from Japan. And she said, "Well, they've attacked
Pearl Harbor, and all airplanes are grounded!" And I said, "What do you
mean, grounded? How can they do that?" And she said, "All planes are
grounded within 150 miles of the coast."

I remember driving home with Jimmy, and Jimmy says, "What's Pearl
Harbor?" I tried to explain to him that the Japs had attacked us, and that
would mean that we were at war with Japan. So I got home, and Dad and
Mother were listening to the radio, and Dad said, "How's this going to
affect your job?" And I said, "Well, it looks like I don't have a job," because
all of our flying is mainly along the coast.

Monday morning [I] drove down to work real early in the morning,
and of course, everyone was excited everywhere. Half of the mechanics and
half the people that worked there had already gone to sign up for the army

or the navy. They were that intense about it. Of course, Europe had been at war a couple of years then. Our boss, Harvey Martin, had been a navy flyer, and he was in the navy reserve, and they had called him. He had his old uniform on, and he couldn't get it buttoned because he had a big pot belly. His wife was there, and he said, "I've got to report in 45 minutes." So he was trying to close out his business and everything. He said, "You gals have a job with me any time you want it after we get out of the war, but I'll be gone during the war." It was just like that.

We didn't know what to do. And you can imagine what it was for a lot of families, like women [who] were home with several kids and all of a sudden their husbands gone. Now a lot of those family men were not drafted if they had children, but a lot of them wanted to go, and a lot of them felt a very strong desire to get in the service right away. It was just like the world had turned topsy-turvy in a few minutes. ○

Like Lauretta Beaty Foy, many Americans had only a vague notion of where Pearl Harbor was, yet most shared her sense that on that "day that will live in infamy," when the Japanese assaulted the Hawaiian harbor, the world had indeed turned upside down. The United States was not invulnerable to attack, as so many had believed, and World War II was no longer someone else's problem.

Oral historian Studs Terkel illuminated these changes and some of the key elements of the American war experience when he reflected on the period for the *Remembering War* spacebridge. He recalled how factories were suddenly full of women "doing things they had never done before," and he noted that it was not the military but the merchant marine that suffered the greatest loss during the first year of America's participation in the war. Drawing on the hundreds of interviews he conducted for his own oral history, *The Good War,* Terkel captured the "topsy-turvy" feelings of Americans as they experienced the highs and lows of the war. Some of those feelings, he recalled, were focused on our Russian allies:

○ Back in those days the Russians were known as our gallant allies. And General Douglas MacArthur spoke of their heroism in the counterattack on the Germans—one of the great moments in military and human history. So this was the spirit of the time. There was a consensus, an overwhelming one. This war had to be fought. And of course, there were dissenters, but very few in number relatively. Strangely enough, there was very little black market. For the feeling was very "gung-hoish" indeed at the time, very much for it. It was a grand alliance in the midst of war. Of course, any war is barbaric, we know that. But in the midst of that was this comradery. The American GIs would hear out at the European theatre, there, about some Soviet counteroffensive smashing the Nazis back. And the barracks would resound with cheers. It was that sort of time.

Naval airbase at Pearl Harbor under attack

Assault *(D. Baltermanz)*

"Fire! Fire!" *(E Yevzerikhin)*

Children of the war *(News Press Agency)*

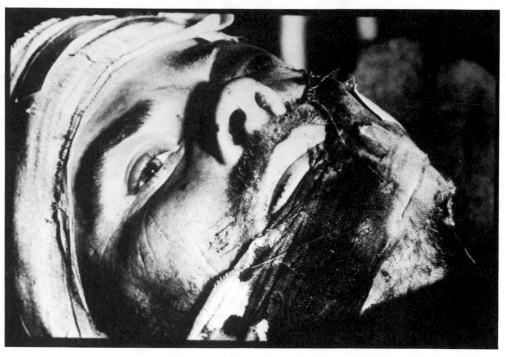

Wounded GI *(Life Picture Service)*

Joseph Stalin at the military parade in Red Square, November 7, 1941 *(News Press Agency)*

FDR *(United Press International)*

One of the most popular of all money-raising groups was called Russian War Relief. And I remember, everyone was chipping in, no matter what their political feelings were. I was making a collection speech for our gallant allies at one of these posh estates, and everybody was so enthusiastic. I remember I was talking and there was a big swimming pool. It was a very elegant estate indeed. I almost fell in the water. But we raised a lot of dough, and people were chipping in. There was that feeling of one ally toward another. ○

Later in his remarks, Terkel noted that the phrase "the good war" was paradoxical because "the adjective and the noun never match." "But," he went on to say, "in contrast to others it was a war that had to be. There was the Axis, there was Hitler, there was the ultimate racism. News of the holocaust was slow in coming in. But nonetheless, a feeling was there that Hitler spoke of—*über alles*, us, as well as his allies. And so in that sense, the feeling was, even though we look at it ironically today, the feeling was that it was good in its execution and its goal. And it's, strangely enough, ideal. The vision was, of course, of a world in which there would be no more such experiences."

World War II was also "good" for Americans because for many it opened vistas hardly dreamed of before. Young men and women, brought up in small American towns and rural communities, traveled for the first time to cities whose names were previously only markers on maps; Americans who went abroad discovered new worlds in the Old World. If World War II was not an end to innocence for Americans, it was, at least, a far more complicated experience than has often been acknowledged; the stories that Americans tell of World War II in the following pages speak to that complexity. There is also in these remembrances, one common understanding: to the extent that World War II was, for many Americans, a "good war," it was also the last time in American history that Americans would conjoin the words "good" and "war."

The Fronts

The Soviet Front: A Soviet Perspective

Almost fifty years have elapsed since that early dawn morning when Hitler sent the world's most powerful fighting machine crashing across the Soviet border, thereby creating the Soviet-German front, more commonly referred to as the Eastern Front. Half a century is sufficient time, one would presume, to weigh all the factors, compare the data, and, setting aside the emotions and passions that inevitably mar our vision when we look at recent events, put things in their proper perspective. So it would appear. Nevertheless, a not insignificant number of people in the West continue either to ignore the significance of what was achieved on the Eastern Front or to write it off completely.

The data are unequivocal. During different stages of the war, the number of German divisions on the Eastern Front was never less than 190 and at times reached 266. During that same period of time, the number of German divisions facing the Anglo-American forces was: from 9 to 20 in Northern Africa (1941–43), from 7 to 26 in Italy (1943–45), and from 56 to 75 in Western Europe (after June, 1944). Simple addition shows that the sum total of the *maximum* number of German divisions in the west (121) is substantially lower than the *minimal* number of fascist divisions simultaneously fighting on the Eastern Front (190). But that is far from all. Six hundred seven enemy divisions were destroyed and captured on the East-

17

ern Front between 1941 and 1945. The number destroyed on the Western
Front between 1939 and 1945 is 176 divisions—not even one third as
many. But even this does not tell the whole story. Over 70 percent of all
fascist casualties were suffered in battles against the Soviet army; the
Wehrmacht lost three-quarters of its tanks, howitzers, aircraft, and artillery
on the Eastern Front. Such are the statistics. Their argument can hardly be
disputed. It was on the Eastern Front that German fascism's fate was
sealed; it was on the Eastern Front that the fascist beast's back was broken.
And we have every right to say that the Soviet army, the Soviet soldier, and
Soviet people played the key role in the victory over Hitlerism.

In the Introduction to this book we touched on some of the reasons for
the staggering Soviet losses during the first stages of the war. Much has
been written about the crimes committed by Stalin and his henchmen.
Much more, surely, will yet be written. We are only beginning to grasp the
scope of these repressions which, in fact, decimated the command of the
Soviet army. Soviet historians have often argued that it was through no fault
of the Soviet Union that the West passively watched the tragedy unfolding
in the east and, in fact, did nothing to stop Hitler, hoping secretly that he
would wipe out Bolshevism. That view is, to say the least, debatable. There
are several reasons why the West might have been anything but enthusiastic
about joining forces with the Soviet Union or coming to its rescue.

One reason pertains to the purges of the 1930s, to the terror of the
Stalin regime that began in earnest in 1934 with the murder of Kirov and
was followed by a bloodbath that decimated the party and the army. This
could not help but cause apprehension in the West; moreover, in certain
respects Stalin's behavior and way of acting was uncannily similar to
Hitler's. The former eliminated his closest supporter (Kirov) because of
his growing popularity; the latter did the same (Röhm) and for the same
reason. The former eliminated the majority of those who had voted for
Kirov (the delegates of the Seventeenth Party Congress); the latter did the
same to those who supported Röhm (the SA). The former packed millions
of people off to the gulags; the latter had millions interned and slaughtered
in concentration camps. Surely, there were differences between the two
men, but the similarity is, nevertheless, striking. Why, one must ask, would
the West wish to come to Stalin's rescue?

Another reason has to do with the secret protocols signed by Rib-
bentrop and Molotov along with the Soviet-German non-aggression pact,
as well as the Soviet-German agreement on borders and friendship and the
protocols of that document. These protocols spelled out German and
Soviet interests not only in Europe but also elsewhere. There is little doubt
that Western intelligence was aware of these secret agreements (although
one wonders why they waited until 1946 to make this knowledge public),
which, among other things, promised the Soviet Union "spheres of interest" in such areas as the Black sea coast, the Baltic states, Finland,

eastern Poland, etc. There was even some talk of dividing up the British Empire once Great Britain was conquered. The spoils were to be shared mainly by Germany, Italy, and Japan, but there was some talk about satisfying Soviet interests as well.

With all of this in mind, one should not be overly surprised at the lack of compassion and aid on the part of the West when the U.S.S.R. was attacked by Germany. As I make that statement, I certainly do not wish to be misunderstood: I find the Western view as expressed by then-Senator Harry S Truman that the two countries be left alone to kill as many of each others' people as possible to be totally repulsive, especially considering the fact that, in the final analysis, it was the Soviet Union that saved Western civilization from Nazi slavery. But one cannot and should not disregard the Soviet Union's domestic and foreign policies under Stalin—policies that were as immoral as they were treacherous. Considering the West's attitude toward socialism in general, the rise of such policies had to have the most negative effect on the West's relationship with the Soviet Union, and the situation at the beginning of the war reflected that point.

While some might take issue with the above, there is no denying the following: that we were not prepared for the Nazi onslaught, which, during the first period of the war (from June 22, 1941, to November 18, 1942), quarantined a territory housing 42 percent of the population and producing one third of the country's industrial output. This was totally, sadly enough, our own fault. We do not attribute it to any fateful position of the heavenly bodies.

By the same token, the fact that we prevailed, that our country found the resources first to check the enemy's advance and then to deal him a knock-out blow, and the fact that the main burden of the war fell on the shoulders of the Soviet people who, ultimately, were victorious, are to our eternal credit. The victory had little to do with the Russian winter, during which Georgians, Armenians, Uzbeks, and Russians suffered no less from the bitter cold than did the Germans. (True, Hitler's army had no winter uniforms in 1941, since its commanders counted on a Soviet surrender before cold weather set in, but that error was a faulty military and political forecast, not a meteorological one.) Nor did it have anything to do with the spring thaw and the lack of roads—the ooze and mud were equally hard on all vehicles and men although many a Western military expert has called these factors nothing less than "decisive." The reason for the Soviet victory lies in the unparalleled heroism, in the indomitable spirit of the Soviet people, demonstrated both at the front and at the rear. It lies in their will to win, increased tenfold by the atrocities committed against the people and their country.

There is a view that attributes the German fascist defeat to Russian ability to fight well on Russian territory. No one would argue that defense of one's kith and kin, of one's home, has been a powerful motivation for all people since ancient times. But during the drama of World War I on the Eastern Front, not even such a powerful motivation as the defense of one's motherland was enough to guarantee victory over a powerful foe. History provides the answer.

The ancient Greeks, hopelessly outnumbered (or so it would seem) by the hordes of the Persian potentate Xerxes, not only stood up to them but dealt them a devastating defeat. Wherein lies the explanation for this? In the superior military art of the Greek commanders? Then what about Thermopylae? What did military art have to do with a handful of heroes being able to hold off an entire army, a fact for which humanity cherishes their memory? The reason lies in what motivated them, gave them their strength, furnished the basis for their dedication. In that most fundamental sense, there is a direct link between the heroes of Thermopylae and the heroes of Dubosekovo, where twenty-eight Soviet servicemen refused to give up and stopped an armada of enemy tanks from breaking through and moving on to Moscow.

In 1776, the people of the thirteen colonies challenged the British Crown. The British had everything on their side: a professional, well-trained army, the best weapons money could buy, the support of mercenary troops. On paper they could not lose. Yet they lost. The colonists were victorious—because they were fighting for their liberty, because they were creating a new, progressive form of government, something unknown to the world of that period, something called a *republic.* That is where they found the strength to stand up to and overcome the British Crown.

The Soviet people's most powerful weapon was the power of their convictions, what they believed in. That is what first slowed the German fascist military machine as it moved on Moscow; that is what dealt it a crushing blow and made it reverse gears for the first time in its history.

Therein lay the answers to how Leningrad was able to resist nine hundred days of siege and why the people of Leningrad, in spite of the shelling and bombing, the cold and the starvation, did not only refuse to break and (counter to fascist calculations) turn into some sort of demor-alized subhuman blob but, on the contrary, continued to read and write poetry, to compose and listen to music, to perform their daily acts of heroism, thereby demoralizing the representatives of the "master race."

Therein lay the answer to why, when Stalingrad was in fact in enemy hands, when endless shelling and bombing turned the city into pure hell, when by all human logic the city could not be saved, it was not taken. What's more, in Stalingrad the fate of the war was sealed—not just of the Great Patriotic War, but of the war in Europe as well. Here fascism was dealt a mortal blow.

That the war created a new generation of brilliant Soviet military commanders who not only were equal but, in fact, superior to their Ger-man counterparts is undeniable. That the Soviet defense industry began to produce not only more planes, tanks, howitzers, and other armaments than fascist Germany but technologically superior armaments is a certified fact. The significance of this can hardly be overstated. Nevertheless, beneath all this lay the main reason for our victory: a motivation, spiritual strength, the Soviet soldier's conscious realization of his mission.

One of the legendary Soviet wartime commanders, twice Hero of the Soviet Union, General Pavel Batov, once remarked: "He who has looked death in the eye, does not lie. And therefore every word of every front-line letter is authentic." The following selection of wartime letters is typical. They render a concise, clear-cut picture of their authors:

February 12, 1943.

Mother, today I leave for the front, though I don't know for which one. We all dream of encountering the enemy as soon as possible. I feel fine. Don't worry about me, I'm a big boy, already 19. Villy (Artillery Lieutenant Villen Poliakov, killed in action in the Crimea in 1944)

■　■　■

July 20, 1941.

We learned quickly. Many had never held a weapon in their lives, never thrown a grenade, never seen a machine gun, could not imagine how you could use a bottle of liquid to put a tank on fire.

We knocked out two tanks and took three prisoners. What naïve do-gooders we were as we appealed to their sense of class solidarity during the interrogation. We thought they would suddenly see the light and cry out "Comrades!" We were well acquainted with the literature of the civil war, but knew nothing about present-day German fascists. After having filled their bellies with our food and smoked our tobacco, they stared at us with expressionless faces and insolently spit out "Heil Hitler!" Who were we trying to convert to class solidarity? These brutes who burn down homes, these rapists and sadists who play harmonicas while murdering women and children? With every new day of battle we understand more and more clearly that a fascist becomes human only when you beat the daylights out of him. (From the frontline diaries of M. I. Berezin)

■　■　■

February 19, 1942. Stalingrad.

Dear Mom, things are hard right now, but we count on help from the Urals. Bullets buzz like bumblebees; shells explode everywhere; everything is on fire, the land and the Volga. But there is no time to think about that—there are many wounded, even more dead. We hide our wounded in the sewer system and the rubble; there we care for them during the day; at night we ship them across the river to our forces. It's not easy. We crawl and slither, float across on logs, do it any which way with one goal in mind: save the wounded. Our boys have taken Mamayev Hill from the enemy several times, but he took it back yesterday. We will consolidate all our forces and, if needs be, will not spare our lives. . . . Night has come. (The last letter written by medical nurse Margarita Sergeyeva)

■ ■ ■ ■

August 22, 1942.

You know, I never loved life as much as now! You remember how I used to complain about how boring existence was?! How ridiculous that sounds today! Here in this forest, in the mud, amid the whining shells and whistling bullets, I thrive on the sunshine, the green grass, nature. How wonderful everything will be after the war.

September 19, 1942.

We fought today. Although man gets used to everything, he still remains human and cannot bear to see others suffer. A wounded tank driver was brought to me—he had had both legs blown off at the knees; every now and then he would come to and ask whether his buddies were OK, how far had his tank advanced. He never said a word about himself. (I. P. Tseshkovsky—a Leningrad school director before the war, a tank battalion commander at the front, killed in action in 1944—excerpts from letters to his wife)

■ ■ ■ ■

Should I die tortured with the pain of my wounds, my final sufferings will be allayed by my being able to reach into my pocket and take out my son's picture; I will kiss it until my lips grow cold and my heart ceases to beat. But maybe mine will be the incredible luck to live for all of you. . . . (Excerpt from letter by K. B. Yurovsky to his wife—he was lost in action in 1942)

■ ■ ■ ■

Some day we may meet. Waiting is hard and to predict the future is even harder. Especially since no one can even be sure of his own life. Today you're alive, tomorrow your head is blown off. Such words may scare you, but we have become so accustomed to death that words convey no fear at all. Tell everyone that I remember them. (Excerpt from Captain R. Z. Vladimirov's letter to his wife—he was killed in action in 1942)

■ ■ ■ ■

Victory, victory, my beloved, my darlings! Today is a great day. I waited, I believed, I carried this with me through the steel and fire storms of war. This is our day; we have paid for it with our blood, with our suffering in the freezing cold, the filth, the snow, insomnia. Now we will soon be together again. I am alive, I am returning to you. There is no limit to my happiness. (Excerpt from a letter by A. A. Yakovlev, commander of a machine-gun platoon)

These letters speak for themselves, as did the veterans of the Great Patriotic War during and after the spacebridge *Remembering War.*

The U.S. Front: An American Perspective

Over the course of World War II, more than sixteen million men and women served in the U.S. armed forces. Nearly twelve million of these men and women saw service overseas. They were deployed throughout the world; from China to Europe, Alaska to North Africa, on the Mediterranean, the Atlantic, and the Pacific, American military personnel served their country and the Allied cause. Of the 405,399 Americans who died in World War II, 291,557 were killed in battle. Another 670,846 American service people were wounded.

Statistics unify the American military experience of World War II, but, in doing so, they obscure some of the meanings of the war by ignoring the extraordinary variety of contexts in which Americans fought, endured, died, and waited out the war years. For Americans, one key distinction of World War II, which may well have impeded their ability to comprehend fully this war, was the multiplicity of experiences it occasioned. Those who fought the war from the air knew a different war from those who trudged through South Pacific jungles, uncertain when the enemy would appear or what he would look like; American soldiers stationed in England may have endured the erratic predictability of aerial bombing but had little sense of what it meant to steer a ship through mined harbors in the North Atlantic. While malaria and sunstroke weakened some soldiers, others, fighting on frontiers thousands of miles away, lost toes and fingers to frostbite. *Remembering War* participant Elliott Roosevelt saw the war from a unique vantage point as the son of the president of the United States; as an officer and pilot assigned to map terrain from Africa to the Arctic, he also saw the war from a distinctive aerial view. In contrast, Charlie Miller, another *Remembering War* participant, spent most of his war on the ground in Europe, escaping from one German prison camp after another. Three years and eight months elapsed between the Japanese assault on Pearl Harbor and the end of World War II, but for the American men and women tending the wounded in the jungles of the Phillipines, manning ships in the Pacific and Atlantic, or fighting town by town from Normandy to Berlin the war seemed endless in time and space.

Those stationed at Pearl Harbor were the first to know the shock of assault; within a few hours of the dawn Japanese attack, 2,400 Americans were dead, and 960 were missing. Those who survived were plunged into frantic attempts to aid the more than 1,200 wounded men and women and to salvage the meager remains of the ships and planes that had comprised most of the U.S. Pacific striking power.

Three days after their devastating attack on Pearl Harbor, the Japanese began their assault on the Phillipines, and here, too, Americans, fighting alongside Filipinos on the Bataan Peninsula, tasted defeat—their often heroic efforts achieving nothing. By spring of 1942, the Japanese were in control of the key urban areas of northern China, of Southeast Asia, and of the western Pacific Ocean. While Americans on the home front repaired the damaged Pacific fleet and accelerated production of new ships and planes, U.S. servicemen stationed in the Pacific had the task of holding onto the widely scattered locations that remained under Allied command. With the Japanese suffering from what they themselves later called "victory disease," a compulsive drive to conquer the entire Pacific basin, the security of the United States appeared to be threatened.

Then, on May 6 and 7, 1942, American sea and air forces unexpectedly arrested the Japanese thrust towards Australia in the Battle of the Coral Sea. It was a strange and unprecedented battle because, although it occurred entirely on the sea, only the pilots of the carrier planes from each side ever saw the enemy. Less than a month later, on June 4, 1942, the American forces experienced a clearer and more important victory over the Japanese at the tiny atoll of Midway; Japanese capture of this little island, situated one hundred miles northwest of the chain of Hawaiian Islands, would have meant Japanese penetration of Hawaiian waters.

While American sailors and soldiers fought—and waited—on Pacific islands and Pacific seas, the American military focused its main attention in the first years of the war on the Atlantic, North Africa, and ultimately, on Europe. Over the protests of many Americans, who viewed the war in Europe as either irrelevant to U.S. interests or as a struggle between the "equal" evils of fascism and communism, American leaders had concurred with other Allied leaders to focus their initial military efforts on the defeat of Germany. These leaders reasoned that, without the participation of the United States, Germany might defeat Great Britain and the Soviet Union; in that case, the United States would be alone against three quarters of the world.

Agreed on the priority of defeating Germany, Allied leaders were at odds on how to proceed in this endeavor. As we discuss further in our introduction to the section entitled "The U.S.–Soviet Alliance: An American Perspective" (Chapter 6), throughout the first six months of 1942, while the Germans continued their intense assault on the Soviet Union, President Roosevelt and British Prime Minister Winston Churchill, along with their military advisers, disputed the timing and location of the opening of a second front in Europe against the Axis. In contrast to Americans who opposed *any* U.S. involvement in the European war, there were strong voices in the United States and England calling for an immediate opening of a second front against the Germans in France. This United States support for an immediate opening of a second front in Europe increased after Soviet Ambassador Molotov came to Washington, D.C., to plead his country's case. Nonetheless, by the end of July 1942, Roosevelt and Churchill had agreed to postpone the opening of a second European front and, instead, to assault French-occupied North Africa, from which they then intended to invade Italy.

Thus, between 1941 and 1943, the United States fought many of its major battles on the Atlantic, struggling to transport men and supplies to England, North Africa, and the Soviet Union. U.S. navy convoys were escorted across the Atlantic by merchant marine ships, planes, and Allied vessels, but, in addition to the dangers and discomforts of tumultuous seas, they were under constant threat of attack by the notorious German "wolf-packs." The dangers only increased as these ships approached their destinations, since the Germans had mined the waters from north of Murmansk to Africa.

Although Atlantic crossings remained grim and frightening endeavors throughout the war years, by the summer of 1943, significantly increased protection provided by air, sea, and radar technology enabled most men and women to survive the journey. By that time, Allied troops, under the direction of General Eisenhower, had conquered North Africa, and definite plans were being made to open a second front in Europe. Once again, however, the invasion of Normandy, which many saw as key to the defeat of the Nazis, was postponed. Instead, in July 1943, a huge combined force of English and American troops made a successful night-time assault on Sicily, which by the fall of 1943 resulted in the surrender of Italy and the Allied invasion of the Italian mainland.

By the summer of 1943, the Allied leaders could speak of the beginning of the end of the war. But for many of the American soldiers and sailors in the Pacific and European theaters, the horrors of war were only becoming fully known. Ernie Pyle, America's best reporter on the battlefront experiences of ordinary soldiers, attributed the fear and vulnerability of American soldiers during the Italian campaign to the constant cacophony of the sounds of war. The sounds of the explosions of shells the Germans were shooting in Italy, Pyle noted, were of such variety that you could not gauge either distance or direction. Writing from an Allied beachhead in Italy in March 1944, Pyle bluntly told what he and the soldiers he accompanied saw, heard, and felt:

> When the German raiders come over at night, and the sky lights up bright with flares, the ack-ack guns set up a turmoil and pretty soon you hear and feel that terrible power of exploding bombs—well, your elbows get flabby and you breathe in little short jerks, and your chest feels empty, and you're too excited to do anything but hope. (*Ernie's War*, New York, 1986)

Like Pyle, those who undertook and survived the Allied invasion of Nazi-occupied France when it finally came in 1944 were marked as much by the lives they saw lost and by the battles that followed as by their military victory. For many Americans who know World War II only from news reports or movies, it is the image of American and British soldiers leaping from boats and approaching the shores of Normandy on D-Day that most vividly represents this war. Less frequently recalled is an image conveyed through one of Pyle's columns of a beach strewn for miles with the unsent letters, toothbrushes, family photos, and "bloody, abandoned shoes" of the dead.

Those who survived the heavily mined waters and the torrent of German crossfire on the beachfront still had many miles to go before their war was over. In the eleven months between the Normandy invasion and the Allied victory in Europe in May 1945, American soldiers battled their way through ancient French towns and fertile fields, dodging snipers at every step as they made their way to the hills and woods of Belgium, Luxembourg, Alsace, and Lorraine. Winter brought a last fierce fight, the Battle of the Bulge, before the Allied forces finally crossed the Rhine into Germany.

In the meantime, as Americans in Europe grew grimly familiar with skies that rained bombs and cobblestone streets dotted with pools of blackening blood, twelve thousand miles away the "other" war continued in the Pacific. Americans stationed on islands like Guam and Saipan, by now firmly under U.S. control, had nothing much worse than boredom and tropical rains to endure, but their fellow soldiers further to the south were still engaged in jungle conflict, and among those who flew the long bombing missions to Japan or heard the sounds of Japanese bombers approaching Okinawa, the loneliness and terrors of war were far from finished.

Most of those who served were young. As Studs Terkel reminds us, they were "pimply-faced kids," a great many of them nineteen, twenty, twenty-one years old. Many had never been more than a few miles away from the small towns or cities where they had grown up. Others were recent refugees from the war-torn towns of Europe. "Suddenly," Terkel notes, "the country boy met the city boy. That's Americans meeting Americans for the first time. And then comes Europe and meeting others from different cultures for the first time, an experience. They came from every stratum of our society. Everyone. So there was Bobby Rasmus, six foot three, 'Too tall for a rifleman', his mother cried out. And Bobby is up front, 'Here I am, the first one in this town that may hide German snipers. What am I doing here? The war depends on me and this moment.' But he also loved music and art. On the way east toward Bonn, Germany, his first reaction was, 'My God, Beethoven's birthplace.' Or here he is in Wherkin forest with all that carnage and horror, saying, 'I could just hear Wagnarian music being played.'"

Americans returned from the battlefields of World War II telling mostly humorous anecdotes and tales of adventures with new buddies, but as *Remembering War* participant Ed Ruff testified, for most soldiers, "there are a couple of things, I don't care who you are, but you can live to be a hundred and fifty years old and you're not going to forget them. You don't think about them, but as soon as something like the spacebridge comes along, they sort of pop back in your memory." Among the things that Ruff and other American soldiers have not forgotten are the images of the dead, as Ruff described in a post-program interview:

○ There are a lot of things you went through, and I don't say you got used to seeing dead soldiers. It was easier to walk past the dead Germans, and I don't think it's callous saying that. There was one battle one day in this town we were in, and after the battle you'd go out and start picking up the American bodies, and that shakes you up. A couple of guys I knew, you'd pick them up, and oh, you don't cry, but you feel so damn bad and think, well, is that going to be me tomorrow? And right away, that goes out of your mind, because otherwise, like a couple of kids did, you'd go totally bonkers. You sort of got calloused to all that death. But the smell, you never forget the smell. ○

Fighting on the outskirts of Moscow *(I. Shagin)*

U.S. infantry at the Makin Atoll (Reader's Digest Illustrated History)

Fighting in the northern Caucasus, 1943 *(M. Alpert)*

On the march *(News Press Agency)*

U.S. soldiers capture
Nazi gun

U.S. soldiers in New Guinea
(United Press International)

Lunch hour, the Belorussian Army Group, 1944 *(M. Alpert)*

Red Cross nurses hand magazines to soldiers on train
(The Philadelphia Enquirer)

"Fiddler on the front" *(Y. Khalip)*

Martha Raye entertaining troops in North Africa, 1943 *(Life Picture Service)*

Stalingrad as it looked after the great battle in February 1943 *(G. Zelma)*

The roads of war *(D. Balterman)*

POWs after the Death March *(Life Picture Service)*

Dead receive honorable burial at sea *(Crown Publishers)*

Dead soldier on Buna Beach *(Life Picture Service)*

Oral Histories

YEVGHENIA
ANDREYEVNA
ZHIGULENKO

1941   **1985**
(News Press Agency)   *(News Press Agency)*

She arrived in Moscow before the war and joined the Dirigible-Manufacturing Institute. This was in the spirit of the time: in those years, the names of Grizodubova and Raskova—two women pilots who had set records—were on everyone's lips. Their exploits suited Zhigulenko's character to a T. She always wanted to fly high, there where the sun shone, where everything was clean and tranquil. (so she said to us).

Yevghenia always wanted to "fix the world." Raised in the Kuban region, she saw succulent tomatoes bend their vines to the ground and break them under their weight. But the sunflowers stood there, proudly lifting their sun umbrellas to the sky. "That's not fair," decided young Zhenya, and she tried to "fix it" by crossing the tomato with the sunflower.

It is possible that many years later this desire to establish fairness in the world led her, not a young woman, to enroll in the All-Union Government Institution of Films, where she finished in 1977. In 1981, her documentary film was released. Night Witches *was about those who had troubled her dreams for more than thirty years, women like herself who had never slept at night during the war. She reminisced about these people, her wartime girlfriends, living and dead, during the spacebridge:*

> These were the girls that were in the woman's regiment. The youngest was seventeen, the commander was twenty-seven. And, you know, these girls flew every night. Sometimes, in the winter nights we had to fly ten to fifteen combat missions. And each time you flew, you thought, That's all, I'm not going to return, it's the last one, it's over. And suddenly you see: your girls are burning, and you can do nothing to help them. And so it was, for 1,100 nights.
>
> Our regiment produced twenty-three Heroes of the Soviet Union.

Right here beside me sits Larisa Litvinova. She also flew a great many combat missions.

But, you know, they flew! It was terrible, but it was necessary, because our homeland was being trampled by an enemy; mothers were crying, children were suffering. It was impossible to endure. You know, I saw one of our planes burning, saw the right wing torn off, saw the face of my friend Galka in the cabin. Her mouth was wide open—probably, in the last seconds she was calling for her mother.

It was impossible to endure.

(She cries.)
Meeting with Vladimir Pozner in the beginning of 1988, Yevghenia Andreyevna remembered her war years.

○ The war found me in Moscow, where I was studying at the Dirigible-Manufacturing Institute. I remember I came running into our plant in Tushino, and a friend met me with the words, "Oh, Zheka,* it's war!" War? What did that mean? We didn't have any idea. The first feeling of war came with the first bombing of Moscow, with the searchlights aimed in the direction of the black sky. But, anyhow, I didn't experience the war then. One day we were sent to dig trenches on the outskirts of Moscow. We were quite cheerful, playing all sorts of practical jokes. . . . Sure, it was war, but we were just kids, only seventeen, eighteen years old. Here we were digging, and suddenly someone yelled, "Hit the dirt!" I and my friend Tanya fell to the bottom of the trench. In fact, everyone ran for shelter during the strafing. The planes flew by, and I raised myself and looked around. Tanya was still lying there, and she had blood oozing from her temple. Understand, we had just been conversing, laughing, discussing this, planning that, and suddenly—she is no more. Suddenly, this human being ceased to exist! At that moment, I understood finally what war was.

When the war started, many of my female peers started writing letters to the government. We demanded to be taken into the army. Of course, they didn't take us. And then Maria Raskova, a famous pilot whom we fondly called the grandmother of Soviet aviation even though she was only twenty-three or twenty-four years old, went to Stalin about this. And, strange as it may seem, this monster told her, "You understand, future generations will not forgive us for sacrificing young girls." It was she herself who told us this, this fascinating woman. She said to Stalin, "You know, they are running away to the front all the same, they are taking things into their own hands, and it will be worse, you understand, if they steal airplanes to go."

And we had just such an incident. There were several girls who had asked to go to the front, and they were turned down. So they stole a fighter

*Zheka, Zhenya—diminutives of Eugeniya.

plane and flew off to fight. They just couldn't wait, because they knew
there in occupied territory were mothers and children; it was said they were
suffering under the yoke of a cruel enemy. It was terrible; we wanted to do
something right away. In a word, there was no holding us back. And
because of this, they formed first a group, then three aviation regiments.
True, only ours was completely female; in the other two some men served.
In the other two regiments they had real fighter planes, but our planes were
flying kites made of plywood and canvas. Our only advantage was that we
were the first to go to the front. You think they were expecting us? No way!
The air-force commander telephoned Vershinin and said, "Konstantin
Andreyevich, how are things with you there?" This was the worst year of
the war, so the question made no sense. "Why haven't you asked me for
help?" the commander went on. What help, thought Vershinin. We have no
planes; our pilots are all lying about in hospitals. But the commander
continued, "Well, since you have been most disciplined and haven't asked
for anything, we've decided to send you some reserves." Here there was a
pause, and the commander blurted out, "It's a woman's aviation regiment."
And he slammed down the receiver to cut off further conversation. Vershinin raised his eyes to the ceiling and groaned, "Oh God, what are you
punishing me for? This is all I need!" He told us about this later himself.

We flew to the front, settled in, but nobody came; nobody received us.
Vershinin came only after a week. Well, we all lined up at attention on the
airfield. We had our hair cut like boys. Imagine, these were girls of seventeen, eighteen, nineteen years of age. They had boy's haircuts, but not like
today; our forelocks were two fingers long, and the rest was shorn off. Well,
here we stood. I stood at the furthermost right of the formation because I
was the tallest. Everyone stretched, stood on tip-toe, puffed out their
chests. We were a funny sight. Well, what can I say—we were kids. We
strapped on our map cases and all the equipment we had. Vershinin walked
along the formations, looked us over, and then, without even saying hello,
turned on his heel and left. But six months later, when we received our first
decorations and Vershinin personally awarded them, he said "I was wrong,
I repent." And we answered, "We did some wrong, too, but we're not
repenting."

If I were to describe everything in two words, it would be these: utter
hell. We could bomb only at night. We flew at an altitude of a thousand
meters at a speed of one hundred kilometers an hour. It was impossible to
fly at such a speed and altitude during the daylight because we were sitting
ducks for German AA fire. Our planes were made out of plywood. Often
the Germans would fire a combination of explosive, percussive and incendiary rounds at Soviet planes. But they fired only percussive rounds at us,
because our planes would catch on fire just from their shock waves. We
bombed crossings, . . . and before an attack, we worked on the front battle
lines.

There was a lot of tragedy and a lot of comedy. Each time we took off on a bombing mission, we didn't know whether we would return or not. When you were over the target, there were so many AA guns and searchlights . . . and when you returned, you checked yourself: is the head still there? Are the arms and legs whole? And then everybody starts unwinding. Honestly, after a difficult mission your teeth chattered, your knees shook, and most of all you wanted just to go to sleep. When it was summer you fell to the ground and breathed deeply, with all your lungs, as if surrendering your entire body to Mother Earth.

The first planes we had were called U-2s, and later P-2s. The bombs hung underneath the wings. They attached a bomb carriage there and led a line which the navigator pulled to the cabin. Everyone sought to get a navigator that weighed as little as possible. The less the navigator weighed, the more bombs you could bring along. The thinnest navigators wrapped themselves with tens of kilograms of extra bombs, which they threw themselves by hand. These were percussion action bombs. For them to explode, they had to hit the dirt or sand and press an explosive mechanism. Thus, in the aircraft these bombs didn't present any danger. Of course, it wasn't mechanized bombing, but when we bombed the front lines, there were three rows of trenches, a very large area that was easy to hit. On the whole, we caused a lot of damage.

The Germans called us "night witches." You have to understand the German mentality: if there is no offensive going on, you are supposed to sleep at night; this is *Ordnung,* order, something sacred for the Germans. But we Russians didn't follow the rules. And suddenly in the middle of the night, we would disrupt their sleep with the sound of our propellers: trak-tak-tak, and then bombs would erupt. We flew at intervals of three to five minutes, so someone was always over the target dropping bombs. The Germans went straight out of their minds. It got to the point where the German command announced that whoever shot down one of those miserable U-2s would receive the Iron Cross. They were terribly afraid of us. They dropped leaflets where we were based. The leaflets said that we were from Siberia, from prison camps, that we had been sent here to expiate our guilt, that by day we sat locked in sheds and by night we were chained to the airplanes that we flew. Yes, that's how much they were afraid of us, of these delicate, tender girls who were seventeen, eighteen years old. One third of them didn't live to see twenty. You know, sometimes on dark winter nights we had to fly ten to fifteen combat missions. After the fifth or sixth flight, especially if it was a difficult target, many of us on the return trip simply fell asleep from exhaustion. I remember that this happened to me not just once. I would fall asleep, but the navigator would give me a shove: "Zheka, Zheka, the plane's going into a spin!" For this reason, we always tried to train our navigators so that, in case we needed it, they could fly the plane instead of us and give us ten to fifteen minutes to sleep.

We couldn't be seen at night; we flew without lights. But to make up for it, we could be heard. The Germans had sound locaters that could determine by intersection the location of any object moving no less than 150 kilometers an hour. On moonlight nights, fighter planes shot us down. We were absolutely helpless before them. True, we had machine guns, but we couldn't shoot to the rear for fear of hitting our own tail fin, and we couldn't shoot to the side because of all the wing material. Our angle of fire was only thirty degrees. Of course, against a fighter plane this was nothing. The machine gun was only good for strafing an enemy column from the air.

The Germans had had so much of us that in the end they decided to get rid of us once and for all. In the day, they couldn't find us, because we dragged our planes into fields and covered them with branches and straw. They couldn't understand it. They were shooting us down, and we still kept flying. But all the same, they resolved to destroy us.

I remember the night. We had to bomb a German airfield. The target was well known; there were a lot of searchlights and a lot of AA guns. In a word, it was business as usual. I was flying ninth or tenth in line. I approached the airfield and saw Zhenya Krutova go in for her bombing run. Then she got caught in the searchlight, but the AA guns didn't fire. I shouted to the navigator, "Let's go to work! The Germans have used up their ammo." Such a thing had never happened before. But suddenly Zhenya's plane caught fire and plunged to the ground. The next plane entered the zone, and once more the searchlights caught it, but again there was no AA fire. But then a red dot appeared, and suddenly the plane blazed up and started to fall, leaving a huge trail of fire. It crashed into the ground, erupted into a fiery mushroom, and went out. While I looked upon this in horror, realizing that there was nothing I could do to help, the next plane entered this sea of light, and only then did I realize that the enemy had adopted a new tactic. They were catching us with the searchlights, and they had one fighter plane up there. Once our plane was pinned by the searchlights, it approached, circled its prey, buzzed it a couple of times as if gloating, drove our girls out of their minds, and then it fired at point-blank range. I remember how the girl before me, Galka, started burning.

I managed to escape, I threw the plane to the right, went into a dive, and approached the enemy from the opposite side, from where he least expected me. Besides that, I gave it some gas and took a low-level flight, about three hundred meters. Bombing at this altitude was risky but possible. The fighter plane couldn't come lower than one thousand meters. I released my bombs and left. But in fifteen minutes, eight of our planes perished.

People often ask, "Why didn't you use parachutes?" What can I tell them? We didn't like parachutes. I am tall, and when I sat in the plane, I stuck way out. If there were yet a parachute underneath me, my head would have been up against the wings. Besides, we were young and foolish and threw the parachutes out. But anyway, the main thing was that a parachute really hindered a pilot's ability to maneuver. If I had flown with a parachute, I would have felt unable to control the plane, especially when I hit the cross section of searchlights and AA fire and had to dodge and weave. But anyway, those with parachutes were dying too. . . .

I've already told you, that it was both tragic and comic—everything was mixed up. First we had cut our hair like boys, but then we let it grow long. It wasn't authorized, but what were you going to do with pilots? They looked death in the eye every day, so nobody could touch them. I used paper curlers for my long blonde hair, and besides that, I used mascara, because I was terribly embarrassed about my unusually auburn eyelashes. One of our more serious girls once said to me, "You should be ashamed of yourself! A war is going on and you are curling your hair and wearing makeup!" But another girl replied, "Don't you understand? I am fighting so that the war will end more quickly, so the sooner I can find my love. Try to imagine this scene: I am flying, flying. I've released my bombs, and I'm returning. I'm already over our own territory when suddenly bullets—tiny, tiny—hit the engine. It sputters and dies, and I land—right on the front line. I land, and from every direction guys run up, from every side, and I take off my helmet, and my hair cascades to my shoulders, and they all fall desperately in love with me. But I see a Georgian boy with a mustache standing there, and suddenly he says, 'Oh, my beloved.'" Here we interrupted her and asked, "But Tanya, why a Georgian?" "Because," she said, "They are very forceful, and I want him to kidnap me." It was beautiful.

Or another incident. We were in Belorussia. We had gone to bed and awoke the next morning to the sound of gales of laughter. It turned out that mosquitoes had bitten us in the night; our faces had ballooned. It was a nightmare! No way, we said, we don't give up that easily! And what do you think happened? We took our gas masks, cut out all the inner contents until only the mask was left, and slept in those. When our commander saw us, she was horrified. "Listen here, what is this?" And we answered, "Sorry . . . but our beauty is more important to us than anything in the world."

As I've said before, our regiment was entirely female. Our commissar was an old bag with a heart of stone. Apparently, she decided that any kind of contact with boys was the equivalent of desertion, and because of this, boys didn't approach us much. But we didn't really care . . . much. It seems that during that time a sublimation occurred, that sexual feelings took second place to something of much greater importance. In other words, we managed to forget that boys even existed.

At this time another division appeared not far away, an all-male outfit. They flew real fighters! We nicknamed them the "Brer Rabbits." Well, the guys were crazy about us. They spread legends about our beauty. They dropped bouquets of flowers on us from the air. Finally, they figured out a way to see us. They would fly back from a mission and ask permission to land at our airfield. When asked for an explanation, they would say, "Comrade commander, we ran out of fuel." Of course, we were all delighted to see them—we had forgotten what guys looked like after all these years. Our commander would order, "Refuel!" So, we refueled their plane. But the next day, somebody had to refuel another one of their planes, and it was this way almost every evening. Finally, our commander said to herself, "Something here is not right." So when another plane came to land and its pilot said he had run out of fuel, she climbed onto his plane, opened the fuel tank, took a stick, inserted it into the tank, and pulled it out—the entire stick was wet, meaning the fuel tank was full. "So that's what's going on!" said our commander. "The next time anyone lands here without fuel, we'll send him off and confiscate his plane." And she did just that the next time. And no matter how much the commander of that regiment swore and cursed, she did not return the plane.

I was such a hot little number, you wouldn't believe it. Marina Raskova took one look at me and said, "Don't send this one into the air; keep her grounded." So at first, I was the squadron's communications leader and later a navigator. I flew, of course, but rarely. But then, when Raskova crashed, I got to fly in the pilot's seat. At first I had fewer flights than everyone else, because I started flying later, but then I outflew everyone. I've been asked, how did you manage to outfly everyone else? It was, believe it or not, because I had long legs. You don't understand? I will tell you. Whenever the PA system called a flight, everyone ran for their planes. Whoever got to her plane first was the first to take off. The flights lasted an hour or two. We'd get back, load up, and run again. I flew twice as many flights as the rest, because my legs were longer, and I could run faster than all the others.

In our regiment, twenty-three people received the title Hero of the Soviet Union. That is a very high percentage. I want to tell you that we had absolutely extraordinary people. All of our girls generally had come from universities. You understand, they called up the boys for service, but we volunteered. We knew with our hearts that we were ready to give up our lives for victory. I remember after one flight one of our girls got out of the cockpit, laid down under the tail of the plane, and went to sleep for five minutes. And suddenly there was a heart-rendering cry. It turned out that in the darkness an ambulance had run over her legs. They laid her on a stretcher and she told me, "Zhenya, give me your word that when I return I'll fly again. Otherwise, I'll die." I said, "Oh God, of course you'll fly!" She was taken to the hospital.

Eight months went by. She had a broken back, had to wear a corset, but she returned to us anyway and reported to the commander. "I'm ready to fly." The commander's eyes widened. Then she said, "Galka, do you want to be my assistant, here, on the ground, so the doctors don't object?" But she refused. And she actually flew again.

We were not crucial to winning the war. They could have gotten by without us. They couldn't have gotten by without the nurses and the switchboard operators. I only later understood why I joined the air force. I apparently thought then, I must get there quickly, quickly, in order to finish everything all the more quickly. And only several years later, when my son was born, did I understand certain things. You see, for a man the important things are courage, heroism, being tough. But a woman is motivated by the feeling of motherhood. I am sure of this. Nature made woman this way. The desire to save one's future children was what apparently moved me and all the women who left the universities to serve in aviation. ○

LAURETTA
BEATY
FOY

1944   **1985**

*Raised in Great Falls, Montana, Lauretta Beaty Foy later moved with her family
to Los Angeles, California. The Great Depression of 1929 affected most American
families, Lauretta's included. After giving up a music career for a marriage that
lasted only three years, Lauretta supported her two sons and parents by working as
a Busby Berkeley dancer for Warner Brothers' studios in Hollywood. She learned
to fly on weekends, while continuing to work at the studios, and eventually
obtained her private, commercial, and instructor's licenses. She left the studios in
1939 when she got a job flying for Piper Aircraft Corporation. As described in this
volume's Introduction, this job ended abruptly on December 7, 1941. In great
demand as the need for trained pilots skyrocketed, Lauretta worked with a CPT
program as flight instructor in California, before signing on with the Women's Air
Force Service Pilots (WASP) in 1943.*

*During the live spacebridge, Lauretta summarized her experience while a
member of the WASP:*

> I was in the WASP—we were all volunteers. We were there because we
> wanted to be. We expected just to be ferrying trainers and light planes
> from factories to points of embarkation, training schools, and so forth. In
> just a few weeks, after going through cadet training, we were flying co-
> pilot on cargo, then on bombers, then first pilot. Then we went to fight-
> ers. We were given advanced instrument training; we went through pur-
> suit school, and finally my squadron was checked out on everything that
> the army had.
>
> The factories were turning out airplanes very fast, and we had very
> few pilots, so we felt that we were able to free some of our men pilots to go
> into combat. We were not allowed to go into combat. We were not mili-
> tarized during the war. In 1979, we were finally recognized by Congress
> as having been in the military.
>
> I was based in Long Beach, California—the Sixth Ferrying Group. I
> would pick up a P-51 at the North American factory, take it across the
> United States to Newark, New Jersey, where it was picked up and put on

boats to England. Then, a Red Cross bus would take me to La Guardia airport [in New York], and I would go by airline up to Niagara Falls, New York, and pick up a P-39 or P-63 for the Russians. From there, I would fly one of these ships across the United States on the northern route, sometimes going into Canada, and take the aircraft to Great Falls, Montana, where the Russian pilots picked them up, went up across Alaska, across Siberia. We thought it was cold going from Niagara Falls to Great Falls, but I used to look at those Russian pilots and think, Oh, they've got a long, cold trip ahead. It was a long, long way, and we really appreciated what they were doing.

In a subsequent interview, Lauretta discussed in more detail one event prior to her experience in the WASP which illustrated her struggle as a woman pilot in a "man's war":

○ Usually, the CAA [Civil Aeronautics Authority—now the Federal Aviation Agency] instructor's rating test would take about an hour and a half. You'd go through all the maneuvers and all the emergencies, then you'd pretend that the inspector was a student, and you'd talk him through some lessons. He gave me about five or six emergencies in just really difficult places, but I handled it all right. Finally, I said to him, "We're about to run out of gas," and he said, "Okay, we'll go back." So we went back and filled up and went out again! He had me do spins about ten different times, and he had me go over and over everything—he was just nasty. Finally, he gave me my instructor's rating, but he didn't want to. "I don't think women should be instructing at all," he informed [the director of this particular program], "but she's done everything, so I'll have to give her the rating." ○

While working for Piper in Pennsylvania, Lauretta received a telegram that read, in part, AIR TRANSPORT COMMAND IS ESTABLISHING GROUP OF WOMEN PILOTS FOR DOMESTIC FERRYING STOP NECESSARY QUALIFICATIONS ARE COMMERCIAL LICENSE FIVE HUNDRED HOURS TWO HUNDRED HORSEPOWER RATING STOP ADVISE IF YOU ARE IMMEDIATELY AVAILABLE. *The telegram was signed by Nancy Love. This was the opportunity many women had been waiting for:*

○ Nancy [Love] wound up with twenty-five girls with whom she was going to start the WAFS, the Women's Auxiliary Ferrying Squadron. So I talked to her. She was a real nice person, and I signed up. I took a test in a PT-19, which was an army primary trainer. I thought, this is great, because I'll be ferrying, and I can get home to see my kids more often. That was the only thing I didn't like about Lockhaven [Pennsylvania]. It was a great experience back there, but I couldn't see my kids. ○

Lauretta, returning to California, ready to begin working with Love in October,
was confronted with the news that she must first attend a training program to be
held in Sweetwater, Texas. Concerned that she could not afford to be unemployed
that long (she was still supporting seven people back home), she called Jacqueline
Cochran, who was setting up a new training program for women in Texas.
Cochran promised her that she and three other women who already had instruc-
tor's licenses would only have to train for two weeks.

When Lauretta reported to the base in Sweetwater, she was confronted with
two more surprises. For starters, the entirely male base was not expecting a class of
women. Lauretta and the other women were summarily kicked off base. Cochran
didn't show up for ten days, during which time the women stayed in town, sharing
rooms to save money. When she did arrive, Cochran, who had managed to acquire
a great deal of clout by this time, not only succeeded in having the commanding
officer transferred but also ultimately rid the entire base of men. The second
surprise came when all the women had been assigned barracks.

○ The four of us [instructors] were left and we went up to her. I said,
"You've got four instructors here; what are you going to do with us?" And
she said, "Well, I don't have enough of you to have that special class for
instructors, so you'll have to go through the regular training." Here I was,
supporting my family at home, and so I said, "I can't stay for that. I can't
afford to do this." [Foy was working for $70 per month.] Cochran said,
"You have signed up for this, and you are not going to fly anywhere else in
the United States if you leave here."

I was furious. I thought, she can't do that to me. How can she keep me
from working in aviation? So I called up some of my friends in the CAA in
Los Angeles, and I told them the story. There was a long pause on the
other end of the line, and my friend said, "Well, the feeling here is that you
better go ahead and do it. Lauretta, I know it sounds strange, but she's
doing all kinds of things that nobody thought she could do. She might get
you involved in court action or something that could go on for years. If I
were you, I'd just stick it out there."

It was awfully tough to take, but once I made up my mind to stay, I
thought, I'm going to be as positive as I can about it.

[The men at the base] were just absolutely against us. The physical
education director said, "well, if we can't get rid of you any other way, we're
going to kill you off with exercises. If you don't do every exercise that I give
you, I'll turn your name in, and you'll get kicked out." And they did try to
kill us off with these awful exercises. We had to march, and it was winter
time, and it was cold; it was bitter cold, and the wind was blowing all the
time.

It was a miserable climate. The barracks were freezing cold—nobody
ever got warm in the winter time—and then, all of a sudden, it was so hot

we couldn't get enough air going through there. We couldn't open the doors because there were snakes outside.

We had about ten minutes between mess and ground school at night. There was another woman there with children at home. We'd go out in back of the hangar and cry. She was talking about her little girls, and I'd talk about my little boys. And we didn't know if we could stand it on account of that. We were both doing all right in the flying and everything, but it was just so lonesome. Then we'd remember pictures of those Russian women and their children in the cold, their homes bombed, no place to go. And we'd decide we could stand it if we could help to stop Hitler.

There were moments when we had a lot of fun, after we'd been there three or four months and after they got rid of all the men. They were scared to death that the men were going to get with the women, and that's why they had guards on us everywhere we went. But after they got rid of all the men cadets, they let us go into the recreation hall, and there was a piano there. We used to play and sing and make up songs and put on silly shows. We had a lot of laughs, but the first two or three months were so grim because they treated us like we were prisoners.

We had seven people in a bay; we had a narrow cot and a locker to keep everything in. Of course, all we had was a flight suit and a pair of pants and a shirt. We couldn't get off the base for several months. Eventually, they let us go into town once in awhile on the weekends. But to be cooped up, trying to study, freezing in the winter, and then all of a sudden, the day that we got out of primary and had been flying in the snow and rain and everything—and this happens in West Texas—it had been freezing cold, and then overnight, it's eighty degrees, and from then on, it's from 80 to 105 every day, and we're in these enclosed airplanes, and they got so hot in the sun that you couldn't touch them with your hand.

It was a miserable climate to be in and a bad situation all the way around. The food got better after a couple of months; the girls complained about the food so much that finally Cochran got a woman cook in there, and they got more help. She made a lot of improvements, and I tried not to be resentful of her, and then I realized that I was going to learn a lot, but it was a very rough experience for me because I felt like I had been tricked into it. I knew it wasn't Nancy Love's fault, because she didn't know that all this stuff with Cochran was going to happen, but I thought, how did I ever get into this mess?

After I got based out of Long Beach, it was much, much different, although we were not wanted there either. I never, never got home on weekends, and all those things I had dreamed about. I worked for two years without a day off, but I managed to sneak home every now and then when the weather would be too bad to fly. By that time, we had learned how to trade things for gas stamps, so that I could get more gas and things like that. ◯

Because most ships went to the East Coast, Lauretta crossed the country many times in a variety of aircraft, under a variety of conditions. Being a woman in what is considered a man's sky didn't help matters:

◯ In a fighter plane, we didn't have any place for any luggage. The only thing you could do, in a P-51, for example, was to open the ammunition box on the wing and stick a pair of socks and one shirt rolled up in the ammunition box. But that was it; we couldn't carry any luggage at all. We always wore pants because we had to climb up into most of those ships.

Many bases we'd land at wouldn't have any facilities for women. And, of course, there were a lot of hotels, especially in the South, where they didn't want women wearing pants—a lot of places. We wore anything we could find before we had our uniforms—mostly white shirts. We'd wash the collar at night in the hotel room and stick it between the mattress and the inner spring, and then the collar would look nice. The rest of the shirt would stink. We did all sorts of things like that because we couldn't carry luggage. We got to looking pretty raunchy sometimes, and there really wasn't much you could do about it. We had a shoulder bag that we could put just a little bit of makeup in. Of course, we usually kept tan enough that we didn't use much makeup anyway.

Our winter flying suits consisted of sheepskin-lined pants, boots, jackets, and caps, and they didn't have any women's sizes. They looked awful, and they were very cumbersome. I could hardly walk with the boots on. But they were warm. And most of the heaters never worked in the airplanes. I look at those pictures of those Russian women flying in open cockpits, and I wonder how they even survived!

We had to be off the ground by an hour after official sunrise, and if we were staying in a city some distance from the air base, a lot of times that meant we had to get up at two-thirty in the morning. We spent an hour pre-flighting the ship, going over everything on the ground and checking a weather report and then filing a flight plan. Sometimes we wouldn't get in to go to bed until ten o'clock at night. Many nights, I had two to four hours of sleep, but you get used to that. If there's a war on, you can do all kinds of things you couldn't do otherwise. I'm sure a lot of people who worked in factories will tell you that, too.

Young people now can't realize how the whole country felt. There was this patriotism that you would call ridiculous now. But it looked like Hitler was going to conquer the world, and all of a sudden, everybody wanted to do anything they could to stop this man and his army; you would just go out and do whatever you could for the war effort. ◯

1943
(News Press Agency)

1988
(News Press Agency)

GRIGORY
YAKOVLEVICH
BAKLANOV

Grigory Baklanov, a well-known writer and editor in chief of the magazine Znamya, *was not quite eighteen years old when the war began. At that time, he was a metal craftsman in an aviation factory in Voronezh. Because it was a defence factory, he was exempted from military service. But he joined, like many did then, and went to the front as a volunteer. He fought in the northwest on the 3rd Ukrainian Front and participated in the battles for the liberation of Bulgaria and Hungary. He finished the war in Austria as the commander of an artillery reconnaissance battalion. During the spacebridge he said:*

> I was an artillery man and saw the whole war from the battlefield. The whole war. I went to the front at seventeen. Each day of the war took away from us more than fourteen thousand of our lives, not counting civilian casualties.
>
> Forty years have gone by. The more you think about that time, the more you are certain that the war could have been averted. This is, of course, a very important conclusion.
>
> I have visited America four times. There are no more similar peoples than our people and the people of America. Today we can reach peace only together.

In his next interview Grigory Baklanov spoke about his war years:

○ I abhor reminiscing about the war. I have grown children, a son and a daughter, and I have almost never talked to them about the war. My growing grandson, who is in the second grade, once asked me, "Is the face of the enemy horrible?" I laughed. If the enemy's face were terrible, it would be easy to recognize him. But there are enemies with charming faces.

I have indeed written about the war, and everything I want to say about it is in my books. Even though, above all, I would rather have forgotten about it. However, here's what has always been interesting to me. When death and destruction can strike us at any minute, life acquires a special dimension. It's in everything: in the light of the sun, in the taste of bread, in the smell of the grass—all of this becomes extraordinarily powerful. The staggering love affairs of the front! I was too young to experience any. But I saw these tragedies; when *he* perished, *she* was left behind. Entire lives were compressed in short bursts of time. I fought as a soldier and then as an officer of a fire direction platoon of an artillery battery. Now, the fire direction platoon, and especially the commander of the platoon, is found, as a rule, with the infantry. . . . He corrects the artillery fire, and this means his place is ahead of the battery. Here you are approaching the most dangerous line, the forward edge of battle. And it's a strange thing. The more dangerous it is, the freer you feel. As they said then, the soul's stature increases. This feeling of the people walking tall, deciding the fate of their country, and, as we thought, of the world, and in some ways that was true, was the feeling of those years.

Youth is a staggering time—as perhaps is childhood. But childhood and youth pass. And no matter how poorly you may have lived, no matter how hard the conditions of life have been, somehow you always remember the good, apparently because of the huge charge of optimism which exists in youth and childhood. Perhaps that's due to not really understanding everything then. Probably those who suffered the greatest psychological shock were those who experienced the front in 1941 and 1942—people like my brother, a student at the Department of History, who left for the front voluntarily even though he had thrombophlebitis and could barely see out of one eye. Nonetheless, he joined the People's Army volunteers and went to the front as a heavy-gun commander. He perished near Moscow. I think that they suffered through the worst psychological stress, seeing how different reality was from what they had been led to believe.

I began fighting in the first months of 1942. Conditions were at their worst. There was, for example, a night when we were surrounded, and we were not sure we would get out. But even then, facing death, I remember myself, remember the people who fought together, and I don't remember anyone who didn't believe that we were going to win. We all knew we might be killed. But no matter how bad conditions became, nobody doubted victory. Of course, there were people who voluntarily surrendered to captivity; there were traitors. Every country has its share of them. But I remember that neither I nor anyone of those whom I knew thought for a minute that we might lose.

At the worst time, when the Germans were approaching Stalingrad, I joined the party. Communists were not taken into captivity; they were killed. But I didn't conceive of another life for myself. Nor did I really think I might die—as I said, youth is a most astonishing time of life, when we think we are immortal. . . .

When I saw the first German POWs at the start of the war, I experienced true wonder, because we had been brought up with the naive notion that no fellow-worker, no proletarian, would ever fight against us. Yet their tank units, on the whole, were composed of German factory workers. At that time on the Northwest Front, I was nearly killed because of my curiosity and desire to understand, to understand who were these Germans fighting against us, because it in no way correlated with the pre-war notions—including the time when I met Germans at the factory in Voronezh where I was working. Anyway, here's what happened. We were in a marsh on a reconnaissance foray, and we ambushed a bunch of Germans. There was a bright moon, so they were an easy target. So they fell down in the bushes, in the water. And I, a young kid eighteen years old, out of stupidity decided I had to see what kind of faces they had. Who were these people? Because they couldn't be the same German workers I had known. And I just missed being killed, because one of them fired at me. . . . He tried to kill me before dying. By then we were familiar with the terrible horrors; we listened to people's stories that chilled the soul; already by then the very word "German" evoked hatred. After the war, after much time, I was able to understand, first in my mind, then with my heart, that fascism was a tragedy not only for the Germans but for all of humanity. One people had suffered through this tragedy, and now they were carrying this terrible disaster to another people. I came to realize it was not a purely German phenomenon, it wasn't just a national feature. It was a tragedy that could happen to all mankind.

There are people who, after the war, lived quite ordinary, commonplace lives. And for them, that time when they performed heroic feats or, as it seemed to them, made history, for them, of course, that time became their finest hour. Many others have gone on in life, achieved success, and so theirs is a more forward-looking view of things. But even I, a successful writer, *must say* that if there was ever something significant that I achieved, it was namely then, when I helped determine the fate of our homeland. That has remained a proud feeling in me. More than anything, it was with this knowledge that my son and even my grandson grew up. Grandpa fought in the war! Not because Grandpa killed anyone, no but because Grandpa fought in the war when it was to be decided whether or not our land and nation were going to exist. Of course, this feeling never disappears; one cannot escape it.

Since the end of that war, many decades have elapsed, and our country has gone through many ordeals. Nevertheless, our nation to a great degree has lived with the legacies left by those people who did not come back from that war, who perished. They left a legacy, a colossal moral force. To not understand them, not think about them, not feel that you are alive because they died for you, would not just be immoral, it would be impossible. Every family suffered, lost someone. In our family, eight people went to the front, and only four returned. How can I forget? ○

1945,   **1986**
with Kay Miller

*Born and raised in Brixton, New Jersey, Charlie Miller entered the army air force
in the summer of 1942. Nine days after his marriage, he was sent overseas to a
base in England. Most of his first years in the service was spent flying decoy
missions over southern France. In May 1943, after his first three days of bombing
missions, his plane was attacked over the town of Wilhelmshaven, Germany, and
was unable to make it back to England. After almost thirty-six hours floating on
rafts in the North Sea, Miller and his crew were picked up by a German patrol
boat. They became prisoners of war, and remained such until their liberation in
May 1945 by Soviet troops. During the live spacebridge of May 1985, Charlie
Miller recalled his encounters with the Soviets during the war.*

I'm the past national commander of American ex-prisoners of war. I
noticed today, from the people speaking up here, a few tears—and rightfully so. At the time of our liberation, we had nothing to eat. Just prior to
the Russians coming into our camp—for three or four days—we heard
gunfire, and naturally all Americans were yelling, "C'mon, Uncle Joe!"
Well, finally Uncle Joe made it. The soldiers came in; they had very few
rations, but they did share it with us, what rations they did have. They
took care of our medical needs that our own camp doctors couldn't
supply, due to the Germans not giving them the proper medication. Another thing I wish to add is . . . seven times I escaped in Germany. Well, I
know that's not saying much for my intelligence because I was captured
seven . . . times, but of all my adventures throughout Romania, Hungary,
and places like that, I was very fortunate with a friend of mine to come
across the Russian forced labor. Now, we hear about the prisoners of war,
how they were treated in Europe, but believe me, no one took a beating
like those Russians. [crying] I can't apologize for my tears. Maybe if there
were more of them, like we saw here today, we wouldn't be having the
summits and so forth.

*In a subsequent interview, Miller shared a more detailed account of his life as a
POW:*

○ That camp [Stalag 7A, 50 miles from Munich] was like a country club. At first, we'd get Red Cross parcels once a week, but that didn't happen too often after Germany started getting bombed more frequently. For a couple of cigarettes, you could bribe a German guard. Sometimes he'd bring an egg or two eggs or a loaf of bread. Or for a cigarette or two, you could bribe him to open the gate, and you could walk out to the French compound, where they kept the Frenchmen, who were also forced labor. One of our favorites from the French was biscuits, just like dog biscuits—hard as a rock. So we'd give them some Nescafe in a 4 oz. can for an egg, or the main thing was biscuits. And we used to get powdered milk from the Red Cross, so we'd soak those biscuits in the powdered milk.

We were never forced to work. But the French, the Russians . . . . Across from us was the Russian compound. In the morning they would take the Russians out, to make them work. [Since] practically anything they did was helping the war effort for Germany, a lot of them would refuse. . . . I think they actually shot five or ten Russians—they refused to go to work. They were starving. That was my first experience with the Russians.

Some nights, you'd get locked in your barracks, and just for the hell of it, a couple of German guards would come up and take the police dogs and let them in. The first guy that would spot them would holler, "Dogs!" and we had three-tier bunks, so the guys on the bottom two would all jump up on the first bunk. And the Germans, you could hear them out there laughing. One time they did it with the Russians. And the dogs didn't come out. The next day, the Germans went in, and they found two harnesses. The Russians had actually eaten those two police dogs! I don't know whatever happened to them [the Russians]; they were probably shot.

There was a dirt road between our compound and the Russians'. We'd take bread and blood sausage, and when the Russians would come to go to work or when they would come home at night, we'd throw it out into the group, but they started tearing one another up—you couldn't believe— trying to get at it. So instead, what we did most of the time was throw it across this little road into their compound when they were out walking. Then they'd still fight but it wouldn't be as compact an area.

In October of 1943, the Americans were moved to Stalag 17B, located near Krems-Gneixendorf. As the Allies tightened the noose around Germany, the prisoners were moved again and again. ○

As Miller mentioned during the live event, he escaped the camps seven times but was always recaptured. His first attempted escape was made after only a month in Stalag 7A:

○ I became friends with a Turkish Indian by the name of Ed Seeborne. He and I decided to escape. At that particular camp, to get out there were two barbed wire fences. I don't know how high they were—eight, ten feet—and maybe about six feet apart, but in between were huge rolls of barbed wire. You've seen it in the movies. Well, we went over the fence and dropped down in this damned barbed wire, and it took us forever—it was also raining—but we finally worked our way over to the other fence and went over that. Mind you, there were guards with lights flashing back and forth, and guard dogs walking and so forth, but being young, and you know, we made it.

We were recaptured approximately thirty hours later. We were walking and went into a little village. All at once someone hollered. It was a cop, an older guy. He had his gun on us, his bicycle in one hand. We walked right up to him and never saw him walking there in the road. He took us to a police station, and from there we were taken by a truck back to Musberg— it wasn't far. There the cops took us into a bar, a typical little neighborhood bar, sitting around drinking beer, you know. That's how we came to talk to this one-eyed bartender.

We were sitting in the corner with these cops around, and this guy came over and was talking to us in English. He told us he just lost an eye. We were thinking, Oh Christ, he's going to poison us. But he was a really neat guy. He brought us some bread. Everything was pretty good until a lady came in. Evidently, she had heard about us. She came in the front door and started to scream. The cop went over and talked to her, but by now everyone else was getting upset. Maybe she had just lost someone in the war, or her house was bombed, or whatever. Anyway, she was hollering, and she got them pretty well upset. Before, they were just sitting around minding their own business. They'd look at us, but . . . . Later they came with a truck and took us a couple of miles back to the camp. That was the first experience. ○

During a subsequent escape that lasted over two months, Miller and his friend learned to look for the Russian forced labor:

○ They [the Russians] would give us little bottles of wine, bread, or whatever they had. They were better fed [than the Russians at our first camp] because they were smaller groups and probably more friendly with the farmers around there. So, when we were walking down the railroads, those were the people we would look for. And one night, they even took us into their camp. I thought, Christ. You know, you're speaking pidgin English. But we got a good night's sleep. The next day, they got us up, and when they went out, we just got in the mob, right with them, and walked right on out through the gate, back to where we found them. One guy had a map he gave us, and they gave us more food to take with us. Wherever we went, we learned to really try to find these Russians, even if it meant getting a little close to a town where we should not be. They never turned us in. They'd probably get a loaf of bread by turning us in. ○

Charlie Miller and his friend were recaptured, again, just before Christmas of 1943:

○ I'll tell you how the German mind works. We were recaptured, and it was either the 23rd or the 24th we arrived back to that camp. Christmas morning they came—we were in solitary—and a guard let us out and took us back to our compound. We spent Christmas with friends; we ate whatever they had to eat, and then they came to take us back and lock us up. You wonder what happens. The next minute they're beating you on the head. ○

During the spring and summer of 1944, the Germans started moving prisoners from camp to camp as Soviet troops advanced from the east. Miller and his fellow prisoners endured a harrowing trip inside a coal barge on the Baltic Sea, followed by an exhausting forced march away from the Soviet lines toward the American lines. The Germans, aware that they might have to surrender their prisoners, preferred to surrender them to Americans:

○ There were 1,200 of us with all our belongings in the hull of the boat. That thing was so crowded that guys were sitting up against the back, against the wall, and other guys were lined up between their legs. It was pretty bad. That trip took two days and nights. Some of the guys volunteered to go up to lower water and stuff down. We didn't know until we got to the dock and all the guys working up top were laughing that the water bucket was the same bucket that they lowered for latrine. Our guys were kidding us. They said, we took care of it. It had a long rope on it. We threw it overboard and let it wash out first, but what the hell it was washing out with sea water and crud and everything else.

We got back, and that's where they handcuffed us. We had to run the rest of the way. It was about four miles to camp. Two guys were handcuffed together. So whatever you had, you either carried it or lost it. They told us, if you drop out, if the guy you're handcuffed to can't carry it, you're both going to be shot.

This guy, Rufus, was a riot, I'm telling you. It's guys like him that kept people going, you know. We were handcuffed together, and we'd been friends for a long time. I said, "Rufe, I can't make it." "What?" I said, "I can't make it. I'm going to fall down. I can't make it." And here we are, handcuffed, and this guy, he turned to me and said, "Jesus Christ, you sonofabitch, you get me shot and I'll kill ya!"

So he reached around and was trying to scoop me up, and I started to laugh. Oh man, he ripped me out! "I should have let you go!" and all that. I remember one English guy who had sixty-five bayonet cuts on him. Some guys ran alone—they ran out of handcuffs. But American ingenuity, some of those guys got the handcuffs off before they got to camp. Somehow or another, they finagled, you know.

We were put in this camp; everybody just flopped. Like a parade gone out. Everybody was pretty disgusted, you know. Getting beat with rifles and everything else. Dogs snapping. We were all really dejected. And all at once a cheer started. Well, you've seen those so-called waves in football stadiums now. Well, that's the way this camp was. We were all on the ground. We looked up, and here comes this guy who was a paratrooper—a poster paratrooper, "join the marines" and all that stuff. He had a big duffel bag with all his personal stuff in it. He wasn't handcuffed. And he was running. He ran right straight up to the other fence and started just flopping right there at the first guys he saw, running around the camp, waving and cheering. In back of him was a German on a bicycle. That German was laughing like hell. And just like that, the morale changed. Everybody started cussing the Germans. ○

Most prisoner of war camps were liberated in April or May 1945 as U.S. and Soviet troops advanced well into Germany. A few days before Miller's last camp was liberated by Soviet troops, the German soldiers and guards deserted. Miller recalled those days:

○ I believe it was May the 5th. According to my memory, it was a day or two after the Germans left the camp. They left. We woke up one morning, and they were gone. We had a colonel. He gave orders that everyone stay in the camp. People were not going to stay, but he was still the boss. Most guys stayed around for about a day, but after that a lot of them went to the village that was near by.

Eventually, the Russians came—a mob of them with women and everything—right with the Russian army. One of the first things they did was turn the side of a truck into a stage and have a floor show! Like what the hell, it's fun time. Meanwhile, their troops were still fighting a little further east, and here we were having a floor show.

I'd become friends with a Russian major. He had a little artillery outfit outside of camp. So I'd go up there and yak with him. He told me that what you do is terrorize a place with aircraft and artillery, and then these people come in, and by then, most of these little areas have already surrendered. They were like guerrillas, no more like an army than anything. It was like a mob. But it terrorized the civilian population, so they didn't have to worry about them. They got them under control for when the troops came in. ○

On May 15, Miller was flown out on a B-17 to Camp Lucky Strike in France, where his plane was met by General Eisenhower.

After the war, when relations between the Soviet Union and the United States soured, men like Charlie Miller and those who had come into contact with Soviet soldiers during the war had to keep inside the good memories they had of these people:

○ If you say that one Russian soldier in forced labor was very nice to me, no American is going to say too much about that. But it's different if you go on day after day about how you were really dependent on these Russian people and how bad they had it—but still they knew we were their friends. We were in those days. They were jeopardizing their lives. If they got caught with us, I'm sure they all would have been shot. [I think they risked so much] because we would have done the same for them. You just say, hey, you're a Russian, we're fighting the same war, he's fighting the same enemy, so I'll help him. There wasn't anything political at all. What the hell did we know what was going to happen following the war? We were in the same boat, and we saw their treatment compared to ours.

The Soviet Union had millions of guys—for every one American that was a POW, there were probably two hundred Russians. But you're not going to sit down and tell the people how the Russian prisoners were dressed, how they got nothing. The Red Cross never called on them. At least the Red Cross came to our camps. But the Russians, they had anything they could scrounge on their feet. It was just terrible, but you're not going to tell Americans, well, the reason the Russians couldn't supply their POWs was because there were so many millions of them. Plus, it was a poor country to start with, and they were being invaded. A lot of Americans would say, "you talk like a communist." So that's why I said during the spacebridge that I was crying because I wanted at least to say something decent about the Russian soldiers.

I had never heard any ex-POW who had any dealings with the Russians, . . . [make] one derogatory remark. Nothing. Politics was never brought up then. Like running into a guy at a convention, and you say, "you remember so and so? That was the name we gave the Russian who lived with us in 17. I wonder whatever happened to him?" Stuff like this, you know? It would be like you trying to find an old schoolmate. You don't care if he or she is a Jew or a Catholic or what the hell. What do you care? Black or white. Only thing you know is that you're looking for a friend you went to school with. ○

VLADIMIR IVANOVICH MIKHAILOV

1945
(News Press Agency)

1988
(News Press Agency)

Vladimir Mikhailov was born in 1922 in the city of Bologoye, halfway between Leningrad and Moscow. He grew up in Leningrad, and graduated from one of the city's colleges, intending to be a professional dock-builder. "I wanted to build huge calvings for ocean ships," he says, "so we could open our country to the entire world. However, nothing ever became of this dream. The war began, the freshman course was disbanded, and I went to an anti-aircraft training school for the Baltic fleet and then to the formation of naval infantry brigades."

Vladimir Mikhailov fought on the Karelian Front until the end of 1944; subsequently, he was recalled and sent to a German language school in Russia. He landed in Berlin on the second day of peace, May 10, 1945, charged with setting up the newspaper Berliner Zeitung. *Later, he served as the head of the news bureau for northern Germany. In the early 1950s he started working for* Pravda *as a correspondent. He went on to head the* Pravda *Bureaus in Austria, the GDR, and the Federal Republic of Germany. Back in Moscow, he was manager of* Pravda's *Department of Socialist Countries and, later, of the Department of Capitalist Countries. Soon after having granted an interview for this book, Vladimir Mikhailov passed away.*

During the spacebridge, Vladimir Mikhailov expressed his opinion concerning the Second Front. But in this post-spacebridge interview, his story is about what he experienced as a soldier:

○ Our naval infantry brigade was formed at Kotelnikovo, where, considerably later, the pincer movement closed around the German armies in Stalingrad. But back then, we had no clue of that ever happening. We were sent to the north. First they wanted to throw us into battle at Rostov, then at Moscow, where things were very hot. But while we were being sent here and there, our troops had already driven the Germans back. So we continued to move north. We were all sure that they would take our brigade to Murmansk, put us on a boat, and send us to England, where together with the Allies we would open the Second Front. However, it didn't work out that way. One night our echelon stopped, and we were told to get off the train. We found ourselves in the far north, beyond the Polar Circle. There were frosts of up to −50 degrees, marshes everywhere. Here the Karel forests gave way to tundra. But the climate and the natural conditions, bad as they were, did not present the biggest problem. The main artery of supplies from Murmansk to Arkhangelsk [Archangel] came through here, the railway for the cargo brought by the convoys of British and U.S. ships, which the Germans had tried to sink in the North Atlantic. The Germans ripped into this area with terrible force. They threw crack troops against us—SS divisions, Alpine divisions—and we had to put up a desperate fight.

However, a minor regression. I was nineteen years old, not yet truly a soldier; nor were my peers. Our most experienced men had served about two years in the navy and had no combat savvy. I come from an academic family. My father was a historian, deeply in love with ancient Rome and Greece, and he talked as though he had lived half his life there. My mother also taught—mathematics—but she was quite carried away with literature. Thanks to them, I was raised in the spirit of brotherhood among peoples, of internationalism. We are often asked why we fought so poorly in the very beginning of the war, why we retreated to Moscow, Leningrad, and Sta-lingrad. We give every reason under the sun, but we sometimes forget one. I cannot recall anyone's ever mentioning it. We were so inspired by the spirit of internationalism that it was hard for me to take aim at a German and harder still for me to pull the trigger. I thought, these are probably the workers of the Ruhr, the dockers of Hamburg. . . . how on earth can this be? It was difficult to understand; we were fighting a ferocious enemy who had been raised like a beast, a beast that had been let loose on our country and looked upon us as though there were nothing that couldn't be changed into manure for the greater glory of Nazi Germany. At the start of the war, it was extraordinarily difficult for us to fight this enemy in moral terms. Though later, our weakness became our strength. We realized how impor-tant it was to do what nobody was going to do for us—to free our country and other peoples from this terrible disaster, from this invasion which could ruin all civilization. This understanding led to victory. As we learned to fight, we did not become as animals. I will furnish but one example.

My mother remained in besieged Leningrad with my father and my sister, who was three years older than I. During the blockade, hundreds of thousands of Leningraders perished. My father died the very first winter. This was a strong, healthy man, it was just that the men did not stand up to hunger as well as the women. My father had an amazingly strong spirit. My sister told me his last dying words. He whispered, "I will save your mother and you." That same day as my sister was going through his things, she found two chocolate bars in his briefcase. We talk about heroism, about people who throw themselves at machine guns. But his heroism was just as great: to die of hunger and know that you have the means to save your-self—to leave it for someone else. . . . I suffered through hunger at the front. As a matter of fact, everybody experienced it. We starved for about five or six months. Per day, we were getting one dried crust and a soup-like liquid in which there were some beets and potatoes. Scurvy started. They told us, all echelons with supplies are going to Leningrad. And we endured. But I remember what a human turns into, consumed by this terrible feeling of hunger.

Well, after the death of my father I received a letter and a small package from my mother. The first part of the letter went as usual—what does a mother write to her son at the front? But then came these words: "I know how much you suffer. But, even so, as you perform your duties, do them without hatred. Remain a human being; do not allow beasts to make a beast of you. You will understand that there are great Germans; there are other Germans." In the package, she sent me some books—Schiller, Goethe. And we all read them. Nobody said, "I will not read these Germans." You understand, this was the kind of humanistic upbringing we had received. We had always learned to relate to other peoples in the greatest respect.

This conviction, that the war would end quickly and on someone else's territory, lasted only until the time when we collided with reality and discovered how well armed the German army was, how much it had surpassed us in military preparedness. It had gone through all of Europe, accumulating gigantic experience, and we realized it would be a long, long struggle. In addition, we faced an army which had all the industry of Europe working for it, while in our country we did not even have two 5-year plans behind us. So, why be surprised that we were forced to retreat. But all that changed after the famous order from the supreme commander in chief. It said, "Not one step backward"; it was issued after our troops had left Rostov. I remember it literally word for word, especially what it said about the troops which, having left Rostov, had covered their colors with shame, for the people had ceased to believe in their own army.

You know, those words stunned us. The people had ceased to believe in us? Did that mean we were cowards, that we fought so poorly? That now it was do or die?

Perhaps we had retreated so lightly because our country is so vast, so we were psychologically geared to feeling secure about moving back. Perhaps we remembered the war of 1812 with Napoleon, when we all knew the Russian generals had lured the French into the depth of the country and then destroyed them. I don't know, but until that moment we had perceived what was happening as some sort of genius plan. But when they told us, "Brothers! What are you doing? The people cease to believe in their own armed forces!"—that shook up the entire army and to a great extent promoted the turning point of the war.

I already mentioned that I served on the Karelian Front, in the far north. Our entire war zone was fought within a space of two hundred kilometers. The entire war. Because the battle was for the railroads connecting Murmansk with Archangel, and that was the main target for us and the enemy. We fought like men possessed. Of course, it helped us that the Germans couldn't use their technological superiority to its full strength. The marshes, the lakes . . . the tanks couldn't get through, only on the main roads. But the fight went on bloodily and desperately.

I was wounded twice. The first, it saved my life, I could say. It was in May 1942. After a stay in the hospital, I returned to the front. Much later I read the memoirs of the C-in-C of the Northern Fleet. It seems that our brigade—something I was not aware of then—had been set up to divert a large group of enemy forces heading toward Murmansk. We attacked them from the southwest. We were seriously outnumbered. But the order was to attack, and we attacked. Many of our men were killed. I was wounded in the arm; I remember running down a road by the marsh and wondering why men were falling all around me. And then I understood: the Germans were firing machine guns from both sides of the road—we had been ambushed.

A month and a half after I was wounded, I returned to the front. I was walking, I remember along a forest road: the golden sand, the sun, the pine trees; it was very beautiful there. And on this road, I met the brigade postman. He told me our battalion was no more. We were about three hundred people. They had been surrounded and destroyed while I was in the hospital. Only I had survived. ◯

1944 **1985**

WILLIAM
BESWICK

William Beswick was working at a paper mill when he was drafted for active duty on May 1, 1941. He was a tank-destroyer driver on the Eastern Front and then a patrol member of an M-20 machine-gunner. It was as "point" on such a patrol that he met Soviet soldiers in Torgau. Mr. Beswick now lives in Westpoint, Virginia, and is the president of the 5,500-member 69th Infantry Division Association. During the spacebridge, Mr. Beswick spoke of his encounters with Soviets at the Elbe. (These comments and his subsequent thoughts on the U.S.– Soviet meeting at the Elbe are included in Chapter 6.) In a post-spacebridge interview he recalled some of his early battlefront experiences:

○ I remember up on the Siegfried Line, it was so called. We were near Zitzen, Germany, not too far from Bastogne. We moved out then, further east. We had nothing to keep us warm except whatever we could get and put on. We put newspaper in between our clothes to help insulate us, make us warm. We were sitting there one day waiting to go out on a firing mission, and the screaming meemies, which were more or less of a harassment type of an explosive, were coming in, and somebody hollered. They make a big whining hum when they start in, and you can't tell exactly where they're going. Anyhow, you run for a foxhole or underneath a vehicle or whatever you can get in to keep from being hit by shrapnel or whatever. And we were in the Huertgen forest at that time, and it was really cold; there were land mines everywhere; we lost quite a few men one night, young men who had just come to Europe as replacements. Our vehicles were ones that looked very much like the German Tiger tank, and they were bringing those young men up there that night. I say "young men"; I was one of them, I guess. And they saw these vehicles sitting up on the side of the road, and they thought they were German tanks. When they went out to go around, they hit some trip wires of land mines that just killed a whole bunch—I guess about forty of them that were just coming up for replacement. They just never even got into combat, really. I stepped on a mine, but the ground was frozen. That's the only reason I'm here today.

Before Torgau, we had met a little resistance one particular morning.

We were driving up the street, and all of a sudden we heard a bunch of guys, and they were waving and hollering, and it was just like you were driving down the street at some celebration right here in the United States. There were about ten houses in which the Germans had held American prisoners of war. And of course, when they saw us coming and they saw the white star on our vehicle, they started screaming and hollering. They had just been let go then; the Germans had just run. I remember one of my guys could see all the American uniforms, and he said, "What in the world are you doing there?" They said, "We're prisoners of the Germans." And he said, "You are like hell." Some of them had been prisoners for two and three years.

I was supposed to go out on a patrol one morning. I was point, and I had a machine gun shot out of my hands that night. We stayed outside of this village. And the Germans were real poor shots that particular evening. I'd say it was about seven o'clock in the evening, and he fired about seven or eight rounds, and all of them went just over the top of us and hit in the fields behind us. Then my vehicle got stuck, and I couldn't get it out of the mud; the driver couldn't get it out. It was one of these six-wheeled armored vehicles. We jumped out for protection, and the old machine gun wouldn't fire; it just didn't work right that evening at all. So after about an hour, hour and a half of firing back and forth, one of the Germans came out of this village. The road was about, I guess, about a half a mile to a mile; the road was wide open, and they came out with a half of a bedsheet on a staff, surrendering the village, and we went up in there. And some of our vehicles had fired in there and set three or four of the houses on fire. That was the first time I'd ever seen people laughing and crying at the same time. They were so happy that their ordeal was over. . . . And we went up, and, like I say, I was point, and I stopped a column, and I could see where there had been some tanks that went straight up the road—some gone down the hill—and just about that time, I saw a German run out of a building. I saw a machine gun in the window, and I fired at the machine gun; I didn't fire at the man. He went on around the other side of the building. I think he was safe; but I fired at the window to keep the machine gun from directing on our people, which it did do. We had quite a skirmish that night. I ran back and got up with one of the other guys, and I had forgotten my personal side arm, and I had to go back and get that. That almost cost me my life. I ran on back then, and I dove into a ditch, and everything has an amusing side to it, it was full of leaves and full of water. The next morning, we went up over the hills, making another line of attack, and one of the guys came up, and he had picked up a German general and a colonel and a driver and the whole bit. This general was trying to dispose of some maps of the area that they had, and he couldn't. So the boy grabbed it and started putting it out on the hood and was making the driver tell about it. The general and the colonel started running up through the woods, and so you can imagine what 150 infantrymen did to them. ○

**VLADIMIR
FEDOROVICH
ROSHCHENKO**

Vladimir followed in the footsteps of his father, a military man who had entered the service before the Revolution of 1917. Vladimir finished school in 1939. He intended to enroll in the Leningrad Military Technical Institute; however, fate intervened in the form of a new military aviation school in Orenburg. Vladimir, like many of his peers, had dreamed of becoming a pilot. So, he set off for Orenburg and passed the entrance exams with flying colors. Later, this school became the Chkalov Military Academy. He graduated in 1941 and was sent to an aviation unit. At the age of twenty, he met the war.

Vladimir Roshchenko fought not only from the first to the last day of the Great Patriotic War but also served in the Far East. After the war, he was stationed on Sakhalin Island, where he taught at the academy. He retired from the air force in 1960, with twenty-one years of service to his credit. He became a civilian pilot and was the first to fly the nonstop Aeroflot flights between the U.S.S.R. and the U.S. He retired at the age of fifty-five.

Vladimir Roshchenko has been awarded the Gold Star of Hero of the Soviet Union, as well as twenty-five other decorations and medals.

○ The war found me in the region of Novgorod. It was a day of rest, and everyone had planned to go fishing. At about five o'clock, they suddenly announced a battle alert—ordered us to get our planes ready on the double. It was entirely unexpected, and it didn't enter into anyone's head that this could be the beginning of the war. Maybe some of the older men had such forebodings, but we kids didn't even think about it.

One June 23, I got my first taste of war: a fleet of German airplanes bombing the neighboring airfield. Only then did I start to understand what was happening. We had been brought up believing that if we ever were attacked, we would repel the enemy and destroy him on his own territory. But as time went on, we suffered huge casualties. On June 27, after a mission to bomb and strafe a German tank column near Vilnius, only two or three of the twenty-seven planes returned. Many of the pilots bailed out and had to fight their way out of German-occupied territory. They got back to us about two months later, and it was from them that we discovered the kind of tragedy that was occurring everywhere. Our reconnaissance was terrible, and when our pilots reached the area of Vilnius, they were met by clouds of German fighters. We didn't even know that Vilnius was already occupied by Germans. To put it bluntly, they shot our planes to pieces because we came in without fighter cover.

I flew my first combat mission sometime in August. It really didn't impress me—it was just like a routine flight. Each bomber had a crew of four people. I was the navigator. We dropped our bombs and returned to our airfield. After this, I flew eight more combat missions. Each time was like a milk run—a piece of cake. But on November 6, 1941, we were shot down over the region of Vyazma. The gunner and the radio operator were killed outright. Three German Messerschmitt-109s attacked us. Our plane started to burn, and we had to bail out. I landed on a field dotted with small haystacks. I had no idea where the Soviet lines were or where the Germans were. I had lost my flight boots and was just in my socks; it was cold, and there was frost on the ground. I listened to the sounds of gunfire from the west and the artillery answering from the east. It turned out that I had landed in a kind of no-man's-land. After about fifteen minutes, I heard voices speaking Russian. Probably our boys searching for us, I thought, but just in case, I reached for my pistol. But these were our boys, thank God. I was half frozen and had dislocated my collarbone; as a result, I landed in a hospital in Tula. I then developed a bad case of pneumonia. After my stay in the hospital, I received orders to fly to the Far East. There, in the city of Komsomolsk-na-Amure, we received twenty-five new planes, tested them, and about a month and a half later flew them back to the region of Ryazan. By this time the battle for Moscow was already over.

I was appointed to the crew of Flight Commander Ivan Prokofyevich Kuryatnik. Our plane was an Il-14. On our very first combat mission, a night flight, we ran into such a thunderstorm that many planes turned back. But we flew through it, headed for our target at Smolensk, released our bombs, and returned home—again through the thunderstorm. How we got through is hard to say. . . . They had already given up on us back at the airfield. When we landed, there was five or ten centimeters of water covering the field. I thought, we're going to catch hell from the commander, but he ran up to us and hugged us and kissed us—anyway, that was my first real test. Seemingly, I passed it well. From that point on, I realized that Kuryatnik had made his decision and that we would be flying together.

We flew missions to such distant targets as Königsberg, Danzig, Warsaw. Such flights took about ten hours. As navigator, I had more space and could move around, but the pilot had to stick to his seat the entire time. It was hard. By the end of 1942, we already had flown about 200 missions. And we had not had a single problem. What is it I consider a problem? When they shoot you down. But being hit with shrapnel—we never thought that was a problem.

In December 1942, I received my first decoration, the Order of

Lenin, while Kuryatnik became a Hero of the Soviet Union. Our bombing had been right on the nose; we had really hurt the Germans—now we were decorated for that. Well, we celebrated the New Year, drank to these decorations, and then went back to flying missions. This was 1943.

As far as our technology of those years was concerned, the bombers we had were basically on the level of the Germans', and our fighters had the edge when our Yak appeared. At the beginning of the war, the Germans had several types of bombers, but we had only one—night bombers. Later, of course, came the P-2, the Tu-2, and the P-8.

In 1942, I participated in the Battle of Stalingrad. We flew a lot there. It was a terrible scene. When Paulus's army group was surrounded, we were allowed to pick our own targets. During one flight, I noticed that a German transport plane, a Ju-52, was making a landing. We circled at about 1,500 meters. I said, "Ivan, let's wait a little bit and circle around; there are no fighters, and the AA guns aren't firing." We circled once, twice, then approached the airfield—I could see nine to twelve planes lining up in a row, ready to take off. Then I said, "Let's hit 'em." We descended about five hundred meters and caught them. They were trying to evacuate the German command. We tore up their flight. As we completed our last bomb run, I saw a bright flash on my right. And then I heard an explosion. I turned—there was a huge hole in the plane. And a cry— shrapnel from an anti-aircraft round had wounded our gunner and our radio operator. When we reached our base, we found our landing gear was jammed. What could we do? We decided to do a belly flop. One wheel came out—and that's how we landed. It twisted us around a few times, but the plane ended up safe. They patched it up, and we started flying again.

Throughout the war, we bombed railroad junctions at Orel, Belgorod, Bryansk. We held up the transportation of German equipment and fuel. I remember once when I was flying a mission where we were supposed to reach the target and hang flares over it. We had to do this just before the approach of the main group of bombers—about a minute and a half before them. The procedure was to take off about ten minutes earlier, find our target, drop the flares, and make room for the bombers. After their first run, we would come back, drop another five flares, and if everything was okay, we would leave. But on this particular flight, when we were into our first run only a kilometer and a half from the target—I opened the bomb-bay doors, and —BOOM—there was an explosion. A piece of shrapnel had hit one of the flare detonators. The flare caught fire inside the plane, and the flames rushed at the gunner and the radio operator. At first we couldn't understand what was going on. Then we got caught in the searchlights, and AA guns pounded us. About five hundred meters from the target, I decided to let the flare go. It fell from the bomb bay, and the flames quieted. But the burning flare's chute caught onto our tail, and we dragged a trail of fire behind us. When we found ourselves over the target at an altitude of eight hundred or a thousand meters, they began hitting us again. . . . We were lit up by our own flare. Things were happening so fast, we were really confused. We called out to the gunner and the radio operator. There was no answer. Looking back at the target against a backdrop of burning flares, we saw two blossoming parachutes. Our comrades had bailed out, because to stay in the plane meant to burn to death. Their fate was not a lucky one. The gunner landed in the center of Orel and was taken prisoner by the Germans. We never heard of him again. The radio operator was killed before he hit the ground.

Our missions were very successful. In July, I was awarded the Gold Star of Hero of the Soviet Union for the battles of Moscow, Stalingrad, and Kursk. And Kuryatnik, he was given the Order of the Red Banner. We were both promoted. I began the war as a sergeant, but became a Hero as a senior lieutenant.

We had two missions to Berlin. I believe it was 1943. They attached extra fuel tanks to the wings, adding one and a half to two hours to our flight, and we headed out. Apparently, they weren't waiting for us when we approached Berlin. The city was lit up; we could see everything. It was like taking candy from babies.

Throughout the entire war, I was wounded only once and then not seriously. I was born with a birthmark, and this is supposed to mean that I am a lucky person. When I went to be awarded the Golden Star, Kuryatnik flew a combat mission without me, with a young navigator. They were going to Serpukhov—this was a restricted zone, defended by our AA guns. Well, our own guns opened fire on them. The navigator gave the signal "I'm one of yours"—we had such a signal: a red, green, and yellow flare— but the flare hit the engine. The plane began burning. Everyone bailed out, but the young navigator was so scared that he opened his parachute while he was still in the cabin. He was sucked in backwards by the airflow, and he perished. After that, Kuryatnik said I was his good-luck charm and refused to fly without me.

Once we were returning at dawn from a raid on Rostov. I looked, and saw an enormous glow on the horizon. I said, "Let's take a look at what's burning." We had to turn back about thirty or forty kilometers. It was Voronezh burning; the Germans had razed it from the air. While we were looking down, we didn't notice that we had entered a zone where barrage blimps had been hung up. The weather was rotten. Suddenly—WHAM! I was hit across the legs; my boots didn't tear or anything, but it hurt. When we landed, we found that half the side of the plane had been sliced off, including most of the navigator's quarters. We didn't know what the hell had happened. And then came the report: we had struck one of the steel cables mooring a blimp. Our propeller had cut it in two. We were lucky. ○

**ALEKSEY
KIRILLOVICH
GORLINSKIY**

1945
(News Press Agency)

1986
(News Press Agency)

The son of a career military man, Aleksey Gorlinskiy got his degree in the Chemistry Department of Kiev University shortly before the war. He intended to become a scientist; however, on June 22, 1941, on the very first day of the war, he volunteered and fought for 1,418 days—from the first day of the war to the last. He began as a lieutenant and finished as a major, always with the artillery. He fought in the Western Ukraine, defended Kiev, escaped the terrible pincer movement around Kiev, retreated to Stalingrad, and was thus a participant of one of the greatest battles of the Second World War. After that, he was among those who fought at the Kursk Salient, forced the Dnieper, liberated the Ukraine, Romania, Poland, eastern Germany, and, finally, Czechoslovakia.

In a post-spacebridge interview General Gorlinskiy remembered the front:

○ You know, in each person's life there are many memorable dates and important events. That is beyond question. But for a war veteran, this is even truer. Some of these events may not have been crucial or central to the war as such. But for the individual, these memories are second to none in importance. I remember, for example, when we were breaking out of encirclement, when our troops were abandoning Kiev. I was a lieutenant, a reserve lieutenant with no experience. Our regiment commander said, "Well, let's try to break through." The pincer movement was not complete. The Germans were trying to block the road and junctions, but in general, it was still possible to travel along them. The regiment commander said, "You, Gorlinskiy, will lead those [who can] make it on foot, and Senior Lieutenant Altman will lead the motorized column." Seven vehicles remained in the regiment. They carried the regiment flag and secret documents. And I remember Altman saying, "But why not the other way around? Why not let Gorlinskiy lead the vehicles?" I realized what he really had in mind: it was possible to sneak by foot but much harder to escape in the vehicles. Well, for some reason I was oblivious to danger then. Only later, after this and other incidents, did I begin to understand what a fine

mess it was. Well, I said, "I agree"—even though agreement is not something they ask for in the army. So they gave me seven vehicles. I had only
one master sergeant. He told me, "Don't worry, comrade commander, I'm
a local; I know all the roads, we'll slip right through." It was night-time, and
with doused headlights but with our engines roaring, we darted through
the clearings in the forests. Apparently, the Germans thought it was one of
their own units moving. Nobody touched us. Those that Altman led never
got out. Some who changed into civilian clothing escaped in small groups.
And here we—in full uniform, with documents, with flags—escaped.

■ ■ ■ ■

Quite unforgettable, of course, was Stalingrad. At many places, we were
only sixty to one hundred meters from the Volga River, sometimes only one
hundred steps. And the Volga's width is one and a half to two kilometers of
water. You really know that there was no place to retreat. As they said then,
"Beyond the Volga there is no land." So we had to stand to the death.
Fighting became second nature, a way of life. For example, they would lob
grenades at us, but we knew exactly how much time they needed to explode, so we would pick them up and throw them at the Germans. This
was run-of-the-mill.

The strangest things stay with you, branded in your memory. In August of 1942, the Germans bombed Stalingrad. It was their first all-out air
raid. The Germans had set fire to our petrol depot. The entire city was
ablaze. Everywhere, there were ashes and smoke; everything was burning.
But what I have never forgotten was this dead horse; it was lying on the
road, staring at me out of its huge glassy eyes, looking at me, looking right
through me. I can still see it.

■ ■ ■ ■

This was in the Ukraine. The Germans were retreating; we were driving
them out, and I remember seeing rows of gallows, the bodies of our people
still hanging from them. All were in civilian clothes. Maybe they were
partisans, and maybe they didn't have any resistance connections at all but
were simply the first people to get caught. I have seen even worse scenes.
When we took the village of Reshetilovka, not far from the town of Poltava,
it was terribly hot, and we were thirsty. So we looked for a well. And we
found it . . . completely filled with children's corpses. The fascists had
conducted a scorched-earth policy there. All the houses were burned.
When we entered villages, we generally found only chimneys standing. And
then it fell upon me to liberate prisoners from concentration camps. The
first such death camp was near Shepitovka. Most of the prisoners were
French. Things were not so bad there. The Germans treated the French
better; I certainly didn't see in this camp what I saw later in camps with our
own people. In short, the first concentration camp didn't leave an especially

strong impression on me. The concentration camp on Slavut left a considerably stronger impression. It was close to Shepitovka, and it was for our people. When we got there, most prisoners were dead; the Germans had machine-gunned them before retreating. Then, the camp at Terezin in Czechoslovakia. The Germans used it as a showcase; they had even brought the Red Cross there. In Terezin itself, the prisoners were not murdered. But two kilometers from the camp, there was a brick factory the Nazis had converted into a crematorium. In 1982, I was a member of a delegation which took part in the first international conference of liberated prisoners from fascist concentration camps. It was held under the aegis of the U.S. State Department; Alexander Haig greeted us. And, you know, one old woman, knowing I had liberated Terezin, approached with a young woman, apparently her daughter, and told her, "Kneel before this man, because he is the reason I survived."

And before Terezin, I remember, was Lignitz, in Polish territory. There were also many Frenchmen there, but there were a great many of ours. When we entered the camp, how these people did meet us! It was impossible to describe. They could barely stand on their legs, merely skin and bones, and from them I also discovered that conditions for the prisoners were unequal. They were especially terrible for the Russians, the Soviets.

You can imagine what kind of hatred our soldiers felt. And it was not simply hatred for an inhuman, sadistic enemy, it was a hatred which rallied the people and helped us fight.

I recall coming across the body of a German officer. He had a wallet, and, of course, you always checked such things for documents or papers. I found a photograph in that wallet. Apparently, this photo came from home. It showed six Soviets harnessed like oxen to a cart, and two Germans boys, about twelve years of age, were driving them with whips. Beside them stood adult Germans, making sure the poor bastards couldn't do anything. I gave this photograph to a correspondent who published it in a newspaper. How could such a thing not evoke hatred? Yes, we took it out on the Germans; we made them pay for what they did to us. ○

The Home Fronts

The U.S. Home Front:
An American Perspective

With the single exception of the assault on Pearl Harbor that officially brought the United States into World War II, no American experienced the war as an attack on his or her own home or town. The battles and bombings, the deaths and atrocities of the war that American soldiers abroad knew only too well never disturbed the American home front. Pearl Harbor had made the threat of invasion real, but the United States remained fortunate in avoiding the horrors of fighting on its own land.

Nonetheless, there was truth in the proclamation of so many American advertisements and posters of the period that the home front was the "first line of defense." Even before the attack on Pearl Harbor, American industry, under President Roosevelt's direction, was gearing up for increased production and for changes in the products it produced. In 1940, the American economy began to shift from agriculture and domestically oriented manufacture to war equipment and supplies, high technology, and service industries. During the war period, the United States spent 186 billion dollars for 297,000 planes and other war materials.

Much of this increased production was delivered to the allies of the United States, including the Soviet Union, under the lend-lease program. Passed by Congress on March 11, 1941, the Lend-Lease Act was proposed initially by President Roosevelt to support the war effort in Great Britain without direct involvement of the United States. In time, the program was extended to include other Allied nations, particularly the Soviet Union. Both Admiral Frankel and Ambassador Olson, whose stories are told in Chapter 5, "Allies," were stationed in the Soviet Union primarily to expedite and oversee the U.S. lend-lease program. The Lend-Lease Act had stated that the President could "sell, transfer title to, exchange, lease, lend, or otherwise dispose of" defense material that was vital to the security of the United States. In return, the United States was to receive "payment or repayment in kind or property, or any other direct or indirect benefits" that the president considered satisfactory. Within two weeks of the passage of the bill, an initial appropriation of seven billion dollars was authorized by the U.S. Congress. By the close of the war, the total expenditure exceeded fifty billion dollars. Reverse lend-lease eventually came back in the amount of approximately eight billion dollars, and returns in kind totaled approximately two billion dollars.

The combination of the demands and financial commitment of the Lend-Lease Act with the suddenly escalating needs for its own defense materials after Pearl Harbor launched the United States into a new era of productivity and social change. In 1939, before the United States entered the war, eleven million Americans were unemployed. Many more were only beginning to recover from the economic hardships and social disruptions brought on by the Great Depression of the 1930s. World War II reversed these unemployment problems. The United States even began to experience a labor shortage, as hundreds of thousands of young men went abroad. Lola Weixel, another *Remembering War* participant, recalls that prior to the war, she had tried in vain to get training as a welder, but after Pearl Harbor, she suddenly received a letter inviting her to start training immediately. Posters, advertisements, and radio announcements appealed to the pride and patriotism of Americans at home, urging them to join the labor force. "You are a production soldier," these ads read, and Americans responded positively, joining the "home-front army" in factories and offices around the country.

Partly because of these shifts in the American economy and partly because of military mobilization, the war years substantially changed the personal and professional lives of American men and women. Many women became heads of their households and had unprecedented opportunities for employment. Between 1940 and 1945, the U.S. female labor force grew by more than 50 percent, as the number of women at work outside of the home jumped from almost twelve million in 1940 to nineteen million in 1945. Thirty-six percent of all women were in the work force by the war's end, a change from 28 percent in 1940. Fewer women were in domestic service, and vast numbers of women took on skilled-labor positions in factories producing defense materials. Women shoveled out blast furnaces, operated huge cranes and drill presses, cleared forests, and loaded ships. While the women who replaced men in aircraft factories, ordnance plants, and shipyards were the most visible, the labor shortage also opened doors for women musicians, airplane pilots, scientists, athletes, and college professors.

Daily life for Americans at home changed significantly during the war years. As men enlisted in the armed forces and were sent from one base to another, some women followed where they could, other women enlisted themselves, and still others remained in their hometowns with new responsibilities and marked changes in their living situations. The forced mobility of Americans in the 1930s, brought on by endless searches for work, was replaced by a different, more intense and unpredictable mobility in the war years. Because gas was rationed and trains were often filled with soldiers, travel for civilians was difficult, but travel they did. Lauretta Beaty Foy, whose testimony appears in Chapter 2, recalled how she was constantly traveling during the war years as a flight instructor and as a Woman's Auxiliary Service Pilot. Because of her work, she was often separated from her two young sons and her elderly parents. Lola Weixel remembers how many women followed their soldier husbands from base to base, often going from job to job and living in makeshift circumstances.

Those who did not travel experienced the war at home as a series of small but continuous sacrifices, despite the end of the depression economy. In addition to gasoline, many food and household items were rationed. American farmers and industrial workers were urged to produce more. Americans who lived in cities responded to the need to ship food overseas by starting "sidewalk" or "victory" gardens to grow enough fresh produce for their families' needs. Children as well as adults collected pots and pans, tin cans, clothing, bedding, cooking grease, and odds and ends of every kind that could be sent to the soldiers and suffering civilians abroad or transformed by American industry into goods useful to the war effort. Americans from towns across the country contributed their pennies and dollars to a variety of relief organizations to help those around the world who were far less well-off than themselves.

For the most part, Americans did not make these efforts grudgingly. World War II was not only a "good war" economically for the United States; it also reunited Americans in a transcendence of the despair and cultural contradictions of the 1930s. As they looked across both the Atlantic and the Pacific to the ravages of war, the oppressions of fascism, the grotesque violations of human life and liberty, the uncertainties raised in the 1930s about the reality of "liberty and equality" for all faded, and American citizens found good reason to celebrate their freedom and the democracy on which it was based.

This renewed patriotism and the relative security and stability of the

American home front were not, however, without cost or scars or hypocrisies. While Americans enthusiastically proclaimed their freedoms and the absence of racism in the United States, they accepted, at least publicly, the internment of thousands of Japanese-Americans. The conditions in these camps were not as terrible as at Auschwitz or Dachau. Nonetheless, American citizens were imprisoned simply because of their ethnic origins. In the media and on the streets, the "murdering Japs" were pictured as nothing less than monsters. More subtly, yet equally troubling, while white Americans rejoiced about living in a land without prejudice, black Americans continued to serve in the armed forces in demeaning positions as cooks and orderlies, and, at home, as *Remembering War* participant Anne Smith recalls, even the social clubs organized to provide recreation for servicemen had clear rules to assure the separation of white and black Americans. The U.S. home front was a place of promise for many Americans—but not for all.

The Soviet Home Front: A Soviet Perspective

Leo Tolstoy's *Anna Karenina* opens with the following statement: "Every family is happy in the same way. Every family is unhappy differently." To paraphrase the Russian classic, while war at the front line is the same for all concerned, the home-front experience is different.

Regardless of what side the soldier is on, the front line meant two things for him: battle and the constant threat of death. Many other elements certainly exist, but those two are, as it were, a common denominator. No such common denominator exists for those in the rear. Nothing could testify to this more convincingly than the wartime situations in the United States and the Soviet Union.

Without belittling in any way the patriotic efforts of at-home Americans, their lives were relatively unscarred by the war (with the exception, of course, of those who lost kith and kin). If anything, war improved their quality of living. At no time before, or after for that matter, have America's industries produced at virtually top capacity; nor has the United States ever come so close to full employment. There were jobs for everybody, including jobs that had never been available. At a time when the issue of the ERA and feminism (modern) were still decades away, women were asking for "men's" jobs and getting them without the slightest resistance from management. On the home front, the money was good, there was no scarcity of products or food, nor was there any realistic threat of bombs spreading death and destruction. In fact, a case could be made for the view that the war was a boon to an America which—President Roosevelt's New Deal notwithstanding—had not fully recovered from the Depression. One is tempted to speculate how the U.S. economy would have fared had there not been a war.

By contrast, the citizens on the home front in the Soviet Union were required to make unbelievable sacrifices and superhuman efforts, to endure such suffering and hardship that, recollecting, it is difficult to understand how it all was possible.

In many cases the Soviet home front was exactly that: home at the front. Leningrad stands out as the most staggering example. During those nine hundred savage days of siege, the Kirov Factory never stopped turning out arms, spare parts, tanks, and artillery pieces, though the plant was often bombed. Far more telling was the iron grip of hunger. There are countless stories of men, women, and children who stood working at their machines and then silently, almost like in slow motion, dropped to the floor, dead of starvation.

Leningrad was both home front and front. It not only manufactured and repaired weapons for the soldiers but also, perhaps even more importantly, it instilled the one element the German war machine could not match: morale, resulting in deeds of heroism beyond the comprehension of the would-be conqueror. According to official figures, six hundred thousand Leningraders died during the winter months of 1941–42. There is reason to believe the total number over those 900 days was closer to one million. Words can never do justice to what the people of Leningrad suffered and accomplished.

While Stalingrad is famous for the decisive battle fought there, it is less well known for its "home-front" contribution. Militarily speaking, that city was of crucial importance. The famed Stalingrad Tractor Works produced a large number of tanks for the Red Army. Much of the oil needed by the Soviet defense industries came from the oil fields of Maykop and Grozny via the Caspian Sea and up the Volga to Stalingrad. Those facts provided the rationale for Hitler's decision, supported by the OKW: Army Group A must take the Caucasus and its oil fields, Army Group B must take Stalingrad and cut off the flow of oil up the Volga River.

The Battle of Stalingrad began on July 17, 1942, when the advance forces of Army Group B came into contact with the 62nd Soviet Army, several hundred kilometers west of the city. By the end of August, the superior German forces, commanded by General (later Field Marshal) Paulus, reached Stalingrad. They stormed the city on September 13 and again on September 26, when they reached the Volga. But the city would not surrender. Not only did every remaining household fight back, but the Stalingrad Factory Works—that is, what little was left of them—continued to turn out weapons. Incredible as it may seem, the workers, who had refused to retreat, repulsed German attacks, fighting side by side with the soldiers, and then returned to their lathes and machines. The aggressor could not come to terms with this kind of refusal to give up in the face of overwhelming odds. Here is just one example:

On October 3, 1942, the Germans stormed a house occupying a strategic corner. It came to be called "Pavlov's House" after the name of the man responsible for its defense, Sergeant Pavlov. The Germans stormed the house for fifty-eight days, and at no time were there more than fifteen men defending it. Yet the enemy never took it. Later, Marshall Vasily Chuikov, one of the heroes of Stalingrad, was to point out that the Germans had suffered more casualties in their assault on Pavlov's House than they did when they took Paris. To this, one of the defenders proudly answered, "Yes, but they *took* Paris."

By November 11, the enemy held 90 percent of what had been the city of Stalingrad, but amazingly enough, that last 10 percent kept fighting— and the civilians who were still alive somehow managed to continue to repair weapons. One week later, on November 19, the mighty Soviet counterattack began. Four days later, Paulus's 6th Army was completely surrounded. The field marshal surrendered on January 31, 1943. Thus ended the most titanic battle in history. It had raged over a territory covering one hundred thousand square kilometers, had lasted two hundred days and nights, had involved two million men, two thousand tanks, twenty-five hundred aircraft, twenty-six thousand guns. The Wehrmacht suffered one and a half million casualties. It was, as Churchill called it, the hinge of fate.

But the Battle of Stalingrad could not have been won—nor could the war have been won for that matter—without the unparalleled heroism of those who worked on the home front, who, deep inside the burning, mutilated city, continued to produce weapons, to repair tanks; of those who grabbed their rifles and submachine guns to fight off every new German assault and then returned to their "civilian" work; of those men who could not enlist because of age, health, or their crucial expertise; of those women who spent sixteen hours a day turning out shells and then nursed the soldiers in the hospitals and cared for their children; of those children who were too small to reach the levers and wheels of their machines and had to stand on make-shift wooden boxes; of those children who overnight became adults, who grew up never knowing toys or games, who comforted their mothers and sisters when the mailman would deliver that dreaded letter, folded in a triangle, which invariably began: "Your son [husband, brother, father] was killed in action. . . ."

The men at the front came back bearing scars that all could see, but the scars of those who had fought on the home front were invisible—in many ways, even more painful, even harder to heal. Today, four and a half decades after the end of World War II, Americans are surprised by the vehemence of the anti-war sentiment in the U.S.S.R. That is understandable, considering the different wartime experiences of the two countries. Had Soviet men fought only on distant soil, had we lost half a million instead of twenty million, had those on the home front experienced a period of good money and good times, then, surely, the Soviet outlook would be different. But this was not the case. In many ways, those on the home front endured even greater suffering and hardship than those on the front itself. All of this ultimately left an indelible mark on the national psyche.

A fourteen-year-old Soviet boy stands on top of a box allowing him to reach the instrument at a plant producing military hardware *(News Press Agency)*

Getting water from the Neva River during the siege of Leningrad
(News Press Agency)

[U.S.] Man hoeing while woman plants *(Wide World Photo)*

Orphans in Rostov-on-the-Don, 1941 *(News Press Agency)*

The poster on the building: "Death to the murderers of children"
(G. Chernov)

Nevsky Avenue, Leningrad's Main Street, 1942 *(B. Koudoyarov)*

"Buy more bonds."
(United Press International)

The streamer on the left: "More tanks for the front!" The poster on the right: "Save us, soldier of the Red Army!" (N. Sitnikov)

"Save it/Sell it"

General Aircraft Astoria Glider Factory, Lola Weixel's crew *(Robert Yarnell Richie)*

Women welders *(Detroit Historical Museum)*

Inspectors of the tank *(Life Picture Service)*

Woman "controls" a vat of molten steel *(Life Picture Service)*

Woman making shells *(King Features Syndicate)*

Aircraft factory

Members of the Mochida family await evacuation bus

Oral Histories

**AGRIPPINA
MIKHAILOVNA
KHROMOVA**

1943
(News Press Agency)

1987
(News Press Agency)

The war found Agrippina Mikhailovna at home. A native Muscovite, she had already worked nine years as a lathe turner in a Moscow electromechanical plant when the Soviet Union was invaded. She continued to work there throughout the war, rising to the rank of forewoman. She gave fifty-three years of her life to the plant, and her work was rewarded with the highest government award—the Order of Lenin. Here is what she said during the spacebridge about the work on the home front:

I started working at the factory in 1933, after finishing vocational school. I worked as a milling-machine operator. When the war started, they took men to the front, and the women had to work the machines. Schoolboys and teenagers arrived at the plant. I worked as a machinist and instructed these boys and girls.

You know, they couldn't even reach the machines! Our director now is Nikolai Sergeyevich Chikirev, but he was an operator then, and they had to give him a box to stand on so he could reach to the machine. Later, in 1944 they called our foreman to the front, and they put me to work in his place. It was hard and cold.

But there was happiness when letters, good letters, came from the front. We waited and waited for the end of the war. And then, when I was working a night shift, they announced that the war was over. You know, there was no limit to our joy! How happy were the people, how glad. . . .

In the name of all mothers, I want to say it must never happen again. May our children and grandchildren produce only peaceful things and never discover war; may the skies over our countries always remain clear.

In a post-spacebridge interview, Agrippina Khromova said:

○ When they declared war, everyone ran to the stores—to buy, of course, to stock up. Well, I thought, you cannot stock up forever. Whatever must happen will happen.

Shortly, within a week, my husband was called up to the front. I was left to work at the plant. Immediately, we started to work twelve-hour shifts and even more. I remember that it was already October when talk went around that the factory was to be evacuated. At that time, we were producing military equipment; we were making supports for the Katyusha rocket launchers, and I milled the side of these beams. Anyway, one morning we arrived at work, and horror, all the machines were lifted from their foundations. In one night they had done it. And right there where my machine had stood was a gaping hole. I asked the foreman, "What happened? Why?" And he said that all the machines were being pulled out so as to transport them immediately to Nizhniy Tagil in the Urals.

I couldn't go to Nizhniy Tagil because I had a small child. Take him with me? Where would I go with him? There were no nurseries or anything, and here I had my parents. The child stayed with my parents while I worked.

When the entire plant left, they organized a special plant in Moscow. We made breech locks for submachine guns. At first I worked at a machine. But later, when they were taking more girls, they made me a master machinist; I had already been a fourth-class machinist. We made these breech locks for a long time.

It was terrible when the enemy approached Moscow. Everyone abandoned their places and dwellings; they panicked. They left their doors open and fled. Again I decided, whatever must happen will happen. What can I do? Where can I take my child? All the more, my father and mother couldn't run anywhere. I slept nights with them. I remember my father dug foxholes where we could hide during air raids. My son used to jump up in the night and cry, "Mama, I'm going to fight the fascists!" And he was all of five years old.

I did not want to think about what would happen if the Germans took Moscow. But when they bombed us. . . . We worked in the shops at night. During the air raids, everyone ran to the shelters. And when you re-emerged from the shelter, you could smell smoke everywhere. I recalled for some reason the book *War and Peace*. It described how Moscow once burned. We are living in the same times, I thought.

We worked, as I said before, in twelve-hour shifts; we had one free day in the middle of the month, and then we rotated shifts. Twelve hours was a workday, and when I became a forewoman in 1943, I had to work even more.

The plant returned to Moscow in 1943, and then they said to me, "Granya, you can go back to your own shop." But nothing remained of the old shop. Only the framework stood. It was dark, cold, and even the emulsion had frozen. We burned campfires every night in the factory. It was hard.

We lived off potatoes. When I worked as a forewoman, they gave me special food rations. We ate in a dining hall and then went home. But the rations weren't given out to everybody. It was a terrible thing. You sat, you ate, and people were standing behind you and waiting; maybe something would be left, and they could eat. They gave the men only four hundred grams of bread. . . .

So it was, when we left for work it was dark, and when we came home it was dark. When the night shift started, even I felt like sleeping myself, and the young kids could barely stand on their feet. It was cold. We had a thermal kiln, where the machine parts went through aging. Usually when they pulled the parts out of the kiln, we asked, "Put them close to the machines so we can feel the the their warmth." And during the dinner break, everyone went to the kiln and laid down and went to sleep.

I trained many boys and girls during the war. Many of my pupils stayed on to work at the plant. I am proud of them. I am proud even now. We worked so hard. We broke records. Later, we got decorations for our labor. And whenever that happened, I always received one. Always. ○

1942   **1988**

Lola Weixel grew up in New York City, where she was a welder during the war. Years later, she became celebrated in the United States as one of the subject-participants in the film, Rosie the Riveter, *a highly acclaimed movie about American women workers during World War II. During the spacebridge, Lola Weixel related the following highlights from her memories of the home front:*

I'm very happy to be here. I hear your people speak, I see the scenes of your struggle, and I remember the great respect we held for the Soviet Union in our hearts. And we still do. That partnership was wonderful. We did it. I'm here representing nearly three million women who came into this army of production in our country. We did it proudly; we did it very well, I think. We had such a good feeling to have jobs of responsibility. This was something new for many, many of us, as we were still in the throes of the Depression and had not held jobs that we could be proud of.

But I remember that, and I'll tell you something else of a more personal nature. My first job was in a little machine shop in Manhattan. And we women, there were eight of us in the shop, made a semicircle of our work place, and we used to sing a lot during our work. We sang patriotic songs, we sang popular songs, we sang love songs, and we sang "Meadowland." I won't try to sing "Meadowland" for you now, but I want you to know that we felt this kinship with you.

Might I have one moment to read a letter from a common soldier to his parents? This is from the Anzio beachhead, April 13, 1944: "Dear Folks, As usual I don't know what to write expect that I'm okay. It must be springtime in Flatbush now. Over here it is getting green rapidly. I received your letter from Leon. I really miss all the kids. I like to see them at this stage. The war news from Russia is very encouraging to us. Perhaps this year we will actually see the finish of Hitler. Love to all, David." I thank you.

The following stories and details were added in a post-broadcast interview:

○ I was a welder during World War II. I worked hard, was an anti-fascist—thought about that every day—and thought about my loved ones in the war. I think that nobody can imagine the passion that we had, first as human beings, as anti-fascists, and, in my case, as a Jewish woman, to defeat fascism and save the world—save civilization from the plans of the Nazis that we all knew Hitler had outlined in his writings and in his ravings. So, I went to school. They had the National Youth Administration set up to train what today we call disadvantaged youth to learn trades. We were all disadvantaged during the Depression. I wanted to become a welder because the boy across the street from my grandma's house was learning to be a welder, and he told me it was the most exciting thing on earth but that women couldn't do it. I wrote to the National Administration, and they agreed that women couldn't do it. Then one day, Herman, the boy across the street, told me that there was a woman in the program and that maybe I should try again. I wrote again, and they said this was an unusual and special woman; She was different than all the other women. She was a protegé of Mrs. Roosevelt. She was going to be a pilot as well, and she was using welding as a means of earning a living and spending her money on flying lessons.

But aha! Pearl Harbor happened. Right away I got a letter, and there were lots of other women there overnight being trained. There were men in the program, too. We had a really good course. We had to take sheet-metal work before we could do welding; we had to learn to use tools. I was very bad. I was pretty dumb, but I was so determined, and they were so kind in that they didn't throw me out. They let me stay as long as it took, and it took me long compared to the other people, but then I got very good. We had two unusual teachers, and they were able to speak and tell me about what the heck I was doing there and what the function of welding was. I was never one who could learn something by imitating; I had to understand the process. Before I knew it, I was not only working as a welder, but I had a certificate that said that I was a first-class welder. Lots of the women got that. We were very, very proud of it. It meant you were capable and could be trusted to work any kind of welding job. . . . Some people thought we were there to meet men. What men? We were there to get that "A" paper.

The women I worked with and the women I went to school with were largely, what we called at that time, working-class women. There's some talk saying that women came from every walk of life, and I suppose it's true, but women who chose to do hard, dirty work were working-class women whose fathers and brothers often were in the trades. They thought it was great. They knew about unions; they knew that they could make more money if they joined unions. Most of them were really down-to-earth, nice; I don't like to say ordinary or plain, but I mean that in the best sense of the words. Women who could be depended upon.

The first job I had as a welder was in a machine shop where they were making targets. We did the metal frames. They were round metal frames, and I understand that a colored sleeve would be put on it. They were towed up in the air on an airplane, and the men would do target practice on those. Now this was really very simple welding, and that made me a little unhappy because I felt that I could do more. I don't want to say that it was boring. It wasn't, because we had a lot of fun in the shop. We did a lot of singing, and the girls were swell. But I really wanted to do more skilled work.

There were some women who wanted to do what they called table work. They would sit, I guess these were some of the older women, and do small parts for the glider. The young ones, and I was among them, wanted to do the climbing all over the glider, working in strange positions and doing more demanding work. That was fun. Now, the last job I had was very strange because they told us that we were making bomb cases. So I say we were making bomb cases. But I wouldn't swear to that. I don't know. They looked like metal coffins.

There were older men, and then, after awhile, wounded veterans . . . coming back, soldiers who had been hurt or whatever. For whatever reason, they were out of the army.

Of the women I worked with, well, there were some more political than others, but they were all very much for the war and against Hitler. I must say that the feelings against the Japanese bordered on the racist. Everybody watched where the Red Army was every day on the maps. Everybody cared about that because they knew damn well we were giving our money, we were giving our production, but they were giving their people. We all knew it; everybody knew it. It hurts me today when I realize that there are so many young people growing up who don't even know that we were a partnership.

At that time of World War II, I had an awfully nice-looking boyfriend, a very quiet, gentle person, and after our courtship, he asked me to get married. I agreed that it was a very good idea. Now, David was in the army, and at that time, although this may sound impossible to people of this generation, he had to get his okay from his officer to get married. You didn't just go and get married because you're a human being and you're in love. The army had to agree that, yes, it was a good thing, you should go get married. David got the agreement of his officer to come to New York, come home and we could get married. And there was a specific date mentioned. Now, that weekend, a Russian heroine, her name was Ludmilla Pavlichenko, a famous woman sniper who had dispatched scores of Nazis to Valhalla, was coming to New York, and they were going to give her a big welcome. I had to choose. Was I going to go get married or go to Central Park and see Ludmilla? Well, my co-workers really thought. . . that I should go to see Ludmilla. But I felt that David had an added glamour, and instead, I missed her.

There was always a question at the time of the war, especially in the earlier stage of our involvement, whether or not it was proper for women to follow their beloved soldiers, husbands, or boyfriends, that is, to the places where their training camps were. I felt that my job was to stay put and do my work. Sometimes, I used to think it would have been better—we would have had more time together. As it was, we were together a pitifully short time.

But I had a friend and a co-worker, and I think that her story is typical of the experiences of the women who went from place to place. Because many times a soldier would be assigned to one place for some training and then go someplace else for another part of his training. My friend was Elizabeth. We called her "Tex." She was a wonderful welder and a woman full of the spirit of adventure and fun. When she and her boyfriend, Sal, got married, she followed him. She went first to Chicago. But she couldn't get a job because the people didn't want to hire women, even though they were trained, if they were following a soldier, because they knew that sooner or later it would be over. They couldn't feel that this worker was going to be someone they could depend on.

That was a very big feature—a lot of women traveling all over the country. I thought about it, but I really didn't want to do it because I felt that my own dignity depended on my own carrying out of my responsibilities. As I said, sometimes I felt I should have; my husband and I would have been closer. But that was Hitler's fault.

My husband wrote to me at one time when I guess he was contemplating how we would get along after the war, because we were not rich people. We were not even comfortable people. We were very uncomfortable people as far as money was concerned. And he said: "You'll be a welder after the war. And you'll make a decent living and I'll do something and together we'll be okay. Don't worry." We did depend on it. So what a shock to find out that it was not to be. I think that the question often is, Well, didn't you women expect to be thrown out after the war? Some women apparently, according to what they say, did. But people I worked with . . . thought we were learning a skill that would last us and be useful all our lives. We were very shocked and angry and hurt when we found that that was not true, that after the war they were finished with us, and we were gone—in spite of being a first-class welder and all that. It was not to be for the future.

I think the testimony of black women was especially touching, in that here they gained so much dignity and a feeling of self-worth from holding down these jobs in difficult situations. They were very good, very good. Black women wanted very much to excel because they had so much to gain. More than the rest of us, I would say. And to hear them say that they had to go back to cleaning somebody's house was really very, very maddening. You can imagine the frustration that went with that.

After the war I got pregnant the minute—I won't say the minute because that's rude, but I would say I got pregnant within a very few hours—of my husband's return.

I kept working through the war, and I had lots of letters and a lot of loneliness. But . . . I don't even like to talk about those years, because compared to what the Russian people went through, we had a picnic. We really had a picnic. I can never forget the stories about how their people suffered. I can think of them now—young women hanging by their throats. I never, never want to see anything like that again. Not for the Russians, not for the Americans, not for the French, not for the Germans, not for anybody. Not for anybody. I want my beautiful grandchildren to grow up without such fear and anxiety. And that's why I am here: to remember war and to tell you that I still do my best. I don't have the old strength left, but I'll do my best. If this is all I can do, then this is all I'll do. ○

**ANNE
SMITH**

1942   **1985**

*Anne Smith grew up in the Bedford-Stuyvesant area of Brooklyn in the 1930s
when that area was racially united and middle class, not the poverty-stricken
neighborhood it has since become. Her father had served with the U.S. forces in
World War I but remained bitter about his experience because as a black man he
was not allowed to fight. At the beginning of World War II, Anne Smith was
seventeen years old. She volunteered to aid her country on the home front by
becoming a hostess at a club or canteen for servicemen. Unfortunately, although
Ms. Smith came from New York to participate in* Remembering War, *and was a
key member of the group gathered in San Diego, she did not have an opportunity to
share her memories on the air. What follows are the recollections she had intended
to contribute:*

○ The war had started, and I had a friend named Muriel. Muriel had a
mother who was a very glamorous lady, who said to her daughter and said
to me, "With the war going on, I think that you should come and do your
bit for the boys at war at the Stage Door Canteen where I am a hostess." So
Muriel and I joined her mother. Her mother was a "senior hostess," and
we were "junior hostesses." The Stage Door Canteen was in the theater
district, Forty-second Street. It was a very exciting place to go to. One
really felt when one walked in that you were entering a theater. It had a
great deal of sparkle, a great deal of glamour and excitement. I think for all
the servicemen who went there, it was a time, if just one night, of exposure
to New York and the glitter of Broadway. It was a pretty place. I don't think
they served alcoholic drinks; I think it was just soft drinks, sitting around a
small table.

I was seventeen, at the most eighteen, years old, and I had hardly been
out of Brooklyn, never mind being surrounded by a lot of military men.
The Canteen was filled with glitter and Broadway stars and a lot of lights,
and yet it was very, very well chaperoned—extremely so. Therefore, my
mother felt that it was safe for me to go. The rules were very tight and very

rigid; one could not date the guys who were there. I followed the rules because I was that kind of person. I did whatever they said to do and did not do what they said not to do. We would go and dance with the sailors and the marines and the soldiers. We met men from all over the world. All the women would be dressed up in fancy clothes, and we would get up and dance. There must have been seventy-five, a hundred, or more women. I went two or three nights a week. I worked from whenever they began having so-called junior hostesses until they ended, until the war ended, I suppose. It was very exciting. It was fun.

Even there it was not really integrated. They had the black hostesses, and they had the black servicemen, and there were Indian servicemen. Anyone who was dark hued, you know, would know without even having it said that you ask someone who was also dark hued to dance. The soldiers talked about home; they were lonesome and just wanted to talk about their families, their girlfriends, their wives, mothers, fathers, whatever.

Most of the soldiers were more interested in a night that would be fun for them, where they could dance and laugh. They talked about family; they didn't talk too much about the war. They didn't talk about the enemy. I guess the enemy was just life around them. I think most of us who were there as hostesses, junior or senior, were just there to lend an ear, which was about all it was. We only got asked to dance by men of color, and they might have been American or they might have been from elsewhere in the world. But they were men of color, and they seemed to know the unbroken rule: you only ask somebody of color if you are of color. And that was America.

I think that my memories are those of a shift between patriotism—real patriotism, and care for what was happening to the country—and resentment at what was happening to young black men, . . . serving their country as well as anybody else could serve, but . . . being ignored, if not maltreated, dismissed as unimportant. My husband was a college grad, and he was with other friends who were also college graduates, and there was a black sergeant who was probably illiterate and who could not stand the fact that here was this group of men who had gone to college. And so this man would make fun of him. He was a sergeant, and they were noncoms, and he would say, "Now, here are the college boys." Then he would say to them, "Hup! two, three, four. Hup! two, three, four. It is did in the following manner!" My husband got so mad. . . . I don't know whether he punched the man out, but I know he kept getting busted.

I don't think that, perhaps, white American women felt the same way. They may have had just one feeling: the patriotism, the sorrow at the loss of life. I don't know that they had the same confusion and or ambivalence that I think we did as black women. That does not mean in any way that there was not the overall feeling of caring about what was going to happen to the country, but trying to identify the enemy became a little clouded in terms of who is the enemy, you know, and what is the enemy doing to you.

We were there, I am sure, because it was an integrated Stage Door Canteen, but they still felt that it had to be populated by people who were black and people who were white so that never the twain would meet. That's where I spent my war years in terms of volunteering, if you will. I didn't wrap bandages, and I didn't do any of those other nice things, but I did do that.

I also lost friends. I remember losing a classmate who had been very dear to me and a boyfriend down the block who had been very dear to me. They died. So I learned that the war was serious; it wasn't all fun and games in terms of going to the Stage Door Canteen and having a nice time.

The war was a painful one, and it was an important one. Even black people felt that we were involved. Then I met my husband, and my husband has helped me understand some of the things that I did not realize in those days. He was a black man who wanted to serve and was in the service but was denied the opportunity to really express his own feeling about the country. He just did what he had to do which was like KP, working in the kitchen, cleaning up the mess, being on, well, being on kitchen duty, basically. He was a man with a masters in music, a man who certainly could read and write English very well. In fact, he had taught English.

I remember anti-German feelings. German butcher shops that my mother had gone to were closing down, and my mother worried about the people who owned the shops and worried about the fact that she couldn't get the good meat that she had bought. We were concerned, or they were concerned—I was still pretty young—they were concerned about what was happening to the Japanese in California, on the West Coast, and the concentration camps that seemed to be coming over and being on this continent, in this country. They were concerned about what was happening in Manhattan, where there was a Bund. I can't remember any hostility about Russians. I think that basically they must have been considered being with us, on our side, and not the enemy. The Germans were the enemy, the Japanese were the enemy, but yet we wondered about, what about the Japanese who were here and are American citizens.

I don't remember that black people went into the war industry as such because there were still barriers in terms of employment, and whatever they had been doing, they just kept on doing. They worked harder, but I don't think their lives changed that much in terms of the war condition. I don't think they went out to factories and did riveting or whatever. Again, it's a long time ago, and it's hard to remember. In some ways it's painful to try to remember. I do remember, when Franklin Roosevelt died, [I was] crying, standing on the stoop in front of our house in Brooklyn, sobbing. Because he was at least symbolic of someone who seemed to speak for all people. You always know there's a flaw, you know, but still, at least if it's there only on the surface, it helps a little bit.

I don't think that some of the pain or some of the feelings of frustration and resentment about the treatment of blacks during World War II have ever left. I don't think they ever will leave. I think that, even today, they still exist in terms of the country and its tolerance and intolerance of a mixed society. I think that's one of the problems that black people felt during that war. I think that we all felt the need to be behind the country and to support the national cause. But then when one turns around and looks at the home cause and you see such divergence and you see such inconsistency, it becomes a little painful. I guess that's the only word I can say, painful.

The Soviets have never been a matter of great concern to the majority of black Americans. Neither pro or con. I think that there have been so many issues within the country that one would not need to go outside your country and try to find somebody to worry about. And I think that with the McCarthy days and the latter days and even the present days that that is not really a concern. I think that most of us are more concerned about how we can survive here with integrity and with honesty, and we don't look for an enemy outside this country. And if we did, it wouldn't be the Soviets. I mean it just doesn't figure; it doesn't enter into my thinking or the thinking of most people whom I know who are my age and are well educated. It's just not a big concern. We don't see the Soviets as Big Bad Brother. There are a lot of Little Bad Brothers right here. ○

Representations of War

U.S. Images: An American's View

For the vast majority of Americans, World War II was not known through personal experiences of battle and destruction but through verbal and visual images from a variety of media. Letters and photographs from soldiers and sailors abroad brought bits and pieces of the war to Americans at home, and the mass media—newspapers, magazines, movies, and radio— provided an unprecedented daily deluge of images of the "overseas" war. Significant changes in technology since World War I, followed by the proliferation of neighborhood movie theaters, the mass production of radio receivers for American homes, and major increases in the speed and quantity of air transport, meant that the events and meanings of World War II could be presented to Americans in ways unimagined in any previous war.

Nonetheless, those responsible for imaging World War II for Americans had a large task. Even after the Japanese assault on Pearl Harbor, the war posed only a remote threat for many Americans. No matter how fast or skillfully projected, it was not easy to bring home the disparate issues, varied geographical contexts, and profound and widespread human suffering of World War II. Even those who fought overseas could not grasp the whole picture of this war: American soldiers stationed in the South Pacific had very different pictures of the war from those who landed on the beaches in Normandy, and few of these men and women could imagine what the war looked like to Soviet civilians in Leningrad or to those imprisoned in German concentration camps.

To help Americans understand why they were fighting and to inspire Americans overseas and at home to support the war effort, the U.S. government and armed services employed tens of thousands of women and men to broadcast and photograph the war, to write stories, to make movies, leaflets, posters, and advertisements. A special department—the Office of War Information (OWI)—was established in 1942 to incite resistance abroad to fascism and to encourage commitment to the war effort at home. The large staff of the OWI not only produced propaganda materials in support of the war but also invested considerable time and effort in research about the requirements for and effects of U.S. media during the war years. The OWI was joined in these efforts by, and occasionally competed with, special media units established within the War Department and within each branch of the armed services; organizations were also formed that created ties between government agencies and private enterprises, from the movie-making industries of Hollywood to the advertising agencies of Madison Avenue.

The men and women who comprised this army of image makers included some of the most outstanding artists of the time. Dick Kent, whose photographs appear in other sections of this book, Robert Capa, and Margaret Bourke-White were only three of the thousands of fine photographers of the war. Walt Disney and the best animators at his studio contributed animated maps that made the tiny islands of the Pacific less obscure and brought to life the movements of ships and troops in the war theaters around the world. In the 1930s, poet Archibald MacLeish turned his pen to radio dramas that warned Americans of the dangers of fascism; appointed librarian of Congress in 1939, MacLeish spent the prewar and war years applying his understanding of art and rhetoric to the U.S. government's war information campaigns.

Among the most evocative images of America's experiences in World War II were Bill Mauldin's cartoons; drawn from the battlefields of Italy and France, Mauldin's drawings captured the texture and fragility of daily life for the ordinary American soldier. His GI Joe and Willy were sketched with an extraordinary precision and fidelity to the grim fatigue and absurdities of war. There was little glamour and not much conventional heroism in Mauldin's cartoons; their tender attachment to the woebegone field soldiers lingered for the reader, while Mauldin's often biting humor was aimed at nature, the army bureaucracy, and the enemy. One typical cartoon, drawn in France, showed Willy and Joe attempting to take cover from heavy rain under a solitary tree; the caption read, "This damn tree leaks." In Mauldin's own words, in the war world of his drawings, "life is stripped down to bare essentials for him [the soldier] when he is living from minute to minute, wondering if each is his last."

While Bill Mauldin accompanied the American GI across embattled seas and foreign fields, from his home state of Vermont, illustrator Norman Rockwell created popular, gentle images of the American home front. His pictures appeared on more than three hundred covers of the *Saturday Evening Post* and were printed and duplicated in dozens of different contexts, from school texts to advertisements. Rockwell painted ordinary Americans in everyday settings, but during the 1940s, many of the moments Rockwell created on canvas were clearly intended to encourage the war effort: Rockwell's Rosie the Riveter is posed high on a stool eating a sandwich during a work break; proud and tough, she dares anyone to question her role. In another painting, a young woman costumed in fabric suggesting the American flag strides forward with all of the tools of "men's work" on her back. Many of Rockwell's wartime pictures depicted a moment in the life of a gangling, freckled, wide-eyed American soldier-boy named Willis Gillis, who wore his uniform proudly and appeared as vulnerable returning from war as he had in going off.

Norman Rockwell's most ambitious project during the war years was a series of four huge canvases called the Four Freedoms. Inspired by Roosevelt's and Churchill's Atlantic Charter, with its proclamation of the "Four Freedoms"—freedom from want, freedom of speech, freedom of worship, and freedom from fear—these paintings took six months for Rockwell to complete and were intended from the start to be a contribution from the illustrator to his native land's struggle in the war. Rockwell's goal was to translate the "noble" language of the Atlantic Charter into terms that everyone could understand. He accomplished this by representing each concept of freedom with a scene from daily life in New England. Freedom of speech was represented by a rural man speaking his piece at a town meeting. Freedom from want was a Thanksgiving dinner. Freedom of worship presents a melting pot of American faces, each engaged in a distinctive form of prayer or contemplation; at the top of the painting are the words, "Each according to the dictates of his own conscience." Freedom from fear presents a mother and father tucking their children into bed (painted during the bombings of London). Rockwell suggests that the image is meant to say, "Thank God we can put our children to bed with a feeling of security, knowing they will not be killed in the night."

Following rejections from several government offices, Rockwell's Four Freedoms were published not as covers but as inside features in the *Saturday Evening Post* in early 1943. Millions of reprints were immediately requested and printed; a nationwide tour to display the original canvases, organized by the U.S. Treasury Department, was attended by more than a million people and brought about the sale of $132,992,539 worth of war bonds.

In addition to magazines and organized tours, the materials created by the army of image makers appeared on billboards that flanked the nation's highways, on the walls of post offices, schools, and town halls, and in newspapers and magazines across the United States. They also appeared in great quantities abroad. Leaflets, often with text on one side and drawings or photographs on the other, were air-dropped behind enemy lines throughout the war; leafletting became particularly effective after the summer of 1944 when a U.S. air force captain named James Monroe invented a tube-like device that could contain at least eight thousand leaflets. With the production of more than seventy-five thousand of these "Monroe bombs" and the dissemination of over two billion leaflets in the last year of the war, cartoons began to appear showing Japanese or German soldiers expressing relief when a U.S. plane dropped a "real" bomb.

There is little doubt that radio was the key American medium of World War II. No depiction of the war years in the United States would be complete without an image of an American family clustered around the household radio. From Pearl Harbor to VJ Day, radio broadcasts kept Americans informed of Allied defeats and successes, of numbers and names of casualties, of the feats of heroes who survived and some who did not. Radio brought not just the words but also the sound of the voice of President Franklin Roosevelt into American homes and work places, and the power of that particular voice at once to challenge and reassure millions of citizens sharing the same moment in time was of inestimable value in creating a sense of public concern and commitment to the war effort. Radio also provided Americans with new songs to sing, and while popular tunes like "Remember Pearl Harbor" and "Praise the Lord and Pass the Ammunition" did not articulate the grief or horrors of the war, they did serve to remind Americans at home that there *was* a war going on.

Americans whose ears were glued to the radio in the 1940s remember two men, Norman Corwin and Arch Oboler, as synonymous with wartime radio. Both were director-writers. Norman Corwin made an art of radio broadcasting with a wealth of scripts ranging from drama to news commentary. *This is War!*, the first dramatic series on radio to openly focus on the war, was directed by Corwin, who also wrote more than half the scripts for the programs. Many Americans will recall the opening announcement by the narrator of the first *This is War!* program:

> What we say tonight has to do with blood and with love and with anger, and also with a big job in the making. Laughter can wait. Soft music can have the evening off. No one is invited to sit down and take it easy. Later, later. There's a war on.

More than twenty million Americans heard these words, broadcast simultaneously over the four major networks of the period and also transmitted by shortwave abroad.

Millions of Americans also listened to Arch Oboler's *Plays for Ameri-*

cans, another series of radio dramas explicitly intended to inspire and inform the American audience about the war and its role in it. Oboler saw radio as having an enormous power to shape the values of the audience, and he was angry that the medium had not been used in the prewar period to call the attention of Americans to the complexities of the war in Spain, the Munich agreement, and other steps that some felt clearly led to war. The scripts Oboler did write created surprising and compelling situations that confronted the listener with the issues of the time without reducing these issues to sermons. In "Ghost Story," for example, Joe, a machinist, complains because he wants to be drafted but has been deferred because his skills are essential to the war effort. Alone one night at the factory, Joe discovers workers from around the world positioned at his machines; they are the ghosts of dead machinists, killed already in the war, who have come to do Joe's work if he insists on going to the battlefields. The message that production work is as important, even if less obviously heroic, than soldier's work is blatant, but its presentation is disorienting and engaging.

Not even the radio of Obeler and Corwin could, however, make Americans *see* either the face of the enemy or the suffering and courage of the men and women on the front lines. Photographs published in newspapers and magazines provided Americans with glimpses of battlefronts, of death and destruction, but within a few months of the United States' declaration of war, it appeared clear to several leading Americans that these still images did not suffice. American generals and statesman judged, probably accurately as evidenced by research during the period and afterwards, that neither the young Americans being sent to the battlefields or fiery seas nor the home front workers being asked to double and triple their production output understood why they fought.

Among the most successful and ambitious responses to this dilemma was a film series entitled, *Why We Fight,* directed primarily by Hollywood filmmaker Frank Capra and produced under the auspices of the U.S. War Department. Capra was charged by General George C. Marshall with the task of creating a series of films that would persuade "young, freewheeling American boys" that there were worthwhile reasons to give up the comforts of home for the "killing cold of the Arctic, the hallucinating heat of the desert, or the smelly muck of the jungle." Capra took this task seriously; by the end of the war he had made seven films: *Prelude to War, The Nazis Strike, Divide and Conquer, The Battle of Britain, The Battle of Russia, The Battle of China,* and *War Comes to America.* With each of these films, the director's overall goal was not only to help win the war but also to "win the peace" by educating viewers in the values and practices of other cultures and by showing the horrors of the exploitation of many citizens by a few tyrants. More specifically, *The Battle of Britain, The Battle of Russia,* and *The Battle of China* were an attempt to acquaint viewers with the cultures of

America's allies and to awaken viewers to the sufferings of people in England, China, and the Soviet Union. The four other films in the series focused on information and arguments about the causes of the war and particular battles; contrasts between the Axis and the Allies emphasize the courage and competence of the Allies compared to the corruption and authoritarianism of the Axis nations. The common motifs of all the films in this series were religion, children and families, the necessity of ending war as a human activity, national history, and the heroism of Allied soldiers. All of the films shared a commitment to the provision of information. Accurate and detailed information hopefully would persuade Americans of the importance of the U.S. engagement in World War II.

Determined to accomplish these goals quickly and efficiently, Capra hit upon the idea of using the enemies' own films to convey the horrors of totalitarianism and fascism. This device, combined with his own uncanny sense of the exact timing and images that would engage the viewer, proved so successful that almost as soon as the first films were released, they were translated and screened for Allied troops all over the world.

Capra went to great lengths to acquire Soviet film footage for the fifth film in the series, *The Battle of Russia,* a film that few Americans in later years would believe was a product of the U.S. War Department because of its unstinting depiction of the heroism, sufferings, and courage of Soviet soldiers and citizens. The film displayed Russia's past accomplishments and noted how the Russians' values were repeatedly marked by invasions of their country. Shots of the wartime situation showed innocent children dying alone in the snow, adults pulling the dead on children's sleds, and a powerful incantation of a vow by Soviet men and women not to rest until the enemy was overcome.

Accused of having approached Soviet Ambassador Litvinov without authorization, and, thus, violating the Articles of War while filming *The Battle of Russia,* Capra defended his actions on the grounds that only the Soviets could provide films of U.S. lend-lease material being used by Soviet soldiers. Capra was allowed to complete the film and had the satisfaction of knowing that it presented Americans with a vivid answer to why we were fighting with the Soviets as our Allies. After viewing the film himself, Stalin ordered five hundred prints to be shown throughout the Soviet Union.

Ironically, while the *Why We Fight* series had a strong impact on millions of people outside the United States and on the American soldiers for whom it was originally intended, only three of the films in the series— *Prelude to War, The Battle of Britain,* and *The Battle of Russia*—were released for theatrical distribution. Americans who went to the movies did see images of war, but much of what they saw reduced the conflict to fights between good and bad people. American popular movies of the period tended to emphasize romantic liaisons or individual heroic deeds, while blurring or ignoring the complexities of history and politics. Several films, most notably *Casablanca,* dramatized the conversion of Americans from passivity or ignorance of the war to active commitment. Other Hollywood films presented caricatured images of the Japanese and German foes or equally stereotyped positive images of the British, French, and Soviet allies. Both during the war years and afterwards, individual characters in American movies might proclaim that "war is hell," but until the 1970s, the dominant film image of war, and of World War II in particular, was war as a great adventure. As projected on American movie screens, war provided unique and appealing opportunities for fraternity among men and for acts of heroism that confirmed the special virtues of Americans.

Underlying the differences between the *Why We Fight* series and the majority of Hollywood war films of the 1940s was a conflict of concerns among Americans in positions to affect the images of war presented to the public. On one side of this conflict was a coalition of artists, academics, and political figures, including then-Senator Harry Truman. This group argued that the overriding goal of all U.S. media for the duration of the war should be encouragement of President Roosevelt's "Four Freedoms"; from this perspective, Norman Rockwell's paintings were the perfect response to the war. In the judgment of these men and women, both federal and private institutions were trivializing the war and deliberately failing to convey its seriousness to the American public. In opposition were business people and conservative politicians, most of whom had long been at odds with Roosevelt's domestic policies; these people were primarily concerned with economic achievement and saw little threat to U.S. security as long as American industry was thriving.

The conflict between these factions exploded inside the Office of War Information, resulting in the resignations of fifteen members of the organization in protest of what they viewed as the manipulation of images to create a picture of the "good war." Those who remained and became powerful in the agency were primarily recruits from Madison Avenue advertising agencies. They had won a curious and unexpected victory in a battle that had commenced well before the war years. With support from the Roosevelt administration, a strong consumer-protection movement in the 1930s had culminated in 1938 in the passage of the Wheeler-Lea Act, which provided for the regulation of advertising content and gave power to the Federal Trade Commission to enact this regulation. As U.S. manufacturing converted to war production in 1940, the advertising industry saw the writing on the wall: a war economy in which consumer goods were scarce would have no need for advertising. By 1942, the worst fears of advertisers were becoming a reality. Senator Truman and others were calling for an end to business tax write-offs that had supported the advertising industry, and other government officials were loudly voicing their dismay at the self-indulgent image of American society portrayed by American advertisements.

At just that time, however, when many in the advertising industry expected a blackout of their medium, the industry came up with a plan to save both itself and the country. Americans needed to be "sold" on the U.S. involvement in the war, and the experts who could accomplish this were the admen themselves. The U.S. government agreed, and as a result, the advertising industry became one of the most influential sources of America's images of war. On one "front," many Americans who had worked in the advertising industry in the prewar years joined the Office of War Information and other federal and military agencies as experts who oversaw the strategies and content of government-sponsored posters, leaflets, and advertisements. The private advertising industry was allowed to flourish with the understanding that it would frame its commercial efforts in terms of the war effort.

The primary strategy used by the advertising agencies to satisfy both their own interests and those of the government was a campaign to "sell" the American Way. The editors of the magazine *Printers Ink* articulated this policy clearly in January of 1943:

> We can keep idealism alive, nurturing appreciation of the values of Peace . . . pointing up the rewards which arise from our way of life. We can keep the Horizons of Tomorrow bright and shining, keeping them clearly before ourselves and all our people as we struggle onward midst affairs and events calculated to dull men's finer sensibilities. We can herald the return of Peace with promises that will challenge the spirit of constructive adventure which feeds in the deep roots of American achivement . . . speaking in truths which flame clearly for all who will see. Oh, what a *mission* for advertising.

Advertising fulfilled this mission remarkably well—in its own, inimitable fashion. As Frank W. Fox,* an authoritative scholar on this topic has argued, the "hard-sell" approach of the advertising industry produced superficial, "supercharged," melodramatic images of the war, images that had little to do with the realities of the conflict but which did succeed in inspiring Americans to buy war bonds, save scrap metal, plant fifty million victory gardens, and enlist in vast numbers in production and armed forces.

Informed by their notions of psychological effects, admen played on two basic emotions—fear and pride. Some of the most strident and threat-

---

*This section is significantly informed by Frank W. Fox's monograph, *Madison Avenue Goes to War: The Strange Military Career of American Advertising, 1941–45*, vol. 4, number 1, Charles E. Merrill Monograph Series in the Humanities and Social Sciences, Brigham Young University, June 1975.

ening ads were those that warned Americans to be wary of hidden spies all around them who might be listening for bits and pieces of information: a casual phrase or word spoken in the wrong place might endanger the safety of the country, these ads suggested, with accompanying gruesome images of coffins and dead pets. The Japanese were portrayed equally melodramatically as monsters and ogres with no respect for human life. Germans were rarely visually represented but were indirectly projected as lascivious tyrants and torturers, who, more than one ad warned, had their eyes on the sexual attractions of young American women: "High Honor for Your Daughter" was the caption underneath an American advertisement image of American girls lined up for projected Nazi abuse.

In contrast, young American soldiers were portrayed as dashing adventurers, cowboys in shining military armor, eagerly taking on—and vanquishing—their foes and rejoicing in the fraternity they found in each other's company. Several ads used the language and visual imagery of sports—football and hunting especially—to convey the challenge of the "game" of war. In posters as well as ads, religious symbolism tended to glorify war, showing figures from President Roosevelt to air-force pilots speaking to Americans from heavenly clouds, while backlit crosses glowed on earth below. Vivid colors, flattened surfaces, and emblematic depictions of guns, flags, and warships called forth cheers for freedom and cries of revenge while situating the war itself in a fairy-tale-like world.

Many of these ads succeeded in simultaneously accentuating the triumphs of American soldiers abroad and insisting on the virtue and goodness of the American way of life. A large number of ads presented images of "Freedom": eagles and airplanes soared unhindered in the skies and American men and machines broke the walls and chains that confined foreigners in other lands. An equal number of images equated the freedom for which Americans were fighting—and making sacrifices at home—with the opportunity to buy and possess the material objects of the good life: American youth happily drinking Coca-Cola and American families displayed proudly in front of their modern kitchen appliances told viewers what they were fighting for and hinted at what would be lost if the enemy should be victorious.

As the end of World War II approached, Americans abroad increasingly witnessed the atrocities of war, as Dick Kent's photographs in Chapter 5 painfully reveal. At home, however, even after American soldiers and journalists had come face to face with the horrors of concentration camps and of cities burned and bombed to rubble, American civilians saw few authentic images of war. Instead, they were presented with pictures of the good life ahead of them and the glories of their past American history. It is not surprising that some Americans were thus left with an image of war as an adventure or romantic challenge that had little to do with daily life in the United States. Nor is it surprising that, bombarded with images of tyrants as undistinguishable foes of a freedom that was equated with material wealth, the heat of World War II should be easily translated into the Cold War that followed.

U.S. war poster

"Your motherland wants you!" *(News Press Agency)*

U.S. Army recruitment poster

'Save us, soldier of the Red Army!'
(News Press Agency)

Post magazine cover, May 29, 1943
(Curtis Publishing Co.)

"We will cut off all routes of retreat for the vile enemy; he will not escape from this noose."
(*News Press Agency*)

P. Korin, *Alexander Nevsky (News Press Agency)*

Life magazine cover, July 19, 1943 *(Life Picture Service)*

A. Plastov, *A Fascist Flew By (News Press Agency)*

U.S. war poster

A Bill Mauldin war cartoon

A scene from the motion picture, *The Rainbow*, "Captured by the enemy." *(News Press Agency)*

S. Gerasimov, *The Partisan's Mother (News Press Release)*

"Willie Gillis returns home safe to Mom"—*Saturday Evening Post* cover for May 26, 1945, by Norman Rockwell *(Curtis Publishing Co.)*

Soviet Images: A Soviet's View

Any government at war will portray a foe as being somewhat less than human—the quintessential beast, murderous, brutal, treacherous; a one-dimensional demon who knows no such emotions as love, mercy, empathy, remorse; a monster that must be destroyed. Usually this process of demonization begins long before war itself. It builds as the hostility grows and gradually affects public opinion. The Soviet government however, on the eve of World War II, did not vilify Nazi Germany for a variety of reasons.

One reason, of course, is the signing of the Soviet-German non-aggression pact in 1939. Politically it would have been not only unwise but also dangerous to stir up anti-German sentiment while trying not to provoke a mortal foe who was looking for a reason to invade. But there was another and more fundamental reason for the absence of what today we call "creating the face of the enemy" and that involved one of the country's basic policies: internationalism.

As soon as they are able to understand, Soviet children are taught to respect all nations, all peoples; we may and indeed do have differences with governments and political systems they are told, but we have a common bond with all people. "Proletariat of the world, unite!"—the closing words of the Communist Manifesto—express the predominant feeling in the pre–World War II Soviet Union. The working people are all brothers, regardless of their country, and none of them would ever take up arms against those who had built the first socialist society, the first land of workers and peasants. Naive though it was, this view reflected the fervor and ideals of the socialist revolution of 1917, the popular dream of world revolution; it was very much part of a Soviet person's makeup—to such an extent, in fact, that when the war broke out, the Soviet leadership encountered an unforeseen problem: the Red Army soldier was not prepared to hate the enemy, was not psychologically primed to deal in kind with an implacable foe. The need radically to change that outlook found its most powerful expression in Ilya Ehrenburg's essay, published in *Pravda* in 1941, under the stark title "Kill!" with its no less stark message: Kill the German wherever and whenever you find him.

Imaging war had, of course, an aim—to contribute to victory. The artist was seen (and saw himself) as a fighting man whose talent and craft served that all-important goal. Literature and music do not directly pictorially image war as do film, paintings, cartoons, and posters; however, it must be mentioned that such works as Konstantine Simonov's poem "Wait for Me and I'll Return," Alexandrov's song "Rise Up, Vast Land," and Shostakovich's 7th "Leningrad" symphony were no less a *moral* stimulus to victory than were physically the battles of Moscow, Stalingrad, and Kursk. They became part of the entire nation's daily existence.

With the country's movie studios evacuated from Moscow and

Leningrad to Alma-Ata (Kazakhstan), Tashkent (Uzbekistan), and Ash-khabad (Turkmenia), and first wartime feature film appeared in 1942 (*The Regional Committee Secretary*, which dealt with the partisan movement behind enemy lines). It was followed by many others, the most internationally acclaimed of which was Mark Donskoy's *Rainbow* (1944), a tremendously moving and powerful epic of Nazi savagery in an occupied Ukrainian village. The heroic and tragic, however, were just two of the basic themes dealt with in Soviet wartime films. Others included friendship, fidelity, and love, probably best rendered, at least in the sense of popularity, in Lukov's classic *Two Soldiers* (1943). This movie provided the unbeatable combination of front-line friendship (typified by two inseparable buddies—Vanya, the strong, silent Russian, and Zhora, the mercurial, joke-cracking Jew from Odessa), love, and heroism (at the end of the picture the two hold off what looks like an entire German army). A song in the film, "Dark Night," became not only an immediate success but also ranks as an all-time favorite and is still sung today. Another theme was the heroic past, a glorification of Russia's former military exploits and leaders. *Alexander Nevsky*, the work of two geniuses, director Sergei Eisenstein and composer Sergei Prokofiev, which appeared on the eve of the war, in 1940, was probably the finest rendering of that theme. A total of 102 Soviet feature films were produced during the war, a reflection of the importance allotted to this genre by the government during a period when the country was fighting for its life.

Paintings had a narrower and less immediate exposure than film; however, through traveling exhibits and countless reproductions in magazines and newspapers, they, too, conveyed the message. In their highest form, wartime paintings attained artistic summits, often having a lasting and powerful impression on a growing number of people. Some examples are furnished in this chapter. Pavel Korin's *Alexander Nevsky*, was painted in the Russian ikon tradition, in which realistic portrayal assumes the scope of generalization. Prince Alexander Nevsky, who defeated the Teutonic Order in 1241, appears as a symbol of Russian invincibility. The link between the thirteenth-century warrior and the partisan Timachov, as portrayed by Igor Serebrianny, cannot be missed. Both stand as stern, calm, confident expressions of their land and people. Sergei Gerasimov's *The Partisan's Mother* deals with a traditional subject in traditional manner—the invader and the unconquerable, the futility of brute force and the power and glory of indomitable spirit. The horror of war and fascist atrocities found a far less predictable expression in Plastov's *A Fascist Flew By*, in which the serene beauty of what at first seems to be a typical Russian autumn landscape turns into a heart-rendering scene of carnage with slaughtered cows, a dog howling over the body of its machine-gunned child-master and, in the distance, almost melting into the pearly-grey sky, the perpetrator of this unspeakable crime. The heroic is the theme of Deineka's larger-than-life painting, *The Defence of Sevastopol*, where the vanquished (the Germans took Sevastopol after nine months) are nonetheless victorious in their refusal to surrender.

The most immediate message, however, to both the soldier and those on the home front, was delivered by poster art and cartoons. "The Motherland Calls" and "Red Army Soldier, SAVE THEM!" are classics with powerful emotional appeal. The message in posters entitled "Blow Them Up!" and "Kill the Fascist Beast!" is clear. That same message, but with far more humor, is conveyed in "Death to the German Occupants," where the foe is depicted as a horde of ugly gnomes about to be crushed by a Soviet tank. Perhaps one of the finest cartoons of the war was produced by Kukriniksi, "The Transformation of the Kraut." Kukriniksi* were also the first to render the theme of the Grand Alliance in a 1942 cartoon depicting a blood-stained Hitler being strangled by agreements between the Soviet Union, the United States, and Great Britain. Similarly, the poster "Europe Will Be Free" depicts the shackles of an enslaved Europe being shattered by the combined blows of Soviet, American, and British swords.

One of Sergei Yesenin's poems has the following line: "Face-to face the face cannot be seen"—the closer the picture, the more difficult it is to discern the details. The somewhat one-dimensional character of wartime art with its single-minded aim of contributing to victory illustrates that point. For a fuller detailed picture, one must back up in time, and the more grandiose the subject, the greater the need to distance oneself so as to arrive at a comprehensive image. The war affected the Soviet nation profoundly, in a way that Americans cannot comprehend. We are still getting it out of our systems, attempting to come to terms with what we went through. This, and not an inherently militaristic or aggressive system, is what underlies the preoccupation with the wartime theme still so evident in contemporary Soviet literature and art. But the imagery of the war produced during the war itself, even though lacking the depth and insight of what appeared in later years, preserves the immediacy, the raw essence, the drama of a monumental struggle that has marked the psyche of an entire people.

*Kukriniksi is a shared pen-name used by three Soviet painters.

Why We Fought

Atrocities were hardly mentioned during the actual spacebridge. The only words that come to mind are those that were spoken during the spacebridge by Vataliy Korotich, who, as a child, lived in German-occupied Kiev:

> I speak to our American viewers as a person who survived the war, who suffered through it, as someone whose country shielded the world from that horror, finally, as someone who rejoices in the fact that the children of America did not experience what we experienced.
>
> I was a child, living in Kiev, occupied by the Nazis. Later, I worked on a documentary film about Babi Yar, where the Nazis destroyed over 200,000 Jews. Every week they transported a truckload of children's shoes from Babi Yar. I don't know why they needed this footwear, but imagine how many children had to be killed in order to fill up a truckload of children's shoes. . . .
>
> We fought for peace in the world; we won that terrible war. We had no childhood. Yet I believe that our unrealized childhood is manifested in the war-free lives of our children—both American and Soviet. For every time we suffer, we learn a lesson. I rejoice that we, our country, saved our future children—that American children were not children of war. And may they never know what war is.

Perhaps atrocities hardly came up because the subject is too painful to talk about. No matter how rich our languages, we find them inadequate to describe what was caught by the indifferent lenses of cameras. Photos are mute. Yet, as we look at these, our eardrums reverberate with piercing screams. These pictures express the inexpressible.

Volumes have been written about fascism. The phenomenon has been studied from every conceivable angle—economic, military, social, political, historical, psychological. Scores of definitions abound, both scientific and not very scientific, beginning with the words: "Fascism is . . ." One definition, however, is without terminology and yet, insofar as we are concerned, is the most exact.

It is expressed by these pictures. This is fascism. Fascism is this.*

Before being incinerated, the inmates of the Majdanek concentration camp had to take off their shoes *(M. Trakhman)*

*Richard Bertal Kent, who contributed his photographs to this chapter and Chapter 7, The Meeting at the Elbe, died October 13, 1988. These photos are published here in his memory.

Nazi soldiers execute their prisoners *(News Press Agency)*

Mother and child being executed by a Nazi soldier *(News Press Agency)*

The execution of Vladimir Shcherbatsevich and others in Minsk, October 26, 1941
(News Press Agency)

A scene on the bank of the Dnieper River, 1943 *(News Press Agency)*

Casualties after an operation near Kerch, the Crimea, in 1942 *(D. Baltermanz)*

German prisoners of war remove the bodies of slain civilians who were killed in Kirovograd, the Ukraine, and surrounding villages during Nazi occupation *(News Press Agency)*

The authorities of the Yanovsky concentration camp set up an orchestra to play during the execution of inmates. Since the musicians were also inmates, they were soon killed by the firing squad. *(News Press Agency)*

The Liberation of a German Concentration Camp

Allies

The U.S.–Soviet Alliance:
An American Perspective

Forty years after the end of World War II, a substantial number of Americans have either forgotten or have never known that the United States and the Soviet Union were allies during the war. (According to several surveys conducted in 1985, more than 40 percent of the American population did not know of the U.S.–Soviet alliance, and at least one quarter of Americans believed that the two countries had been enemies during the war.) Yet, most historians would agree that the efforts of the two sides were mutually indispensable. The "Grand Alliance" of Great Britain, the United States, and the Soviet Union merited its colloquial name not only because it united three powerful countries but also because the complementary contributions of each nation to the defeat of the Axis powers allowed for a joint effort that was more than the sum of its parts. For the United States and the Soviet Union especially, the subordination of individual interests to the common goal of defeating the Axis powers was not only a crucial political act but, for a brief time, also provided a model of social and cultural alliance.

The wartime U.S.–Soviet alliance was not, however, an easy union to accomplish or sustain. Although a number of Americans were attracted to the Soviet Union in the 1920s and early 1930s, it was not until October

1933 that the United States accorded diplomatic recognition to the Soviet government. Ironically, by the mid-1930s, many Americans who had sympathized with the struggles of the post-revolutionary Soviets and had supported Soviet socialist policies had turned against the Soviet Union in reaction to the notorious Stalin "purge" trials that resulted in the executions and imprisonments of numerous Soviet citizens, many of whom had been famous figures of the revolution.

Further American disillusionment with the Soviet Union occurred in 1939, when on August 23 the Soviet government signed a treaty with Nazi Germany providing for mutual nonaggression and prohibiting either side from lending support to any third power hostile to the other country. Rumors that this pact contained a "strictly secret protocol" that divided a large part of Eastern Europe between Germany and the Soviet Union seemed to be confirmed when the Soviets followed the Germans in an invasion of Poland in September 1939. As eventually became known, under the terms of the secret protocol, the Soviet Union was to take control of Estonia, Latvia, and Finland, as well as the former Russian province of Bessarabia, which had been incorporated into Romania after World War I. When the Soviet Union invaded Finland, two months after the invasion of Poland, American public opinion turned strongly against the Soviets, and the Soviet Union was expelled from the League of Nations. By the summer of 1940, the Soviet Union had formally annexed the three Baltic republics of Latvia, Lithuania, and Estonia and approximately 10 percent of Finland's territory; Rumania had, meanwhile, also conceded Bessarabia and northern Bucovina to the Soviets. A few Americans defended these Soviet moves on the grounds that rejections by England and France of several Soviet overtures for an alliance had left the Soviets with no choice but to make a pact with Germany that would postpone, if not prevent, war between Germany and the U.S.S.R. Most Americans, however, were unable to perceive the pact as a peace-keeping gesture and concurred with Eleanor Roosevelt that "it just lets Germany do its will."

Ironically, both views of the Soviet-Nazi pact eventually proved to be at least partially correct. In June 1941, Germany did "do its will" and invaded the Soviet Union, evidencing the validity of both Soviet fears and American skepticism that the agreement between the Soviets and Nazis would, in fact, constrain the war. Some historians, including Soviets and Americans, would subsequently argue that the Soviets were even more skeptical about Germany's rhetoric of nonaggression than were Americans and that the Soviets had, therefore, agreed to the treaty only to buy time to prepare for war with the Nazis.

These arguments were superseded, however, by the fact and fierce intensity of the German invasion of the Soviet Union. Great Britain, led by Winston Churchill, who had consistently been more sympathetic to the Soviets than his predecessor, Neville Chamberlain, immediately welcomed an alliance with the Soviet Union. The invasion also provided the occasion long sought by President Roosevelt for the United States to take steps towards more effective cooperation with the Soviets.

The first of these steps was the extension of lend-lease appropriations to the Soviet Union. Despite resistance from some American isolationists, the U.S. Congress approved lend-lease aid to the U.S.S.R. in October 1941, even before the United States formally entered the war. Spacebridge participant Samuel B. Frankel was one of the first Americans sent to the Soviet Union to work with the lend-lease program. Transported as "super-cargo" because the United States was not yet officially in the war, young Navy Lieutenant Frankel arrived in Moscow, on his way to the seaport at Murmansk, just as the Nazis were approaching the outskirts of the Soviet capital. Ambassador Clinton Olson, another spacebridge participant, was flown to Moscow at about the same time, in the fall of 1941, as part of a U.S. delegation to negotiate lend-lease arrangements. Both men experienced a disconcerting mixture of mutual suspicion and support upon arrival. Their stories of the fall of 1941 are marked by memories of ordinary events—playing cards in the Moscow subway stations, the city's built-in air-raid shelters—and extraordinary moments such as the dinner given by the Soviets for the British and American delegations following the signing of the protocol for the lend-lease program. Forty-five years later, in a post-spacebridge interview, Ambassador Olson remembered that dinner vividly:

○ It lasted from six in the evening until almost dawn the next morning. We saw not only twenty-six courses but thirty-six toasts, and we drank every toast to the bottom. After we finished the dinner, we had coffee and brandy and cigars, and then we were escorted to Stalin's personal movie studio, where, after all that food and drink, we saw not one but two films.

Being the lowest ranking guy present by far, I was by a side door and everybody was gathered in a horseshoe around a couple of double doors through which they expected Stalin to appear. Instead, he came through a side door and I was the first one to be introduced to him by Constantin Umansky, who was the Russian Ambassador to the United States in those days and who had flown over with us. Stalin looked at me and then said something to Umansky, and Umansky said to me in English [Olson later learned Russian], "Well, that star on your shoulder patch, I guess he thinks you're pretty young to be a marshall." Wallace Cale of United Press overheard this—he was one of the few correspondents present—and that made headlines all over the United States—of how Stalin mistook an American lieutenant for a marshall. ○

The lend-lease agreement that occasioned this incident provided an important bond between the two nations, but even after the U.S.–Soviet alliance became official following the Japanese assault on Pearl Harbor and the U.S. declaration of war, cooperation between the Soviet Union and the United States required considerable effort on both sides. Neither the United States nor the Soviet Union provided the other with the detailed information concerning military and economic conditions, customary with other lend-lease countries, and several of the American contributors to this book recall situations during the war in which their Soviet colleagues were unwilling to reveal certain kinds of information. While each country produced propaganda for its own citizens that lauded the war efforts of the other, Americans who actually worked with or encountered Soviets testified to deliberate constraints imposed on their interactions from both governments. More than one account suggests that Soviets and Americans were actually better allies in their day-to-day encounters than was intended by official policies.

Most of the interaction between Soviets and Americans occurred in or near the Soviet Union, and with the exception of journalists and diplomats, most of the Soviets and Americans who actually worked together during the war were associated with the lend-lease program. No place better embodied the alliance than the Soviet port city of Murmansk, situated far to the north of the Arctic Circle on an unusual inlet that does not freeze solid because the Gulf Stream runs right by it. As the only Soviet port open during much of the war, Murmansk was the destination of hundreds of ships carrying U.S. war materials and basic goods to the Soviet Union. The route from Scotland, around the northern tip of Norway, and down to Murmansk was treacherous even in ordinary times due to foul weather and ice-clogged waters; in addition, during the war years Allied ships on the "Murmansk run" were under constant assault from German U-boats, surface raiders, and aircraft. One convoy lost seventy out of eighty ships, and between June of 1941 and September of 1943 one fifth of all supplies intended to reach Murmansk by convoy was lost. Sometimes referred to as suicide runs, the voyages to Murmansk cost thousands of lives, as men froze to death in minutes in the icy Arctic waters.

Those who did survive were welcomed and aided by Soviets even before they reached the port, since Soviet icebreakers came out to clear the waters beyond the Kola inlet for arriving Allied ships. Studs Terkel relates the story of one such arrival by an American merchant marine named David Milton. Milton remembered a Russian ship pilot, his chin, eyebrows, and nose covered with icicles, coming aboard the U.S. ship as it sailed into Murmansk; while everyone else huddled in the ship's cabin, the Russian pilot stood out on the deck in the wind "like a statue." The moment they arrived in Murmansk, Russians began to unload huge U.S.–built locomotives onto railroad tracks, and within a remarkably brief time, the locomotives were speeding out to the front, pulling Soviet flatbed cars loaded with American tanks that had also been brought by the convoy.

Murmansk itself was one of the few places where Soviets and Americans actually served side by side over a sustained period of time. (Given the large geographic area and simultaneity of events in World War II—in particular, the Nazi invasion of the Soviet Union and the Japanese assaults on U.S. and Allied territories in the Pacific basin—the Soviets and Americans were fighting on the same side politically but in different theaters throughout most of the war.) Admiral Frankel, who was stationed in Murmansk for almost four years, and Ambassador Olson, whose lend-lease responsibilities took him to Murmansk for the spring and summer of 1942, have a common memory of watching the whole town disappear around them as the result of continual German firebombing. As long as ships continued to arrive, however, Soviets and Americans had tasks to do on shore, and if weeks sometimes went by with little for the men in Murmansk to do but check cabled lists of incoming commodities and requests, there were also times when their presence meant the difference between life and death for those who had barely survived the run and for those who awaited supplies and equipment on the Soviet front.

Such cycles were not unique to Murmansk; American soldiers halfway across the globe in the Phillipines and New Guinea also knew the erratic rhythms of war. What made Murmansk uncommon was that whatever the situation of the moment, it was shared by Soviets and Americans. In part because of its remoteness from Moscow as well as Washington, Murmansk provided a context where Soviets and Americans could get to know each other despite policies that discouraged personal liaisons. For Americans stationed at Murmansk, it was a rare if unsought opportunity to comprehend the experience of invasion and what it took for Soviets to resist the German assault. Ambassador Olson could only describe ironically the "lovely experience" he had when he found himself in a tank in −40 degree weather, teaching Soviets how to use and repair U.S. tanks. To imagine him out in the winter field he describes, surrounded by Red Army soldiers learning to maneuver U.S. tanks, is to gain access to a portion of the war experience that has been unavailable to most Americans and perhaps to Soviets as well.

Murmansk linked the United States to the Soviet Union symbolically and empirically during World War II. But while Americans and Soviets needed to cooperate at Murmansk to effect the lend-lease operation, the contributions of each side were separately conceived. This arrangement may not have been ideal, but it was not surprising in the context of the difficult relations between the two countries during the 1920s and 1930s and the continuing hostility toward the Soviet Union in powerful segments of American society.

In this context, a little-known air base at Poltava in the Soviet Ukraine took on a symbolic importance comparable to that of Murmansk. Like Murmansk, Poltava instantiated the U.S.–Soviet alliance because it was a place where Soviets and Americans worked side by side and depended on each other in daily ways. What made Poltava unique was that it was established as a joint operation to provide a base for U.S. B-17 and B-24 bombers and reconnaissance aircraft.

Remembering War participant General Elliott Roosevelt was intimately involved with the creation of the Poltava base. General Roosevelt attests to a spirit of cooperation that informed each stage of the endeavor. Poltava was suggested by the Soviets because it had an airfield and some accommodations already in place, but Roosevelt remembers his first visit to Poltava as marked by the Soviet's willingness to make any necessary changes at Poltava or to find another site. The real work came after selection of the site. Accommodations were not sufficient, and materials to build and furnish living quarters, maintenance sheds, and airplane shelters had to be brought in from Iran through the Crimea. Once the requisite physical structures were in place, Soviets and Americans had to work out a system through which they could accurately differentiate between American and enemy planes. This required an unprecedented sharing of detailed information about military schedules and targets.

Unfortunately, many of the achievements of Poltava were buried under ascriptions of blame when on June 21, 1944, the Germans attacked the airfield in a surprise raid, destroying forty-seven B-17s and damaging nineteen others. This attack raised tensions between the two allies, primarily because the Soviets had agreed to protect the base but had no radar-directed night fighters. Rather, their anti-aircraft defenses consisted mainly of machine guns mounted on trucks, and their fire-fighting equipment was nothing more than buckets and shovels.

In reflecting on Poltava, the anger of Americans after the German raid seems ungenerous if not inappropriate, given the toll the war had taken on Soviet resources and equipment. Both the positive and negative aspects of the joint endeavor at Poltava are better understood, however, if placed in the context of larger issues that occasioned conflict not only between the United States and the Soviet Union but also between the United States and England and among U.S. military and government leaders.

One key source of distrust and tension among high government and military officials was the long dispute among the Allies over the opening of a second European front. After the June 1941 German invasion of the Soviet Union, Stalin urged the Allies to begin a military effort in Western Europe as soon as possible to relieve the pressure on the Red Army in the east. Stalin wanted this second front to begin in 1942; he argued that a serious Allied effort somewhere in Europe would divert sufficient German forces from the east to allow the Soviets to defeat quickly the remaining Nazi forces. This, he urged, would shorten the war and ultimately save many more Allied lives than would be lost on the second front.

Both the United States and England assured the Soviet Union that a second front would eventually be attempted, but although some American civilian leaders and much of the English public supported the opening of an Allied second front in 1942, American military leaders rejected the idea on the grounds that U.S. troops were insufficiently prepared for a major effort at that time. American General Dwight D. Eisenhower and others proposed an Allied invasion of Europe in 1943, but the British successfully opposed this recommendation, urging instead that the Allies focus on the war in the Mediterranean in 1943. As the son of President Roosevelt and a close friend of General Eisenhower, General Roosevelt had intimate knowledge of the ongoing U.S. discussions of a second front. When, during the *Remembering War* spacebridge, several Soviet participants raised the issue of the delay of a second front in accusatory terms, General Roosevelt wanted to respond but was prevented from doing so because of a time constraint. In a subsequent interview, he told his side of the story:

○ You see, the Russians felt that they had borne the brunt of the war, and that in resisting the Germans, they had pulled a great number of Nazi divisions away from the western part of Europe and that, therefore, we should go in and open the front in the west by a big landing operation in France or the lowlands. Churchill wanted to do it, but he didn't want to go into Europe per se. He wanted to go up through Greece, and he wanted to make a big attack through the Balkans and up through Romania and Bulgaria and all through Albania and Yugoslavia. All the American military people said, first of all, we weren't ready; we weren't combat-prepared to open a big second front. Our troops were too green. We were training and getting lots of experience in North Africa and Italy and Sicily, but we'd been taking our lumps pretty well, too, during those campaigns. And we knew that we had shortcomings, that we were not yet a really smooth military operation. We weren't about to go in and sacrifice hundreds.

Well, really, from Stalin's point of view, it wouldn't have hurt us to sacrifice millions of lives on a second front because it would have taken the heat off him. But our point of view was that you don't go in until you've got a chance of succeeding. We waited until we had what we felt was a knockout punch available to us. As it was, it was nip and tuck. ○

The United States and England were still waiting in November 1943, when the "Big Three"—Churchill, Stalin, and Roosevelt—met for the first time in Teheran, Iran. According to General Roosevelt, who attended the Teheran conference, the big argument was over "when are you going to do it?" General Roosevelt recalls his father and Churchill telling Stalin that an invasion could not be scheduled in under a year, and then it had to be a time when all of the troops were in the right spot and when the initial landing could be made with an element of surprise so that the Germans did not have a concentration of troops waiting. This was agreed upon.

The "Big Three" also agreed at Teheran to set May 1944 as the target

date for the European invasion, and with Roosevelt siding with Stalin
against Churchill, the three finally concurred on a landing in northern
France as opposed to Churchill's Mediterranean strategy.

England and the United States fulfilled their promise and landed on
the beaches of Normandy in June 1944, just one month after the target
date. Most historians now agree with General Roosevelt that the Allied
invasion was, indeed, "nip and tuck." Many Allied lives were lost on "D-
Day" as the initial landing came to be called, and some historians argue
that it was only by extraordinary good luck that the invasion succeeded. It is
also true that, however belated from some perspectives, the opening of a
second front in Europe did significantly weaken the Germans in the east,
allowing the Soviets not only to expel the enemy but also to move rapidly
into Eastern Europe and Germany.

In the end, it is impossible to say what would have happened had
events been otherwise. While the issue of a second front is often reduced to
assessments of the comparative loss of lives, the issue was more complex
than that, since decisions about timing and location were intertwined with
disparate projections of each country's territorial claims and postwar intentions and with disputes about the role of the Soviet Union in respect to
Japan and the war in the Pacific. As Allied leaders began to foresee the end
of the war and successive high-level meetings were held—first at Teheran,
and later at Yalta and Potsdam—concern grew about Stalin's postwar ob-
jectives in Europe and about the strength of the Soviet commitment to
President Roosevelt's vision of a new United Nations organization to pre-
serve the peace. At the second meeting of the Big Three at Yalta on
February 4, 1945, the leaders of the three nations agreed to synchronize
their final attacks on the German army. They decided that a defeated
Germany would be divided into four occupation zones, and they also
agreed to a new provisional government for Poland that would include both
Soviet-sponsored communists and representatives from the Polish government in exile in London. Free elections were pledged for Eastern Europe,
and the Soviet Union was promised the return of all lands and concessions
lost in the Russo-Japanese War of 1904–5.

In addition, three other secret accords were drafted and signed by the
conferees at Yalta. The leaders agreed to exchange liberated prisoners and
to repatriate each other's civilians as they were rounded up in Germany.
The second agreement arranged for a voting formula with a veto for permanent members of the proposed United Nations. In the third understanding, the Soviet Union formally promised to enter the war against
Japan three months after Germany surrendered. The secrecy of these
agreements was dictated by both military and political concerns—distrust
of Chiang Kai-shek's willingness to hold to these agreements, the military
advantage gained by the Allies in keeping secret the timing of the Soviet

entrance into the war in the Pacific, and controversies among American and British leaders about Europe's postwar future.

In his fourth inaugural address on January 20, 1945, President Roosevelt had made clear that he would approach the Soviets at Yalta as authentic allies. "We can gain no lasting peace," Roosevelt warned his fellow Americans, "if we approach it [the end of the war] with suspicion and mistrust—or with fear." Stalin appeared to echo Roosevelt, while realistically acknowledging many Americans' distrust of the Soviet Union, when in a toast to his guests at Yalta he observed that it was easy for allies to maintain unity during a war but that "the difficult task came after the war when diverse interests tended to divide the allies." Stalin concluded that he was confident that the "present alliance would meet this test."

In retrospect, however, many Americans saw the Yalta conference as the setting for the final act of the alliance and the opening of the adversarial relationship of the Cold War. Many of the same issues discussed at Yalta were raised again at the Potsdam conference in late July and early August 1945, but by then, the leadership of the United States had passed to Harry S Truman. Disputes over representation at the United Nations and the Soviet occupation of Central and Eastern Europe set the stage for subsequent claims by some Americans that President Roosevelt had "sold-out" American interests at Yalta. Truman informed Stalin at Potsdam of the development of a weapon of "unusual destructive force," and according to Truman's *Memoirs,* Stalin expressed his hope that the United States would "make good use of it against the Japanese." Only days later, Stalin issued orders to Soviet physicists to begin work on their own atomic weapons. Many Americans today recall their quiet bewilderment when at the end of the war the leader they had come to think of as "Uncle Joe" suddenly became an evil tyrant and their Soviet Allies—as quickly—became their enemies. Instead of the continuation of the alliance that some had seen as the basis for long-term world peace, the ties that had united the two countries were soon unraveled, and the nuclear race was on.

The Soviet—U.S. Alliance: A Soviet Perspective

The story of the U.S.–Soviet alliance during World War II is, to say the least, one of contention. When debating hard-liners on American television, I have on many occasions pointed to the U.S.–Soviet alliance of the war years; in response to my insistence on our having been allies, I receive at best the grudging reply: "We were . . . sort of." This is often followed by a recitation of Churchill's famous statement, "If Hitler invaded Hell, I would make at least a favorable reference to the Devil in the House of Commons. No one has been a more consistent opponent of Communism that I have for the past twenty-five years, I will unsay no word that I have spoken about it. But all this fades away before the spectacle now unfolding." The least one can say about Sir Winston is that he was consistent, for a quarter of a century earlier, as the driving force behind the Entente move against Soviet Russia, he had called for smothering (or was it strangling?) the Bolshevik baby in the cradle. He had never had any other desire. What he was saying now was that he was prepared to take the Devil himself as an ally, provided Beelzebub fight Hitler—and in this concrete case the Devil was the Soviet Union.

Speaking on the same subject at approximately the same time, Franklin Delano Roosevelt expressed a view that, while less patently anti-Soviet, could hardly be interpreted as being pro-Soviet: "Any defense against Hitlerism, any rallying of the forces opposing Hitlerism, from whatever source they may spring, will hasten the eventual downfall of the present German leaders and will therefore rebound to the benefit of our defense and security."

So when today's right-wingers (the descendants of those who financed, supported, and appeased Hitler in the hope that he would turn East and destroy and kill Bolsheviks) speak of a "sort of" alliance between the U.S. and the U.S.S.R. during the war, they are not totally wrong. At the governmental and decision-making levels, it was "sort of," and this sort-of-ness became apparent on many occasions and in many ways. These must be investigated. But before doing that, one point should be stated with utmost clarity: at the level of the fighting man, the alliance was anything but "sort of." It was real. It was built with the strongest of all materials—friendship—and cemented by the most powerful of all bonds—common blood.

The men who sailed on the convoys to Murmansk and Archangel and met an icy death in the waters of the North and Barents seas will never be forgotten. Every year on the same day, a ship sails out of Murmansk harbor. Men and women stand on deck, some old, most young; some in military uniform, most not. When the vessel arrives at a certain point, the horn sounds a mournful blast, and a wreath is laid on the grey-green waters, a wreath in memory of those who died bringing food, ammunition, and weapons to the Soviet Union during the war; in memory of those who tried to protect those ships from the U-boats and the Stukas; in memory of the American, British, and Soviet sailors who share a common watery grave and whose memory is cherished and sacred in the Soviet Union.

Nor will the fighting men forget the airfields of Poltava, where the famous Flying Fortresses landed to refuel after bombing Germany from bases in Italy and Britain. There was nothing "sort of" about the relationship of the pilots, the navigators, the men and women who risked their lives and fought shoulder to shoulder.

But while this is true and has not been and will not be forgotten in the

Soviet Union, the U.S.–Soviet alliance was a troubled one. Many years after the war, we hear statements about the "vital role of lend-lease," the "key factor" in the Soviet ability to stand up to Hilter. On the other end of that spectrum, I have heard Soviet statements that lend-lease was inconsequential. Neither view is true, which is usually the case when dealing with polarized opinions. The truth lies closer to the middle—although not exactly halfway between the two views in this case.

Lend-lease.
The Lend-Lease Act was passed by Congress on March 11, 1941, with Britain to be the main recipient. The U.S.S.R. was granted lend-lease privilege on October 1, 1941. This was *three months after* the German surprise attack. However, concrete agreement on goods and deliveries was not reached until June 11, 1942—that is to say, *one year* (minus eleven days) after Hitler's attack. The Soviet Union had been fighting without any aid from the West, particularly from the United States, during what was probably the most crucial period of its existence. Hitler and his general staff had planned to conquer the U.S.S.R. in five or six months, so clearly, that first year was the do-or-die period for the Soviets.

By the fall of 1942, the Nazis had seized a territory that housed two thirds of all Soviet industrial facilities. Without the military production of these factories, the Soviet Union's continued resistance was severely limited. That, in part, was precisely what Hitler's military planners and strategists were banking on. What could not be foreseen—and in that respect their understanding (better said, lack of understanding) fully coincided with that of Western leaders—was the moving of fifteen hundred factories from the western European territory of the Soviet Union to the east. They were dismantled, packed, transported, and reassembled in just six months—something like moving all the industries of Detroit and Pittsburgh to California in the same period of time. Thanks to this incredible endeavor, by early 1942 production had picked up, and by winter the Soviet Union had outstripped Nazi Germany in the production of tanks, planes, and long-range guns. By the end of that same year, lend-lease was still only a trickle. In 1942 the Soviet Union produced 24,700 tanks. The total number of tanks provided by lend-lease for the entire war was 6,000.

One of the statistics most often cited in Soviet studies concerning the role of lend-lease is that it accounted for a mere 4 percent of Soviet matériel. Four percent is not an untrue figure, and it does shed light on the actual role played by lend-lease. It does not, however, tell the whole story. True, quantitatively lend-lease was not a decisive factor, but it was qualitatively important. For example, bomb sights are among the plane's most important features. They are also one of the most technologically complex elements, calling for highly specific know-how in optics. When compared with the entire mass of a bomber, the sighting device certainly comprises even less than 4 percent. But without sights, bombers cannot function efficiently, cannot hit a target with precision, and so the bombs that have been produced will be wasted. The superficiality of the 4 percent to 96 percent comparison is clear. There is not the slightest doubt that lend-lease was an important factor in the Soviet war effort, one that contributed to the Soviet victory. However, it is no less certain that lend-lease was a typical example of too little coming too late to be the decisive factor in saving the U.S.S.R., let alone being the key factor in its victory. The Soviets could have done without it—but they would have had to make even greater sacrifices and suffered more deaths. We do not regard the help we received as "sort of." We see it for what it was: an assist, but not crucial.

The Second Front

In 1941, when the Soviet Union was grimly hanging tough, Stalin sent Churchill the following message: "A front in Northern France would not only serve to detract some of Hitler's forces from the East, but would exclude a German invasion of England. I understand the difficulties involved in creating such a front; however, I feel it must be created. Not only for the common good but in the interests of Britain. The best time to do it is now, while Hitler's forces are tied up on the Eastern Front."

This proposal was rejected out of hand. Later that same year in Washington, Churchill presented Roosevelt with his own plan—Operation Torch. Far from having anything to do with a second front in Europe, Operation Torch provided for the invasion of North Africa. Much to FDR's credit, his initial reaction was negative. The United States supported Operation Sledge Hammer, an Allied invasion of Europe in 1943 or, if possible, even in 1942. In May 1942, when Soviet Minister of Foreign Affairs Molotov arrived in Washington to meet with Roosevelt and Churchill, he was informed of their intention to implement Operation Sledge Hammer, information that was received in Moscow with delight and enthusiasm.

On April 1, 1942, Roosevelt had written to Churchill: "Your people and my people demand the opening of a front that would relieve the pressure on the Russians. And both our peoples are intelligent enough to realize that today the Russians are killing more Germans and destroying more equipment than you and I put together." That view had been the motivation behind the announcement made to Molotov concerning Operation Sledge Hammer. But only a few days after Molotov had departed from the U.S. capitol, FDR was forced to change his mind under pressure from Churchill, as well as from other sources. The final decision was for no second front in 1943.

Not surprisingly, the Soviets were extremely disappointed. This was reflected in the letters Stalin wrote to Roosevelt and Churchill. Knowing of FDR's initial desire to have a second front, Stalin wrote: "Need I stress how disappointing this news will be to the Soviet nation, the soldiers and civilians, this repeated putting off of the second front which leaves an army to fight on after such enormous sacrifices without any significant support from the Anglo-American forces." Stalin's letter to Churchill was far more blunt: "I must state that the issue is not only the disappointment of the Soviet government but rather the preservation of trust in the Allies, a trust that has been severely taxed."

Final agreement on a second front in Europe was reached in Teheran, where the Big Three met in November 1943. There, Operation Overlord was endorsed and planned for May 1944. For a variety of reasons, the plan was delayed a full month to June 1944. *By that time, Soviet territory had been almost completely liberated, and the Germans were on the run.*

Does that mean D-Day was not a great achievement of both military planning and execution? Most certainly not. However, D-Day came much too late to help the Soviet Union, much too late to relieve the pressure exerted by Hitler's forces, much too late for the Allies to claim to have saved the Soviet Union. It came after Hitler's fate had been sealed, when the outcome of the battle on the Eastern Front was a foregone conclusion.

The Battle of the Bulge

On December 16, 1944, just six months after D-Day, with Allied forces deep in Belgium, the Germans launched a devastating counteroffensive. It caught the West by surprise, as testified to by the British military expert and historian Sir Basil Liddell-Hart: "The blow was staggering for the Allies. The situation was nightmarish. Concern was expressed that the Germans might reach the Channel and repeat a second Dunkirk."

The German plan was simple enough—repulse the Anglo-American forces, push them into the sea, so as to be able to concentrate all forces on the Eastern Front and stop the Russians. The German onslaught continued, forcing Churchill uncharacteristicly to ask the Soviet Union for help. At the beginning of January 1945, with the Wehrmacht still advancing in the Ardennes, he sent Stalin the following message: "The battle in the West is very heavy and at any time large decisions may be called for from the Supreme Command. You know yourself from your own experience how very anxious the position is when a very broad front has to be defended after a temporary initiative. I shall be grateful if you can tell me whether we can count on a major Russian offensive on the Vistula Front or elsewhere during January. I regard the matter as urgent."

I would give anything to know what thoughts passed through Stalin's mind when he read that message or what the Soviet supreme command thought when they read it. We will never know. However, less than two weeks later, on January 12, 1945, the Soviet armed forces began their winter offensive a full month ahead of schedule, forcing the OKW to pull twenty divisions from the Western Front and thereby taking pressure off of the Allies. On January 27, Churchill wrote: "We are delighted at your splendid victories over the common foe and the powerful forces which you have put forth against him. Please accept our warmest thanks and congratulations on your historic achievements."

The War Against Japan

Cooperation between the Soviet Union and the United States had many facets, some well known, others less so. The Soviet contribution to the victory over Japan falls in the latter category.

One of the issues discussed at Yalta in the spring of 1945 was Soviet involvement in the effort to defeat Japan. This issue was brought up by the Americans, not by the Soviets. There was good reason for discussion. According to U.S. military experts and assessments by the Joint Chiefs of Staff made at that time, it would have taken at least another year, if not two, to defeat Japan. What is more, an invasion of Japan would have cost a minimum of one million American lives (all of these evaluations were made without consideration of the A-bomb). Facing those prospects, the United States asked the Soviet Union to declare war on Japan.

The Soviet answer was clear enough. Even though it might be difficult to convince soldiers who had been fighting for four long years to go off and fight an enemy who had not invaded their country, they would do it. In exchange, the Soviet Union would expect the return of certain territories annexed by Japan in the war of 1905; the U.S.S.R. would declare war exactly three months after the surrender of Germany. Germany surrendered on May 9, 1945. The Soviet Union declared war on Japan on August 9 of that same year—exactly three months later as promised.

British Prime Minister Clement Attlee greeted the news by saying, "That war declared today by the Soviet Union on Japan stands as a decisive proof of the solidarity between the main Allies and will shorten the period of struggle and create the conditions conducive to establishing general peace. We salute this great decision of the Soviet Union."

In what is probably one of the most authoritative works on the subject, *The History of the War in the Pacific*, written by a group of Japanese military experts, we read: "The news of the U.S.S.R.'s declaration of war on Japan was a staggering blow for the leaders of the Japanese government. Even the atomic bomb in no way changed the state policy as determined by the Supreme Council for the Direction of War. However, the U.S.S.R.'s coming into the war shattered all hopes of continuing the war."

While having no desire to overstate the case of the Soviet contribution to Japan's surrender, the facts certainly seem to fly in the face of the following statement made by President Harry S Truman in the early 1950s: "The Russians made no contribution in the victory over Japan."

■　■　■　■

As a boy living with my parents in New York City in the 1940s, I remember such things as Russian War Relief—the money, the clothing, the toys, the watches that people contributed. I remember the mass rallies. I remember the Soviet delegations hosted by the summer camp I was at in the Catskills. I remember the genuine love Americans demonstrated for the Soviets, the enthusiasm they had, the praises they showered on the Red Army. I remember the jokes—like the one about Soviet Marshal Timoshenko really being Irish: Tim O'Shenko. All of this was not "sort of." It was real.

In my own country I have seen Soviets recount with tears in their eyes how they received parcels from America: Spam, powdered milk, powdered eggs, Hershey chocolate bars, woolen socks. Army songs relating to the war years still echo praises to the Studebaker trucks and the Jeeps that were the pride and joy of every army driver. No Soviet has forgotten that and other aid. The feeling is not "sort of." It is real. We *were* allies, we *did* fight and conquer the common foe; together *we* saved the world from fascism.

Arm in arm; U.S. and Soviet soldiers

Churchill, Truman, and Stalin at Potsdam *(Imperial War Museum)*

American support for lend-lease *(Fox Photos)*

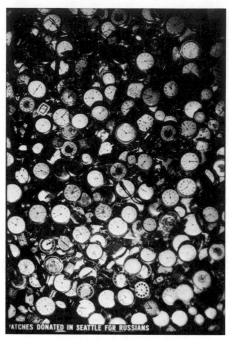

Piles of watches donated for the Soviets *(Life Picture Service)*

U.S. ship filled with supplies

An American ship off-loads at Murmansk *(News Press Agency)*

American pilots at the airbase near Poltava

An American war veteran makes a visit to the Babi Yar war memorial *(I. Mikhaliov)*

Oral Histories

1942,
with Soviet child

1958

Raised in New York City, Samuel B. Frankel graduated from the United States Naval Academy in 1929. He had what he terms "a normal tour of duty" that included Nicaragua in 1931 and China and the Philippines through 1934. In China he encountered several Soviets who sparked his interest in going to the Soviet Union and studying Russian, which he subsequently did.

While there, he met and fell in love with his wife of fifty years, who worked at the U.S. embassy. Once finished with his studies, Admiral Frankel found that there was not much interest in a Russian-speaking naval officer, so he returned to his destroyer until war broke out in Europe. The navy went through its records, discovered that Frankel was a qualified, Russian-speaking officer, and, as a result, he was sent to the Soviet Union during the early fall of 1941.

During the spacebridge, Admiral Frankel remembered his time in the Soviet Union:

I was a captain in the U.S. navy. I was stationed in Murmansk for four years of the war, and I'd like to remember and have you remember the intense activity that took place in the icy waters of the Arctic Ocean where we had thousands of men on hundreds of ships fighting their way through the submarine-infested waters during the bombings of the Nazi aircraft to arrive at Murmansk. We welcomed those who came, who arrived, and we mourned those who were lost. A tremendous number of people were lost there. I remember the intense cooperation given to us and also extended by us to the workers of the port and the defenders of the port. I remember particularly the sacrifices on the part of the hospitals and doctors who actually moved their patients out into the corridors to make space for our survivors who numbered into thousands. I shall never forget my activity in Murmansk. I shall never forget the friendships; I shall never forget the support of Ivan Dimitrich Papanin and Admiral Golovko and their many assistants. I have returned to Murmansk, and I still feel the same feeling about Murmansk that I felt during the war, and I have been told that I am an honorary citizen of that city.

In a subsequent interview, Frankel discussed the events just prior to his engagement at Murmansk as well as the difficulties and personalities he encountered there. He arrived in Moscow at the same time that the Nazis approached its outskirts. As a result, the embassies and much of the Soviet capital had been transplanted downriver to the city of Kuibashev. While he was there, Pearl Harbor was bombed, and the United States officially entered the war. The British, who had been handling the lend-lease program out of the northern ports of Murmansk and Archangel were having trouble with the captain of the American-controlled patrol ships, and Frankel was sent to Murmansk:

○ I was up there for a long period of time—almost four years. I wore a lieutenant's uniform (I had yet to advance to captain), but I was dealing with a Soviet vice admiral and a British rear admiral. I asked permission to wear a commander's uniform, but word came back, "no." I received what they called a temporary promotion just for that job. I was the youngest captain in the navy. I probably ended up the oldest captain before I was promoted again. But by that time I had established myself and was given full authority by our ambassador in Moscow. If anything happened up there, whether it be with ships or lend-lease, I would handle it, and there would be nobody I would have to refer to in Moscow.

I got along very nicely with the Russians. We were out on an outpost, right in the thick of things—it wasn't political in that respect. The political types didn't go up there early in the war—it was too dangerous. So I got along beautifully until towards the end, when it got safe [for people to go] up there, and more of the political people, like the KGB, were coming up. I was warned by my friends up there that if the government people asked me how I was getting along to tell them, "terrible, we don't get along at all." I would say, "Regarding anything that is necessary for the U.S.S.R., [the Soviet captain] cooperates fully, but when it looks like it might be more helpful to the U.S., he drags his feet. But he'll do what he has to to get what the U.S.S.R. needs." They didn't want the Russians to get along too well with or become too much like the Americans.

The town was almost wiped out. Wooden structures . . . were fire-bombed; a lot of damage was done. We were lucky and very cautious. They had bomb shelters, but I never went in them. They were not very efficient. It was safer to go in an open trench where you could at least watch the planes. If the planes looked like they'd passed the point where they could hit you, you knew you were all right. ○

Admiral Frankel worked very closely with two Soviet heroes, Admirals Golovko and Papanin:

○ Papanin was a very unusual man. He was a great Arctic explorer. He was a man who floated around on ice floats for months at a time and took various observations. He was in charge of the northern sea route, the route from Murmansk across the northern part of the U.S.S.R. to Vladivostok. He was a rather interesting gentleman in that he hadn't much formal education. He was an expert in Arctic matters though, and he had a very persuasive manner. He ran his organization like a feudal lord. People would come to him on certain days and say they needed money for an operation for their child, and he would give them money. ○

Although he got along well with the officials, Admiral Frankel found himself learning in unanticipated ways about Soviet rituals and protocol. One such lesson occurred when he tried to give a party for all the personnel at the base:

○ I thought I'd give a housewarming party, so I invited everyone with whom I had contact, starting from the girls who translated to Admiral Golovko, the commanding chief of the northern troops. I invited them all. There were food and drink for man and beast starting at five o'clock. At five, the operators and such came, then the higher echelons came through. Finally, the chief of staff for Admiral Golovko arrived. His station was about two hours away, so I would understand why he couldn't come, but he sent someone. Then I got a note from Admiral Papanin that he was ill. I knew that this was a 'diplomatic illness,' so the next morning, I got some oranges and went to his place, where I'm sure he quickly hopped into bed. I went to his bedside and said I was sorry he was ill and here were some oranges. He told me to sit down. "You know that was a mistake, your party. If you had invited only four or five people, we would have been able to come and let our hair down because we wouldn't have the subordinates around. ○

Frankel never had the opportunity to throw another party. And although he did not forget his discoveries about Soviet codes of decorum, he also remembered the extraordinary cooperation among Soviets and Americans that was possible during emergencies:

○ We had one convoy where the whole ship was lost, way, way up north. The survivors painted the side away from the ice white with flour paste. They lighted a tar barrel or something to give the [enemy] planes the idea that they had already been hit. We had to go up there, and both Papanin and Golovko were very good in that respect. ○

At the end of his tour, Frankel asked Golovko for an aerial photo of the town of Murmansk as a souvenir. He was told they did not have that:

○ That was their way of saying that it was not something they *could* give me. When I went back to Washington, I found out that I would be returning to Murmansk, so I wanted to take back a present to the admiral. We had a plane, a German plane that was shot down. I happened to be looking through the portfolio, and I saw that there were a group of aerial photos of Murmansk. I took two of them, had them framed, and when I went back, I paid a call on Admiral Golovko. I told him, "I was worried. Here you are, commanding this post and you don't have any pictures of Murmansk. I decided you ought to have some." So I brought out the pictures, and he looked at me and said, "You sly son of gun, where did you get these?" He thought it was the funniest thing he'd ever heard. But he did not exhibit them. It might have looked like the U.S. and the U.S.S.R. were exchanging secrets. ○

NIKOLAI IVANOVICH IVLIYEV

1944 **1987**

Nikolai Ivliyev was born in 1918 on a farm, the youngest of thirteen children in a peasant family. As a boy, he went to live with his uncle in a village near Stalingrad, where he finished high school. In 1937, he was sent by the Young Communist League to the Naval Academy in Sevastopol, from which he graduated in 1941 on the eve of the war. Through the course of the entire war, he escorted Allied convoys from Great Britain, Canada, and the U.S. to Murmansk. He finished the war with the rank of lieutenant captain, continued to serve, and retired with the rank of rear admiral.

During the spacebridge he spoke (in English) of his experience with the Allies:

> I participated in convoys in a sector between England and our northern ports. It so happened I was sent to Iceland to meet the ships, which were built in the United States for the Soviet naval forces. They weren't big ships; they were called "small sea hunters."
>
> I had to participate in the repair of these little ships, which had before this crossed the ocean, and then go together with them to Murmansk.
>
> I well remember the meeting in Iceland with the American sailors. The meeting was quite excellent, very friendly; I met people who were united in a single goal, a single cause: to overcome the common enemy, Hitler's fascism.

In a post-spacebridge interview Nikolai Ivliyev said:

○ I met the war on a battleship based at Sevastopol. That night, when our people still were unaware of the treacherous assault of the fascists against our country, we were already under attack. We were bombed. The Germans wanted to bottle up our fleet in Sevastopol Bay. But most of the mines they dropped fell on the embankment where they blew up. Our fleet opened fire. The first German planes were shot down over Sevastopol in the early morning hours of June 22, 1941.

That's how the war began for me. We were taken from the ship back to the Naval Academy, where they formed battalions that guarded the northern part of Sevastopol. I was one of a small group that was sent to Moscow for further training, which included learning a language—in my case, English. After about half a year, I was sent to England, to our military mission, the Department of Naval Convoy Services. The officers of this service were then stationed at ports and naval bases. I wound up at Hull Naval Base. And there I arrived, the first Soviet officer in this city. Naturally, I was the subject of interest, because up until then they had never seen a Russian. I lived in a hotel, but when the hotel was destroyed—there were a lot of air raids—I moved to the home of an English family and was received like one of their own family members.

I had an acquaintance, a local postmaster; he was already over sixty. One day he said, "You know, I told my mother about you, and she wants very much for you to come visit us." I went. He brought his mother out in a wheelchair, and she asked me, "Come closer." I did. She asked me to bend over, and she began feeling my head. I said, "What are you doing?" And she replied, "You're from a communist country, I'm searching for horns!"

There were many such incidents. I remember, for example, one of the convoys arriving at Murmansk. I was being ferried from an English ship by an English launch. I was talking with this sailor, and I was interested in how long he had been stationed here. "I've been working on this launch," he said, "for three months." I asked, "Well, how do you like our country? Only don't judge Russia from Murmansk, it's a very far away place, and the buildings and supplies are poor." And he said, "Are you kidding, sir? I was surprised to discover *any* buildings here." I said, "Are you pulling my leg?" He said, "No, we are taught in geography classes that Russia is a huge country, covered with snow, full of wolves, and summers never come; that Russians live like nomads and have lots of children. They eat everything in sight, and then they move to another place. The wolves come after them, so they throw their children to the wolves to escape. It was only when I arrived here and discovered normal people living in brick buildings that I understood how I had been fooled."

Outrageous, to be sure. But these are some of the more preposterous notions people had about Bolsheviks. I remember my first combat baptism by fire. It was aboard an English torpedo-boat escort in 1942. We had met a German ship, and we blasted away at each other. There was a heavy storm, and it hindered the attack quite a bit. In the end, we managed to torpedo the enemy. We came so close that we poured heavy machine-gun fire at each other. I stood with the English commander, on the deck. I was proud and excited finally to see real combat on an English ship; I also wanted to see how the English conducted themselves under fire and how they fought. Of course, I felt responsible—indeed, I represented the Soviet navy. The British officers conducted themselves in different ways—some showed no fear, others ducked behind the wooden box where the compass was mounted, as if that wooden box would save their lives. I liked the ship commander because he took off his service cap, ordered his men to open fire, and in the course of battle, he conducted himself courageously and commanded coolly, even when the ships came so close to each other.

Our torpedo struck the central part of the German ship; it was torn in two and started to sink. A huge column of fire shot into the sky. . . . The ship had been carrying mines on board, and they exploded. Sailors were jumping overboard. The storm suddenly abated, and we started to pick up the German sailors. The British commander and I later interrogated the German captain. He didn't want to talk and answered only in German. I knew a little German, the commander likewise, but we understood each other poorly. The German captain was wrapped in a woolen blanket, because the water was icy cold; we gave him as much whiskey as he could drink, and then he started talking—in perfect English.

First, he said, he was indignant that there was a Soviet officer on an English ship. The commander told him, "Why not? We're allies." And he said, "You should be allies with us against Russia." What a thought. Unfortunately, even among the senior officers some shared that view. But . . . the majority of sailors I sailed with . . . they simply idolized the Soviet army, which many Englishmen then considered as having saved England. . . .

I can say that when I reached England—there they idolized the Russians as much—that they considered it possible to criticize anyone they pleased, even Churchill, but the queen and Stalin under no circumstances. I must say that I was an altogether careless, light-hearted young man. I'd wear out a pair of socks, let's say, and I would buy another pair and throw the old ones out. My landlady, with whom I lived, would darn them and return them. I said, "Why are you bringing me back these socks? I'm still a young man, ma'am and I can buy more." And she would say, "You are too extravagant! I will write Stalin, I will write Stalin!" For them, there was no higher authority than Stalin. ○

Recalling his attitude toward Stalin in connection with the repressions of 1937–1938, which resulted in practically the entire leadership of the Soviet armed forces being destroyed, Nikolai Ivliyev said:

○ Then, of course we could hardly imagine what was happening. I remember when the commander of our academy disappeared we were in confusion, because we dearly loved this person. And then came the rumor that he was arrested. Not one of us thought it was just. These incidents were numerous, and it was impossible to believe that all these people were enemies. We thought they were victims of slander. At the same time we didn't know much about our government, least of all Stalin. ○

Although Admiral Ivliyev had more dealings with the British, he also had meet-ings with the Americans, about whom he formed the following impressions:

○ It always seemed to me that the Americans had a lot in common with us—undoubtedly more than the British did. The English were good when they got to know you closely. The Americans became friendlier more quickly; they were open spirits. If they didn't like something, they said so openly. The Americans treated us cordially, but a little bit arrogantly. The thing was that our navy wasn't powerful; our ships couldn't escort the convoys and stayed within our zone. Well, because of this, because of lend-lease, they considered us dependent upon them and not them upon us, that they were helping us and that we could not help them. But England looked upon us like saviors. ○

The opening of the Second Front occupied the minds of literally all the Soviet people, and Nikolai Ivliyev was no exception:

○ The opening of the Second Front caused anxiety for us all. We knew that the British were still not ready for this in moral terms after Dunkirk, where they were driven out. But they were preparing. There at Hull, for example, they were building artificial piers, which later proved useful. But the decision makers were in no hurry. Let the two tigers fight it out was their view; let the Russians and the Germans kill each other. Of course, that was a sore point with us. The Second Front became a kind of fixation for us. This led to a funny story that in fact could have had dramatic consequences for a comrade of mine who was also stationed in Britain. When the Allies finally landed on June 6, 1944, early in the morning, he got a call from a local Glasgow paper. "How do you feel about D-Day?" he was asked. We had become so disillusioned that he said, "Fuck off, all you do is promise; you never do anything!" And he went back to sleep. When he awoke, they brought him a newspaper. In it was a story about the Allied landing in France and about this Russian officer who had said nothing would come of it. In short, it was a scandal. As for the landing, I feel it happened only when it became clear that the Soviet army was rapidly advancing. The Allies started to get nervous and decided the time to land their troops had come.

They could have landed a whole year earlier. Soon after D-Day, I had the opportunity to inspect Omaha Beach and the German fortifications along the coast. The so-called Atlantic Wall was not so formidable. I think the British knew this, for their reconnaissance was very good. Nonetheless, they kept putting it off, wishing to spill as little of their blood as possible, allowing the Soviets to die wholesale. It was only when we moved into Europe that they decided it was time to open the Second Front. ○

CLINTON OLSON

1942 **1985**

Ambassador Clinton Olson graduated in 1939 from Stanford University with a degree in physical sciences and engineering and was in his second year of Stanford Business School in January 1941 when, as a reserve officer, he was called to active duty. By the middle of June 1941, he was a production control officer, concerned with U.S. machine-gun production. He crossed Siberia twice, once by train and once by bomber, and spent part of the spring and summer of 1942 in Murmansk. During the live spacebridge, Ambassador Olson recalled his service during the war years:

I was a young lieutenant in 1941 who went to Russia with the Harriman-Beaverbuck commission and was a member of the military supply committee which negotiated the military supply program with the Russians, together with the British in the conference of September 1941. I remained there in 1941, '42, and '43, and then moved to Iran in 1944 and 1945. I was a member of the Persian Gulf command which was also helping to deliver supplies to the Soviet Union.

I'm reminded of a story brought on by our WASP, Mrs. Foy, about her delivery of Air Cobras or P-39 aircraft to the Russian air force. I was at Moscow airport on one occasion, and some P-39s were taking off, and I asked the Russian general standing there how the Russian air force liked our P-39 Air Cobras. He said, "Very good." I said, "What do you like about them?" "Oh," he said, "they have a big cannon." The P-39 had a 37-mm cannon which shot through the propeller drive shaft of the airplane. It was the biggest cannon on any aircraft at that time. I said, "Is there anything else you like about the P-39s?" "Oh," he said, "they are very strong. The wings are made of metal, the wings on our MIG-3s [their best fighter plane at that time] are plywood sections, and when our pilots would run out of ammunition, they would fly the wing across the vertical stabilizer of the German bombers and knock them down that way. Then, usually, the pilots would have to parachute." So they liked our P-39 because it had a metal wing, and with that they could knock off two or three tails from German bombers before they had to parachute out of their own planes.

In a subsequent conversation, Ambassador Olson elaborated on the story of his arrival in Moscow in 1941 and related several other remarkable incidents of the war period:

○ In September 1941, I received a call from the Office of the Secretary of War, asking me to report to that office by noon. It was about ten minutes of noon at that point. In those days, you could get a taxicab in Washington very easily, and I rushed out and got a cab and went over to the secretary's office and was ushered into a side office, and that's how I met the man who introduced himself as Averill Harriman. I said, "Yes, sir, what can I do for you?" He said, "Lieutenant, you've been selected to go on a special mission to the Soviet Union." And I gulped. That was like going to the moon in those days. And I said, "Yes, sir. When does it leave?" And he said, "The day after tomorrow."

So, there I was. "The day after tomorrow" I went out to Andrews Air Force Base and climbed into the bomb bay of a big bomber, the type of which I'd never seen before but which was a "Liberator." Crossing the Atlantic in those days was quite a flight. You think the tourist sections of planes are uncomfortable today, why, try sitting on wooden stools in the bomb bay. We landed at Prestwick and flew to London where we had ten days of conferences with the British. And that was the Beaverbuck part of the Harriman-Beaverbuck mission to Russia. In the course of events, this second lieutenant had luncheon with Churchill at Ten Downing Street. I sent my fiancée the cigar butt that Churchill laid down at that luncheon.

After our time in London, we flew across the North Cape of Norway, off the Shetland Islands, where we were mistakenly attacked by three Spitfires who quit firing before they got in killing range. Then we flew around the North Cape, and at the North Cape, why, there were all these little mosquitos that started coming out at us, but those mosquitos were Messerschmitts. So, we dove into the clouds and made it to Archangel, where we were really supposed to land. We took a look at the airstrip there and decided we could get the B-24 in, but we'd never get it out again. We had no agreements with the Russians at that point, and we weren't about to turn over our latest bomber, not knowing what was coming up ahead of us. Anyway, we flew into Moscow nonstop, setting the world's over-water distance record on the flight, about 3,300 nautical miles.

We started to land in Moscow, and all of a sudden the wheels were about to touch down when the pilot gave her full throttle, and we started to take off again. There was a horrible crunching of metal sound, and I could look up in the cockpit and see them fighting the controls. We were flying along like a wounded duck. After we got up a ways, why, it finally leveled off. It turned out that a Russian had pulled a plane across the runway right in front of us with a tractor, and so we had to take off. We had had enough of this plane already, and as we landed again, all four engines stopped. We were completely out of gas. We got out and kissed the ground.

We were taken to the Hotel National in Moscow and treated very handsomely. Then we began negotiations with the Russians and the British. I was the highest-flying second lieutenant you ever saw in your life. The British delegation consisted of Lieutenant Colonel Sir Gordon Macready, Lieutenant General Sir Hasting Ismay, and Major General Mason Macfarlane and Colonel Greer. The Russian delegation of this committee consisted of Colonel General Yakovlev, Lieutenant General Golikov, Major General Khoklov, Major General Ivanov, Major General Lalushenko, Engineer Brigadier Chichulin, Engineer Brigadier Bushmalev. The U.S. delegation consisted of Major General James Burns, Colonel Bundy, and Second Lieutenant Olson. So I was in some kind of company. . . .

After we finished the conference and signed the protocol that set up the lend-lease program to Russia . . . and were getting ready to depart, or so I thought, Harriman called us all together and said, "General Thamonville, you will be the chief of the American supply mission to Russia. Lieutenant Olson, you will be his deputy for now." I gulped, and he said, "Well, you know since we've reached agreement, some of you must stay behind and administer this." At that point, I was a little homesick, and I had seen all of Russia I wanted to see for the moment. He also named another lieutenant, Lieutenant Cook, who was with us. So we were the nucleus of the first supply mission to Russia.

. . . On the fifteenth of October, the German troops were getting very near to Moscow, and we could hear a lot of artillery fire in the distance. I was talking with the general, chief of our mission, and I asked, "What's going to be our position? We're not in the war, and if the Germans come in, do we go to the east with the Red Army if they move to the east? Or do we stay here when the Germans come in and go home through Europe?"

We both agreed that our duty was to stay with the Red Army. Some hours later I had a telephone call. My nickname was "Olie," and the general said, "Olie, don't alarm anyone, but Stalin has ordered us to be ready to leave Moscow in four hours." That morning, while we were discussing all this, a tremendous snowstorm came up, so the group of us had to trudge to the railway station carrying our baggage. Moscow was panicking. The streets were full of people, and when we got close to the station, there was a mob scene. The Kremlin Guard had to make a corridor for us to get through. It looked exactly like you'd expect an evacuation to look: refugees from the front, a blizzard raging away, eerie lighting around, a crowd held back by bayonet. We walked through this corridor in snow knee-deep, and I started laughing. One of the guys said, "What are you laughing about?" And I said, "Well, I think I'm having a dream. This is surely 1812 all over again."

We all crowded aboard the train, finally, and sat there for a long time. We were not sure, but we thought we were going to Klebishev, on the Volga at the edge of Siberia, which became the temporary capital. The entire diplomatic core, the Russian foreign office, the Bolshoi Ballet, the opera and the artists of the Soviet Union were all on these couple of trains that were moving out. They would stop sometimes for almost a day, so it took six days to go six hundred miles. We passed troops from the Far East divisions of the Red Army, heading to the Western Front. We didn't have too much to eat; we had some canned goods with us. But we had lots of booze, and that helped the morale situation a bit, if not the morals. By the time we got to Klebishev in six days, why, all the cars were mixed up, and we were very well acquainted with the ballerinas of the Bolshoi Ballet. They were great fun, and we were able to continue to see a group of them after we got to Klebishev, where they put on some performances.

One incident I recall during the evacuation involved Charlie Thayer, the third secretary of the U.S. embassy, and John Russell, later Sir John Russell, the British third secretary. Third secretaries in embassies were jacks-of-all-trades; they did the coding of the telegrams, the housekeeping chores. They'd arrange that you get coal, food, this sort of thing. A poor, old peasant woman came up to the train with a goose, a cooked goose, trying to sell it. Things were really scarce. She figured she could make a killing from these trains with her geese, and I'm sure she did. In this instance, John Russell and Charlie approached this old woman at the same time, each one trying to get the goose for his ambassador. Imagine John ahold of one end of the goose and Charlie the other, having a tug-of-war. I never understood why John wanted it for his ambassador, who was Sir Stafford Cripps. Sir Stafford Cripps was a vegetarian.

We arrived at Klebishev on the Volga, which was really a mudhole. Charlie Thayer and John Russell managed to acquire a house in which several of us were invited to live. We decided we were going to have a big party on New Year's Eve, so in the middle of December, we sent a guy named Morris out to find a suckling pig. Well, trying to find a suckling pig in Russia in those days was really something. Morris was gone about two weeks, but he came back, and that was the first I ever saw a suckling pig being shaved. I said, "Morris, where did you get this pig?" "Oh, from a friend of mine." "Morris, how much did it cost?" "Oh, it didn't cost anything." I said, "Don't try and kid me." It was worth a small fortune in those days. He said, "Oh, yes, I got the pig because the owner couldn't feed it, so all we have to do is give him one back next spring." Next spring came, and it cost us $225, which is about $2,000 today, to get a suckling pig.

The party was worth it. It went on for about a day and a half. The ballerinas had lost much of their clothing, so they appeared in their Sunday best. But when they left, they were all arrested by the secret police and given the choice of contact with their American and British friends or their careers in the ballet. Soon after this, the secret police saw that we were getting the front-row seats at the ballet, and so we weren't even able to get the seats. These were the little touches that showed the strains in the alliance.

There were other instances, too, tensions between us as allies. Admiral Stanley was our ambassador, and he became very annoyed about the fact that the Soviets wouldn't give the United States credit for the tremendous amount of aid we were giving to them. You'd have these long columns of Studebaker trucks going through the streets, and the propaganda people were passing on information, so the people were saying, "Look at all the German trucks our people have captured." Stanley made a big issue of this, and we did get a bit more credit after that. We were always held at arms length by the officialdom.

We were there supposedly to help the Russians, but they really didn't work with us very closely. They were terribly suspicious, and over those two years that I was there, I was arrested in American uniform thirteen different times by the secret police, including one time for a short session in Lubiyanka prison. But I always had a sure way of getting out. They didn't pay much attention to the diplomatic passes we had, but I had collected some copies of the menu of the dinner that we had with Stalin [see page 143]. I was out at the R.A.F. mess one night and had changed my uniform and left my passes behind. Curfew was underway, and about midnight I was arrested by a lady gendarme and asked for "dokumenti, pozalsta." "Let's see your documents, please." I reached for them, realized I didn't have them, and thought, boy, I'm in a pickle. Then I reached in my pocket, and my hand closed on this piece of cardboard. When I realized what it was, I said to this sentry, "Wait a minute, comrade. I'm a personal friend of Comrade Stalin's." And that was like saying you're a friend of God's. She thought, this man is crazy, and she started laughing and stuck the gun in my ribs a little harder. Then I said, "Ah, so you don't believe me. Well, I had dinner with him not too long ago, and I have a copy of the menu here." I pulled this thing out and showed it to her under a hooded streetlight. She turned white and saluted and said, "Izvinitya, pozalsta. Izvinitya, pozalsta." "Excuse me, please. Excuse me, please." I walked out and never traveled again without that.

Another time, I was walking in American uniform around the main corner in Moscow at the Hotel National, and two tommy-gunners came up and shoved their tommy guns in my ribs and gave me the *dokumenti, pozalsta* business. I showed it to them, but that wasn't good enough, so they walked me the few blocks over to the Lubiyanka prison. They started interrogation, and they were starting to get a little rough, and I could have gotten out easier, but I wanted to see what they would do. I was experimenting a bit. I wanted to see how the menu would work under these conditions. All of a sudden, I had had enough of it, and I said, "You better knock this off, comrades, or I'm going to have your neck," and drew my finger across my throat. And I went through the same routine, and they went pale and said, "Excuse us, please. Excuse us, please." I walked out using some very choice Russian cuss words.

In Murmansk we were checking off what was coming in—the tanks, planes, and all those military supplies we were shooting in. We were not allowed, quite frankly, to work very hard in our liaison with the Russians. A typical day would be spent mostly checking the cables in from Washington about this commodity or that commodity: do they need this? and do they need that? We'd provide answers, make recommendations, and send in Russian requests. The Soviets submitted some enormous requests which we really couldn't supply; our own troops had to be supplied, and even before we were in the war, the British and Canadians and the Dutch were depending very heavily on us for machine guns and airplanes and everything else. We were the arsenal of democracy, and we were not able to comply with a lot of the Soviet requests, so they were very disappointed. They thought we could supply anything overnight, almost. Just like they expected the Second Front to open immediately; they kept that pressure on us to open the Second Front long before it was a realistic possibility.

Some time later, I was back in California to be married, and the day of our wedding, my fiancée got a call from a Captain Rudnick—whom I had met in Vladivostok and asked to carry some letters to my fiancée because he was sailing across the Pacific. He couldn't believe that I could have gotten back to Moscow and flown across Siberia and was there in Los Angeles. Anyway, it was arranged that he would come to the wedding, and he came in Russian naval uniform with a chest full of medals. In addition to the bride, he was the hit of the wedding. He set people on their ears a bit by drinking a toast of champagne to his good friend the major and his bride and then throwing the champagne glass in the Russian fashion against the garden wall and breaking it. So everybody else tossed their glasses, too. The gossip columnist of Los Angeles had our wedding as one of the featured items the next day and talked at length about this glamorous Russian naval captain who was there. He sailed back to Vladivostok and got into great trouble because of his attendance at our wedding and all the publicity it got, and last I heard, he was running the coal barge up and down the Siberian coast. So you could see why I was a little sour on this so-called alliance business. ○

VLADIMIR
IVANOVICH
MIKHAILOV*

From the conversation during the spacebridge:

The opening of the Second Front—it was the dream of all our people. I want you to understand. In 1941 we dreamed that you would stand with us in Europe against Hitler. We suffered terrible hardships. But our dream did not come true in 1941, nor in 1942, nor in 1943. And yet, if the Allies had landed a year earlier, the war would perhaps have ended a year earlier. Maidanek and Dachau would have "functioned" fewer years, and every year the fascists destroyed from one and a half to two million people. Our cooperation was born in pain and torment; it must be revived. The seeds we planted then must now give forth new shoots. Otherwise, a new catastrophe is inevitable.

Recalling the wartime collaboration, in a post-spacebridge interview, Vladimir Mikhailov said:

○ I was among the participants of the victory parade in Berlin. It was quite a parade when the Western Allies entered the city and Allied troops marched through the main street to Brandenburg Gate. I stood on a small platform, somewhere to the side, of course, because in the center stood the generals, and I was just a lieutenant. Beside me stood an American captain. I didn't speak English, and he didn't speak Russian, nor German. But how happy we were! When our column marched past, . . . he clapped me on the shoulder, said something, and smiled. And when the Americans marched by, I slapped him on the back. And there was such a sensation of brotherhood, even though it wasn't expressed in words. It was more than a brotherhood of arms. Much more. And, word of honor, if anyone had told us that soon we would be set against each other, we wouldn't have believed it; we would have simply laughed. ○

*Introduced on page 61.

1942   **1986**

General Elliott Roosevelt, the second son of President Franklin Delano Roosevelt, was born in New York City in 1910. After completing his formal education at Princeton University and Columbia University, he ran a small airline out of Burbank, California, and then became both the aviation editor for the Hearst papers and the personal pilot for William Randolph Hearst. In this capacity, he often flew guests to Mr. Hearst's unique mansion at San Simeon, the model for the site in the classic film, Citizen Kane. *By the late 1930s General Roosevelt had purchased the Texas State Radio network, and subsequently, with the encouragement of his father, he enlisted in the army air force in 1940. Commissioned as a captain, he soon became head of a joint army and navy exploration team that was responsible for finding airfields and weather stations in the Atlantic Arctic. As General Roosevelt revealed during the spacebridge, he later became responsible for one of the few joint U.S.–Soviet endeavors in World War II: the air base at Poltava:*

> My name is Elliott Roosevelt, and I am the son of President Franklin Roosevelt. I commanded the British and American Allied reconnaissance during World War II in the European theater. I helped to found the air base at Poltava. We flew our shuttle missions, and I flew in there in advance and followed the bombers on their trans-European missions into the Soviet Union and out of there on several occasions. I can say that we had perfect friendship between the Soviet and American soldiers who were together at that air base and that we worked with perfect coordination throughout that entire operation. It's just a shame that that kind of cooperation doesn't still exist.

In a post-spacebridge interview, General Roosevelt provided more detail about Poltava and about other key endeavors in which he was involved:

○ I was shot down three times in Africa. The Germans reported me captured for one week; they thought they had me, and they were broadcasting that they had me. But then some Arab nomads took me up in the mountains and all the way around the front, and I got back to a British unit. It took a week. They took me on a burro.

In 1943, I went into Cairo with General Eisenhower and then flew my own plane from Cairo to Teheran. Teheran was the first meeting that ever took place between what they called "the Big Three"—Stalin, Churchill, and Father. For security's sake, my father stayed in the Russian compound, and so I stayed there with him. That was the conference where they determined that they would open a front in Europe at the earliest possible moment. Of course, Stalin had been after them for almost a year to open this up. We weren't really prepared to do it then. . . . As it was, it was nip and tuck from D-Day in June of 1944 until the breakthrough months later; we were in danger of not pulling if off and really being shoved right back out. The Germans were a much more effective fighting force and knew how to maneuver their troops much better than we gave them credit for, or than Stalin gave them credit for. Stalin won by the weight of numbers, and he won by weather getting on his side. The weather got so bitterly cold over there in Russia that the Germans just about finally froze to death.

So at Teheran, the Russians put a lot of heat on Churchill and Roosevelt to open the Second Front. The big argument was, "when are you going to do it?" Churchill and my father said, well, we can't see that we'll get in in under a year, and then it's got to be a time when we have all of our troops in the right spot and we've got to be able to make the initial landing with an element of surprise so that they don't have a concentration of troops there. We, of course, were trying to get Stalin to agree to step into the Japanese war and help us. And, of course, he refused.

So the net result was that Stalin got what he wanted out of Teheran. He got his front almost within a year of that meeting at Teheran. And he never did come through with an agreement. It wasn't until after Father had died that the Russians said they would join us in the fight against Japan.

Well, this gets me to the Russian part of the story. In part because I had been there at the Teheran conference and had met with Stalin, later in 1943 I was sent over to Moscow with several other officers to meet again with Stalin to request a place where we could establish an air base for B-17 and B-24 bombers and for our reconnaissance aircraft to fly ahead of the missions and behind them to assess the damage, to be able to land and refuel and regroup and come back on another mission.

The Russians had expressed a desire to cooperate, and they then asked for a team to be sent over who would look at the site that they had selected and determine whether it was adequate. If it wasn't, they were prepared to make whatever changes were required or choose another site. When we were negotiating in Moscow, I had to negotiate one-on-one, first of all with Stalin, then I had to negotiate with the air-force commanders.

Stalin was very congenial, very pleasant. He was a gruff sort of person but very prone to rather boisterous laughter, and he laughed at his own jokes a great deal. During the war years, he was, to my way of thinking, quite smart. He was much more educated than I expected. I had always thought he was kind of a peasant. You know, you heard about him killing six million people, sort of cold-heartedly, but I found that he was extremely well educated. My father and Churchill were both fantastic historians. Stalin knew his history, his geography. He knew English. He understood English perfectly, but he wouldn't let on; I didn't find out about it until I was interviewing him, and by that time, I had gone to school to learn a little bit of Russian so I would be able to know what they were talking about sometimes when they were talking in front of me. I found out that he knew as much English as any of the casual people around Father, except for the expert people who were interpreters. Stalin was absorbing everything that either Churchill or Franklin Roosevelt said at these meetings and then waiting and listening to the interpretations, and he had all that time when he knew perfectly well what had been said. He had that advantage over both of them, and he never let on to them.

So, after meeting with Stalin, we were taken to Poltava. They had an airfield there. They had a certain amount of accommodations for personnel but not enough, so we had to arrange for stuff to be brought up from Iran into the Crimea to Poltava, where we established our Nissan huts and all of our maintenance sheds. We had around four thousand troops in the permanent maintenance of that operation, and they, too, were brought in overland through Iran. Then we had to work out with the Russians a system whereby they would recognize and know when we were coming in.

As a matter of fact, I had a situation where they got it mixed up. When I was flying by myself down the corridor ahead of a group of bombers that were coming in after bombing Warsaw, a Russian pilot flying an American-made P-39 came up and shot me, shot one of my engines out. There was no radio communication; there was no way I could tell him. Although they were supposedly briefed and I had the only twin-boomed and twin-tailed airplane in the whole air force—both enemy and Allies—and they should have known that this was a friendly aircraft, they didn't. The pilot was green, I guess. I force-landed on a Russian air base. The Russian pilot came into the same air base after me. They arrested him, and they treated me like I was liquid gold. They were full of apologies. Anyway, he caught it; he was shot for getting mixed up.

Then, of course, a lot of things happened—like one man jumped up [during the spacebridge] and wanted so much to talk to me because he was at Poltava as a liaison officer from the Russian air force. He had been on some B-17 missions and wondered if I remembered him. Well, I vaguely remembered someone by that name, but he didn't look much like he had then. He probably didn't recognize me!

We had missions out of Italy and out of England, across the continent, bombing a target like Budapest, for instance, and then on into Poltava. That experience was the closest experience I had with the Russians. We did develop all of our maintenance crews. We had a sergeant who was a maintenance sergeant on the P-38 airplanes, and I found out that he could speak Russian, not very good Russian, but adequately. I set him up with a group of other kids, and they would show our type of maintenance to the Russians. The Russians would send all their mechanics from their squadrons; they'd come in in groups, and they would watch how our boys would take care of the planes after they came in from the mission and how they got them ready for the next mission.

We tried to work very closely with them. But they were very adamant about not allowing us a great deal of freedom to get out into the countryside and talk with the people in that area. They wouldn't let any of the Americans mingle with the local population because of our way of going out and fraternizing.

It was a tough duty being over there. You couldn't go anyplace, and the surroundings weren't very pretty. There wasn't anything to do, except just stay right there on the base. So they tried not to make the tours of duty there too long. Almost everybody I knew that was stationed there was very unhappy; after they'd been there about thirty days, they'd about had it. But most of them had to stay well over six months.

There was a certain amount of time when we were permitted to get together, at mess time or in the officers' club, where we could overcome the language barriers—it was quite interesting to me how quickly and easily they did start to fraternize and have good times together. Then, of course, there were times when we had our bombers coming in, and the German fighters would come in after the bombers, and the Russians would not realize what they were. The Germans were able to get in and do a lot of damage to our aircraft. There were some real bad snafus in the chain of the command and the ability of both sides to coordinate well.

Soviet soldiers were all around, and we were very open in saying come on in and see how we do things. So they were having hundreds and hundreds of officers and enlisted personnel in there all the time, soaking up all the information that they could get. And it seemed sort of one-way, because they never did open up that way to us. Top officers were allowed to see what had happened at Stalingrad, to see the carnage, and it was pretty much of a hellhole. The Germans were on the point of engulfing the whole area, when suddenly the Russians brought in fresh divisions, armed with American lend-lease guns, equipment, and trucks. The Germans didn't know what had hit them. The Russian army just rolled right over them and sent the Germans back in such complete consternation; they just broke and ran.

That wasn't the end of it, however. The Germans regrouped and started back in, and it was a real bitter fight from there on out. But the

Russians felt that they had won a huge victory, and that was the turning
point in the war. I believe that it really was in many ways the turning point
in the war, but the truth of the whole matter is that probably the turning
point in the war was the gradual weakening of the ability of the Germans to
resupply their troops in the field with new equipment, because we kept
bombing, aerial bombing, and wiped out the German ability to manufacture. As a result, the Germans weren't able to replace anything out in the
field. Gradually, this drove them into an ever-smaller sphere and finally got
to the point where there wasn't any point in fighting any longer.

When the world got into World War II and we found out that we can
mobilize, that we can do these fantastic things, that we are capable of
rapidly developing annihilation machines, it was the beginning of a new
kind of mentality. We said that we had to have an over supply of weapons so
nobody would dare attack us. Now the other side, they're doing the same
thing. It all started when Truman asked his people, "Should we use the
atomic bomb as an international weapon to guarantee the peace of the
world?" And his people said, "Yes, but not as an international weapon. We
have a 25-year advantage over all the rest of the world, including the Soviet
Union." Truman bought it and said, "We are going to use the atomic bomb
in order to be the policemen of the world." Within five years, the Soviet
Union had caught us and started to pass us. Not twenty-five. Not twenty-
five.

Now if Franklin Roosevelt had been alive, the atomic bomb would
never have resided as just our little thing. It would have been the ultimate
weapon to make sure that the United Nations would work. Because we had
to have world government. They all call people cuckoo who dream of world
government, but boy oh boy, if we don't have world government, how are
we ever going to come together? There's only one way right now that we
could do it. That's if we got attacked by little green people from another
planet. That would bring us together. But not until that happens are we
going to come together. ○

VLADIMIR
FEDOROVICH
ROSHCHENKO*

*Recalling the combined war effort against Nazi Germany, Vladimir Roshchenko
said during the spacebridge:*

> Mr. Roosevelt spoke of his stay in Poltava. Maybe you remember how we,
> three Soviet officers, arrived for a joint flight with your crews; these flights
> were a "first" in our wartime collaboration.

*Introduced on page 67.

I flew with an American crew, and our relationship was always good; I never experienced anything but kindness. Once I had to make a flight to Italy to reconnoiter a German sea force. The flight almost ended tragically. We were hit. The co-pilot was wounded. I had to to move over to the right seat, and together with the U.S. commander, we landed the plane in Naples.

What did I bring away from the meetings in Italy, from the meetings at Poltava with your people, our allies in the defeat of German fascism? That they were kind, good, hard-working people.

And I hope for us all, that the skies over our planet remain peaceful for all time.

In a post-spacebridge interview, Roshchenko described the shuttle operation that brought Soviet and U.S. air-force men together:

○ In 1944 we were based in the region of Kiev. We retook Kiev in November of 1943, I believe. At that time, we received a shipment of American B-25 bombers.

Then, out of the blue, Strategic Air Commander Golovanov summoned me to Moscow. I flew along with two other pilots to meet Golovanov. He gave us this mission: fly to Poltava; you will take part in a joint flight with the Americans there. Watch them work, share experiences, and we will make use of everything you learn.

We arrived at Poltava and presented ourselves to our command. The American planes were not there yet. In about five days, a group of B-17 Flying Fortresses arrived from England. The bombers occupied two airfields: Poltava and Mirgorod. We were there to greet them. We had no idea about U.S. pilots. We watched them closely. All landed excellently. Then our base commander presented us to the American command. There was, for example, Roosevelt's son. After this, each of us was assigned to one of the U.S. crews. We talked a little and then went to bed.

It was a beautiful night, not a cloud in the sky. I was lying in my shorts, when suddenly the whole sky lit up. Flares on parachutes were in the air. "What the hell is this?" I thought. Well, it was a German raid. The garrison was half destroyed. Only one house remained intact, the one with our pilots and the American crews. Well, everyone started running. I managed to grab my leather flight jacket, yanked my boots onto my bare feet. I ran out, threw myself into a ditch where about five Americans were already lying. About then, a German bomb hit approximately one hundred meters away from us. It smashed the communications center. One bomb fell on the converted railroad car where our correspondents were—they were all killed. The Germans began dropping "frogs"—this was a type of tin-can bomb. When they struck the earth, a spring made them leap back into the air and explode. They started fires.

In short, we lay in the ditch for about three hours. The sun was already rising. The last plane came, photographing everything, and then the Germans left. We couldn't hit them back—our anti-aircraft defenses were too weak. The Germans had burned or damaged thirty Fortresses. It was a sea of fire. The planes had been tanked up with about twelve tons of fuel. Dawn came. Lying next to me was an American kid, and all he could say was, "Okay, okay." He was happy to be alive.

The raid was over, and one of our commanders said to me, "Volodya, let's go take a look." We went. The grass was high, and our soldiers ran ahead, but the Americans stayed behind. Suddenly, we heard an explosion. We looked, and one of our soldiers had disappeared. We went further and came across a severed hand lying on the ground. I said, "The hell with this. Let's get the fuck out of here." Which is what we did. But many of our soldiers who had rushed to save the American planes were killed. They stumbled on 'frogs' that had not yet exploded. Some fifteen Americans also perished. We buried them together—their boys and ours.

Around noon, the commander of our air base summoned us. The order: head out immediately to Mirgorod and bring the Fortresses to Kirovograd. I flew there, met the American command, told them about the airfield at Poltava and what had happened. In less than two hours, the entire B-17 squadron took off. We had thirty planes. We flew in to Kirovograd, landed, and spread the planes across the entire airfield instead of leaving them bunched in formation as they had been in Poltava. We slept outside in sleeping bags. That night, the Germans bombed the airfield in Mirgorod. But the planes were already gone. Still, they destroyed the fuel depot and blew up the ammunition dump.

After this the Americans flew in reinforcements; Fortresses arrived from Teheran. We began to fly joint missions, and I was included in the leading crew. Before that first flight, we decided to put on our best flying togs; it was a way to celebrate the occasion. Our target was a large oil refinery and fuel cistern in the region of Drogobychi. My job was to scout and direct the squadron across our territory. The B-17s had an automatic radiolocation device for bombing. We Soviet pilots were not allowed to see it—it was classified information. But once they let me see. It was a great device for bombing—completely automatic. The navigator calculated the run, punched it up, and no one could change the course, even if they were scared stiff.

As we approached Lvov, German AA guns started firing on us. Our plane took some shrapnel, but nothing terrible happened. We flew in tight formation, in two groups—one from Mirgorod, the other from Poltava. At Lvov, we hooked up with American fighter planes—P-51 Mustangs. They circled, covering us. Then we proceeded toward our target. We bombed excellently, on target. Then we flew on. It was over Hungary that we encountered German fighters. Immediately the American fighters were ordered to go around to the opposite side of the formation and let the Flying Fortresses open fire on the Germans. They were approximately a kilometer away. A Flying Fortress was exactly that; it was armed at every point with five heavy-caliber machine guns. We opened fire. It was like a wall of fire going at the Germans; a continuous avalanche of fire. So what did the Germans do? They turned around and fled.

We landed at Foggia. That was in Italy. The front had moved somewhere up toward Rome. We landed, got out of the plane, and I looked— people were running toward our plane. They had never seen Russians before. They hugged me and threw me up in the air. And they started trading immediately—give me your flight boots, and I'll give you mine. They put me up for the night in a separate tent. But before going to bed at two a.m., I was the guest of honor at a dinner to celebrate our safe arrival. I was treated with great warmth and got a good deal of attention; they questioned me about everything.

At about three or four p.m. the next day, they summoned me to the air base, put me on a Fortress and transferred me to Bari. There I met two of my Soviet comrades. We were given accommodations in a hotel room. I don't know why, but we found ourselves in a hotel filled with Englishmen. Living in the same hotel, one floor higher, was Shornikov and crew. Shornikov had been awarded the Gold Star of Hero of the Soviet Union. He had helped Tito break out of a German encirclement . . . . Anyway, three or four days later, the Americans suddenly realized we should be staying with them, not with the Brits. So they got us into their hotel. And that was the beginning of a real friendship. They took us around the headquarters and showed us everything. They took us to Naples and showed us the ruins of Pompeii. The air force commander received us in the royal Neapolitan castle and hosted us. He gave us a tour that included the famous golden royal Neapolitan bathroom. Then we flew back; we put the plane on autopilot and had a party—I don't know how much we drank, but it was enough to float the plane. We were just like happy little kids. We landed at a military air base. There we got acquainted with living conditions; the Americans showed us some stunts, such as a group of planes flying at a height of ten meters—twelve planes flew over. We all ducked.

Then suddenly I saw an old friend—a B-25. They told me it was going on a reconnaissance flight. Well, I asked to go. At first they said no, but then they decided to let me go. I went as I was, climbing in without a uniform or flight boots. Off we flew. The mission was to reconnoiter a formation of German ships, which was supposed to be not far from the region of Rome. There were clouds around us as we went. We approached the sea coast . . . the clouds broke, and we found ourselves flying over the shoreline, and two or three kilometers ahead of us, there were about fifteen German warships. One, as I remember, was a biggy, either a cruiser or a battleship. Well, they opened up on us. Our altitude was not great. Our right engine caught fire. The co-pilot was wounded. We thought that if we could gain altitude, we could somehow push the co-pilot out and open his parachute from here. But we decided not to risk that. I transferred to the co-pilot's seat, because I already had flight experience in the B-25; I had flown them in the Soviet Union. So far, so good. Finally, we approached our airfield, but the engine was still smoking. The commander—he knew some Russian—said, "Bail out. I'm going to land it alone." I said, "What sort of comrade would do that?" In short, I refused. We landed the aircraft together; the ambulance arrived and took away the co-pilot.

What surprised the Americans most of all was that I had 220 or 230 combat missions to my credit, whereas they flew about 25 flights and then got to go home. We stuck to it. Throughout the war, I flew a total of 298 missions. My dream was to hit 300, but the command forbad me to fly; they said, "you are alive, be happy, you've worked enough."

In September the shuttle flights ended. The Americans said, "We can't fly you across the front lines; we can't ensure your safety." We flew to an airfield in Cairo; from Cairo we made our way to Teheran, and then we flew to Poltava. We had reached home. I wrote a detailed report to my command, but I never heard a thing about it. It was lost, apparently, somewhere in headquarters. That was in 1944. ○

**STANISLAV
MIKHAILOVICH
MENSHIKOV**

Stanislav Menshikov is a professor of economics and history. His father was Soviet ambassador to the U.S. During the spacebridge, when the military wartime alliance between the Soviet Union and the United States was the subject of discussion, he rather sharply criticized America for putting off the opening of the Second Front for so long:

During the war I was just a kid. But I remember the feelings of our people towards Roosevelt, the president of your country. And the chief reason of our respect toward him was that, in our eyes, he was a personal symbol, a symbol of the understanding the American people had of our common goals, our common interests in the overall struggle.

However, one should not idealize the past. Our alliance was formed with great difficulty in those years. There were those who did not believe in this alliance; there were those who delayed the opening of the Second Front. But the alliance took place anyway, and the Second Front was opened anyway. And this was thanks to the fact that at the head of the United States and at the head of the Soviet Union stood realistic, intelligent statesmen who understood the commonality of our interests, understood that we were fighting for one goal. And I would hope that we can pause and think a minute about what unites us.

What unites us above all is the struggle to make sure that the horror which we saw on the screen today shall never be repeated.

Reacting to Professor Taubman's statement (see page xiv), Menshikov said:

I want to support this theme. I believe it's necessary to study history, not only for young people but for diplomats and seasoned diplomats as well. Each time that I think that in Geneva the latest rounds of negotiations has once again been unsuccessful, I wish that the diplomats would look at old treaties—not yet that old, but those of the end of the Second World War.

Three months before the end of the war, Roosevelt went to Yalta. At that time the war was already won, its fate was pre-determined. Many of Roosevelt's advisors were saying, "You don't need to go; our main enemy now is the Soviet Union or will be the Soviet Union in the near future."

Roosevelt didn't listen—went to Yalta; later, Truman to Potsdam. And agreements were reached which set up a very serious basis for postwar peace and security. Some say we have not fought these forty years because we are afraid of each other's nuclear weapons. In my opinion, this is not the only or the chief reason. The fact is that we created the basis for security then and again later, in the '70s. And it's necessary to ponder over these experiments, to ponder a little bit more about the things in them. In my opinion, this relates to what you call political will, realism, and understanding of the security interests of other countries. Roosevelt understood very well the security interests not only of America but of Russia, and he was very clear about it. That is very important. Let them use this positive experience more frequently.

1943   **1988**

**GHEORGHI
ARKADYEVICH
ARBATOV**

A member of the Academy of Science of the U.S.S.R., director of the U.S.A. and Canada Institute and one of the Soviet Union's leading experts on America, Gheorghi Arbatov made the following comments during the spacebridge about Soviet-American collaboration in the war years:

As a veteran of the war, I am deeply moved by this meeting of ours. Like many others, I was eighteen years old when I left for the war. At eighteen, I commanded a rocket artillery battery. You saw footage of them firing, today. However, now I think about everything, not only as a participant in those distant events but as a historian, as a researcher of politics. And here is the thought that comes to mind: apparently human nature is such that people are lazy; they do little unless there is great pressure. That applies to our relations. Indeed, it is easier not to have any relations at all and not know anything about each other and not to do anything to help things adjust for the better. And only necessity makes us act. That happened during the war. We had to act together. And here, in this communication link, I see an urgency that is no less as great.

Be that as it may, look about at how many people are sitting in our auditoriums who fought in that war. They all survived, even to this day. But in a future war, there will be no one to return, and there will be no veterans.

I live with this thought every day. Of course, it is good to see all of you. It is good to assure ourselves of the things in which we deeply believe—that many Americans remember the war and don't all wish to pay homage to the SS and think about us as allies and not as evil enemies, not as targets to shoot at, not as the reason for increased defense spending. But we must do very much very quickly, because the need is just as great, the threat not a bit less than it was then.

GRIGORY YAKOVLEVICH BAKLANOV*

In a post-spacebridge interview, Grigory Baklanov touched on the theme of military collaboration, although he did not link up with any of the Allied forces during the war:

○ We thought a lot about the Americans. There were many reasons for this. First of all, at the end of 1942 when I was on the Northwestern Front, then later at the military academy, and in 1943 when I went to the Southwest Front—which became the 3rd Ukrainian Front—we received American supplies: Spam, boots. . . . Finally, even our battery received tractors that had been converted from American tanks. They had very narrow tracks and were very fast. However, they ran only on aviation fuel, and so they would burn like matches when hit. Nor were they suited to bad winter conditions. In the battle for Hungary, for instance, they couldn't climb the icy slopes. We had to unwind the winch, hook it to a tree, pull the tractor up, and then pull the gun itself. Our slower-moving CTZs were much better suited for this work. Anyway, I want to say that we saw concrete American help and therefore thought about it. But to us, fighting at the front lines, this kind of help seemed less important than the opening of the Second Front. We expected the Allies to land in Europe in 1942 rather then in 1943. We thought it was high time. But it happened in June 1944, and, by then, things were going very well for us on the front. We had a superiority in tanks and planes, and our artillery at that time generally surpassed the Germans'. I don't want to say that this help wasn't needed, no. Simply, that by the summer of 1944, we were not in a desperate situation, like when the Germans were at Stalingrad or, even earlier, approaching Moscow. ○

*Introduced on page 51.

The Meeting at the Elbe

A U.S. Perspective

On April 25, 1945, seven jeeps full of U.S. soldiers under the command of Lieutenant Albert L. Kotzibue reached the German town of Strehla on the Elbe River. Overcome with curiosity about their Soviet allies, Kotzibue and his patrols were out looking for Soviet soldiers, despite orders from higher-ups that U.S. army groups were to stop their movement eastward considerably west of the Elbe River. After encountering two Polish soldiers, whom they initially mistook for Soviets, Kotzibue and his patrol used hand grenades to loose two sailboats and a barge from chains that bound the boats to the west bank of the Elbe. Then Kotzibue and five of his men paddled across the river to the eastern shore. There they were met by three Soviet officers, one of whom was a press photographer.

Four hours later, another small patrol of three U.S. soldiers under Second Lieutenant William D. Robertson reached the German town of Torgau, sixteen miles upriver. They had started out to round up German prisoners, but, as with Kotzibue's patrols, curiosity led Robertson and his men to the banks of the Elbe, across which they guessed was the Soviet army. Robertson climbed a three-hundred foot tower and signaled his allies across the river with a makeshift U.S. flag made of a bedsheet daubed with red and blue paint. At first, the flag drew small-arms fire, but after greetings were shouted in German across the river, the firing stopped. From the

west bank of the Elbe, Robertson inched out across the girder of a shattered bridge; a Soviet moved toward the American from the other side.
The two met and embraced near the eastern shore. Later, after several
hours of drinking and exchanges of watches and other small articles,
Robertson persuaded four Soviets to return with him to the U.S. camp
across the river.

Starting from the banks of the Dneiper and the coasts of Normandy,
two thousand miles apart, Soviet and American troops had finally and fully
vanquished their common enemy, and in so doing, had unexpectedly come
together. Because Robertson and his men had had the foresight to bring
Soviets back to their camp with them, they received the historical credit for
the first U.S.–Soviet meeting in Germany. Kotzibue's group never received
appropriate recognition for at least sharing in this occasion, in part, ironically, because having decided to confess to violating orders, they uninten-
tionally misreported the coordinates of their location to headquarters. In
yet another irony of the historical moment, this fulfillment of the U.S.–
Soviet alliance also marked the beginning of the division of Germany into
two parts, one to be controlled by the East and the other by the West.

The soldiers of both countries either ignored or were unaware of the
political ramifications of their encounter. American soldiers had heard
numerous stories of the heroism and the fury of the Soviet troops, and
among the American forces in Germany in the early months of 1945, there
was daily gossip about the possibility of meeting the Soviets. When the two
nations' soldiers did actually meet, they stood on a riverbank littered with
the bodies of German civilians who had perished in a nearby bridge explosion. Profoundly distressed by the human carnage surrounding them, the
Americans and Soviets took an oath, pledging to do all in their power to
prevent another war. The oath is still remembered as a symbol of the
wartime alliance between the United States and the Soviet Union—a
symbol of hope for a world at peace.

During the several days they spent together at Torgau, Soviet and
American soldiers celebrated the approaching victory and the alliance that
had made this victory possible. They shared food and drink, and despite
language barriers, managed to share stories of the war they had all endured. Newspapers and radios all over the world quickly reported this first
meeting of the two great armies.

To commemorate the fortieth anniversary of this historical meeting, a
contingent of U.S. citizens, led by World War II veterans, met a group of
Soviet citizens at Torgau on April 25, 1985. The two groups included men
who had met as soldiers at the Elbe. For many, it was the first reunion in
forty years, and they took the occasion to renew the oath some of them had
made in 1945—an oath never again to make war. That oath, initially a
spontaneous oral declaration, had been widely publicized by journalists
who made the oath stand for the union of Soviets and Americans for peace.

They also laid a wreath on the grave of Joe Polowski, who, at his request, was buried on November 25, 1983, at the site of the Elbe meeting. Polowski, a taxi driver from Chicago, was one of the Americans with Lieutenant Kotzibue from the 69th Division that met the Soviets at Strehla. He had made it his life's crusade to impress on the minds of his fellow citizens the meaning of the oath of the Elbe, an oath that had become a key symbolic gesture of both nations' desire to avoid war.

The hundreds of U.S. soldiers who soon followed Kotzibue and Robertson across the Elbe remember those first short days of "unofficial" U.S.–Soviet meeting as a unique moment, a punctuation point between the virtual end of one war, the Good War and Great Patriotic War; and the beginning of another, the Cold War. The generosity of the Soviet troops, the conviviality of the occasion, and the ability to communicate despite language barriers have not been forgotten, even by those who, in subsequent years, came to question the willingness of Soviets and Americans to live up to the Elbe oath—"that all nations will and must live in peace."

A Soviet Perspective

Speaking in strictly military terms, the Soviet-American linkup at the Elbe River was relatively unimportant. It was, however, of the utmost political and psychological importance, especially considering last-ditch efforts on the part of the German high command to achieve a separate agreement with the Western Allies. Keeping that fact in mind, we must conclude that while the actual linkup was indeed insignificant in the military sense, the operations that led up to it were more than significant: they were decisive in sealing Hitler's fate. Just what were those operations?

By the end of 1944, the Western Allies had liberated France, Belgium, Luxemburg, and part of Holland. They enjoyed a two to one superiority in men, four to one in tanks, and a six to one advantage in aircraft.

On the Eastern Front over the summer and fall campaign of 1944, the Soviet Union had put 1.6 million of the enemy's men out of action, but enemy troops were still on Soviet soil, in Latvia. On the one hand, Soviet troops had crossed the German border in eastern Prussia but, on the other, the territories of Poland, Hungary, Austria, and Czechoslovakia still lay between the Soviet forces and fascist Germany. These were not simply buffer zones. They were sources of raw materiel and military production for the Wehrmacht.

At this point in time, the German supreme command (the OKW) made the following decision: hold the line on the Eastern Front, launch an attack in Hungary, and strike the Allies in the Ardennes with the aim of shattering the front, bypassing Brusells in the east, and coming on Antwerp, thereby destroying twenty-five Allied divisions. This, they hoped, would disrupt the Allied plans and make them more receptive to the idea of a separate peace. The plan was even more far-reaching, as testified to by the following directive signed by Hitler on December 10: "Destroy the enemy forces north of the Antwerp-Brusells-Luxemburg line, thereby radically changing the character of the Western campaign and, possibly, that of the entire war."

The Nazi offensive began on December 16. In response to an Allied request made by Winston Churchill, the Soviet high command (the Stavka) decided to begin its winter offensive nearly a full month ahead of time—on January 12. The combined forces of three military groups headed by Marshalls Zhukov, Konev, and Rokossovsky attacked. By the beginning of February, they had advanced from five hundred to six hundred kilometers, to the Oder River, only sixty kilometers from Berlin, putting five hundred thousand men and thirty five enemy divisions out of action and, in effect, forcing the OKW to call off its western offensive.

The Soviets paused at the Oder to regroup for what would be the last major offensive of the war. By mid-April, they were ready. So was the enemy. The OKW had 195 divisions on the Eastern Front and 70 on the Western. That deployment spoke for itself: do anything to stop the Russians. But when the Soviet forces came blasting out of their Oder River position on April 16, they cut through the German defenses like a knife through butter. Only five days later, on April 21, Soviet long-range artillery lobbed its first shells into the German capital. Thus began the battle of Berlin.

No less than three hundred thousand men defended fortress Berlin. "Men" is perhaps not the correct word. Many of them were teenagers—members of the Hitler Youth, thirteen and fourteen year olds who had been trained to use the anti-tank Faustpatron and to sacrifice their young lives for the Führer—and old men, even veterans of World War I. Hitler's dream of a one-thousand-year Reich, of a German master race ruling the world, was going down in flames, and according to Hitler's plans, no one would be spared in this final scene of Götterdämmerung.

Much of this was reflected in the matter-of-fact tone of the official OKW diary:

> April 22. Hitler finally takes the ultimate decision not to escape to the South but personally to guide the Battle of Berlin and remain in the Imperial Chancellery. He calls a meeting in the Chancellery at 15 hundred hours during which he acknowledges that the war is lost. Hitler arrives at the decision to divert all forces from the Western Front, presently facing the Anglo-Americans, so as to use them in the defense of Berlin.
>
> April 23. The Battle of Berlin has assumed a particularly violent character. At 10 o'clock Field Marshal Keitel met with General Wenz near

Wiesenburg and discussed with him the plan of moving on Berlin in the direction of Pottsdam so as to join up with the 9th Army. This finally frees the army from the impossible task it was faced with, namely, that of fighting on two fronts. It may now fully give itself to fighting the Soviets.

On April 25, the Soviet pincer movement was completed. Try as they might, the German forces could not break through. The fate of Berlin was sealed. And on that same day at a place called Torgau, on the Elbe River, Soviet and American troops linked up in what was one of the most symbolic events of the war. In Moscow the linkup was celebrated by 24 salvos from 324 guns.

Among the first to meet on the half-destroyed bridge spanning the Elbe were Lieutenant William Robertson and Lieutenant Alexander Silvashko. This is how the Soviet veteran recalled that great moment forty-three years later:

○ When war came to the Ukraine in 1941, I was working in the regional Komsomol committee. I suffered all the horrors of fascist occupation. I first fought the enemy as a partisan. In December 1942, I was able to join the army and enlist.

Soon after that, I began to serve with the 8th Rifle Platoon of the 173rd Rifle Regiment. Ours was a machine-gun company, and that is where I served to the very end, always at the front lines. I was wounded twice and suffered one contusion, but no hospital could hold me long, and I always returned to my company. I fought in the battles, terrible battles. And then came Germany. The fury of the fighting! The fascists resisted to the last man. But they could not stop us.

In the spring of 1945, as we neared the Elbe River, our platoon time and time again encountered the almost insane resistance of retreating German forces.

On the evening of April 24, 1945, we fought our way into the city of Torgau. My company was up front, followed by the main forces. The Germans opened up on us with artillery fire, forcing us to dig in and send out reconnaissance.

On April 25th, we forced the Germans to retreat. That was the day we were to link up with the Americans. It was a special day, one I will never forget. Lilacs were blooming; it was warm and sunny. The morning mist was lifting over the river, and firing from across the other bank had stopped. We all felt the war was almost over. . . .

But the fascists had a diabolical plan. They came out on the bridge wearing white arm bands. Well, we figured that means they want to surrender. So we signaled them to come over, that we would not shoot. They waved to us, motioning that we come to them. So two of us started inching across the bridge—and suddenly they opened fire. It was real hell. It's a miracle I was not killed.

194

Sometime later, a group of soldiers appeared on the outskirts of Torgau. They were wearing uniforms we had never seen before. I thought to myself: this must be another Nazi trick. Meanwhile, these soldiers hung a flag from the belfry opposite us. Then, four of them came toward us—we could see they were not looking for a fight. They yelled, "Moscow!" "America!" "Don't shoot!" We crawled across the bridge towards each other and met right at the middle. We shook hands. None of us spoke the other's language, but soldiers can communicate in their own special way.

I noticed one officer among the Americans who turned to me and said, "William Robertson." I answered, "Alexander Silvashko." I spoke no English, and he no Russian. We used sign language but quickly agreed to report to our commanding officers. Robertson wanted me to take him to our regiment commander and then take us to his division commander as the living proof of his having actually linked up with the Russians.

We all sighed a great sigh of relief. The soldiers ran down to the river's edge to wash and shave. Some even tried to swim in the cold water. There was a tremendous feeling of joy in the air. I remember one of our machine gunners came up to me. He was the old man of the company, close to fifty. He started talking about his family, his native village. He'd received a letter the day before telling him his daughter was getting married. There were tears in his eyes. . . .

No sooner had I reported on the linkup than Major Larionov, second in command, came running to my dugout with captain Neda, the battalion commander, and Sergeant Andreyev. Robertson invited us into his jeep, and the four of us drove off to the U.S. divisional headquarters situated some forty-five kilometers away. It took us about an hour to get there. Along the way we passed what was left of the German forces, destroyed on the Eastern Front, moving west to surrender to the Americans. A group of German officers and noncoms stopped our car to ask directions. They were astonished to see us together—Soviets and an American officer. The Germans were wearing medals and carried weapons. They all seemed to be in surprisingly good spirits as they lined up in front of the divisional headquarters and neatly stacked their rifles, submachine guns, and machine guns into piles. These "POWs" sashayed around, clearly feeling very much at home. The four of us, armed only with handguns, were somewhat concerned the Germans might try to pull a fast one, especially the SS.

. . . Late that evening we arrived at the U.S. regimental headquarters in Würzen. No one was expecting us—as demonstrated by the hulabaloo our arrival created. Soon we were on our way again, this time to the U.S. divisional headquarters in Trebsen. They had been informed of our arrival. Although it was very late, we were given a very cordial welcome; in fact, it was like a festive occasion. News reporters were all over us; it took some doing to get rid of them and finally have something to eat. Our late supper somehow merged into an early breakfast. . . .

We were received by the commander of the 69th Division, Major General Emil Rheinhardt. We raised toasts to our armies, to our countries. After that, there was a picture-taking session, and then accompanied by the division command and riding thirteen jeeps, we rode back to the Elbe where the Americans would meet their Soviet Allies. ○

Hands across the Elbe *(Press Association)*

Soviet and American troops meet on the Elbe near Torgau *(G. Khomzor)*

Celebration at U.S.–U.S.S.R. linkup on the Elbe River *(Dick Kent)*

Sgt. Dick Kent and Soviet soldier toast the victory at Elbe River linkup *(Dick Kent)*

Sgt. Dick Kent with Russian women soldiers *(Dick Kent)*

Soviet and American soldiers have a friendly chat near Torgau *(G. Khomzor)*

Hodges, the commander of the 1st U.S. Army, awards the Legion of Honor, the highest U.S. decoration, to several officers and generals of the Soviet 5th Army, May 1945 *(News Press Agency)*

Bear hug at the Elbe *(Dick Kent)*

Oral Histories

**ALEKSANDR
VASILYEVICH
OLSHANSKIY**

1945   **1986**

This retired major general, a participant of the meeting on the Elbe, evoked the memory of this important event during the spacebridge:

> I see in your studio Bill Beswick—he's a veteran, and chairman of the committee of the famous "Fighting" Infantry Division. This division met with us, with our recon platoon of the 125th Regiment of the 58th Guards Division on the 25th of April. It should be said that the meeting on the Elbe was not only a historical event. It was a very important operation, brilliantly conducted by the unified command of the anti-Hitler coalition in the complicated battle conditions. There was heavy combat on the left and right, and you could expect anything from the fascists any minute.
>
> It was here, in close to Torgau, at 10:27 a.m., that we met. It was just beautiful. The meeting was great. We vowed to struggle for peace and never to allow war again.

Aleksandr Olshanskiy visited the United States with a delegation of Soviet war veterans in 1986. Their trip took them to Washington, D.C., Chicago, Detroit, and Dallas. Recalling his impressions, General Olshanskiy said:

○ We had the opportunity to meet with different groups and organizations. We wanted to know how Americans felt about April 25, 1945, when our forces linked up on the Elbe. We wanted to know whether American vets still remember it, what American youth think of it. People were very friendly, showed us respect. Many said that the Soviet-American cooperation during the war should serve as an example for today's leaders. But, at times, we encountered the most amazing ignorance on the part of Americans. One man told us that his son believes that the United States fought against the Russians during World War II. Many young Americans did not seem to know what the linkup on the Elbe was about; many had not heard of it. Once they were informed, though, they all agreed that the spirit of that linkup must be preserved and developed. ○

WILLIAM BESWICK*

William Beswick was one of the first American soldiers to meet Soviet soldiers at Torgau, Germany, on the Elbe River in April 1945. During the spacebridge, Mr. Beswick recalled the meeting at the Elbe River in 1945 and his return to Torgau for the funeral of fellow Elbe veteran, Joe Polowski:

I was on the end with Lieutenant Robertson. He came to the Elbe about fifteen kilometers north of Mr. Kotzibu's patrol, which Ed Ruff here was a part of. Although that Kotzibue patrol made the first linkup with the Soviets, Lieutenant Robertson got the credit for it because he came back with the first Soviet soldier. I believe that Ed can verify that.

Anyhow, to go back just a bit. We were at Islandburgh, and we were having quite a time there for a little while. I think it's maybe fifteen kilometers from Torgau. We were advancing on, and when we got to the limits of Torgau, they held us up. Well, we didn't know exactly what was going on, but in a few minutes, word came down that we were meeting the Russians. . . . One of the patrols that had gone out had made contact. So, of course, as soon as they made contact, they sent back somebody with proof that they had a Russian with them.

I'm sure that all of you recall the incident of the flag that Lieutenant Robertson and his crew made. They got a sheet and some dye out of a drugstore, and they made a makeshift flag, and they hung it out of the tower on the castle there on the banks of the Elbe. Well, as soon as that word came back and we were sure, then the rest of us went on up. I say rest of us—there were a whole lot of us went up, and there were maybe two to three hundred on the riverbank at that time. None of us, of course, spoke Russian, and the Russians never spoke English, but at a time like that you don't need to. There was a lot of backslapping. [He weeps.] I'm sorry. . . .

In a post-spacebridge interview, Mr. Beswick described the context of the U.S.–Soviet meeting at the Elbe and provided more details about his experiences during this encounter:

○ First we went into the village of Wittzenhausen and spent the night. We

*Introduced on page 65.

met with quite a bit of resistance and were held up there for about another day. Then we continued on to east of the Werer River at Wittzenhausen. We were the ones that liberated the prisoners at Buchenwald concentration camp, just near Folda. Some went in, but I elected not to go after I had heard some of the other people talk about it. After Folda, we went into Lutsen and then Leipzig. From there, I was on another patrol, and we went out toward Torgau. Torgau looked like a little foreign village that you might have read about in a book. The streets were all cobblestone. I can't really say they were any different from the little farming villages that you see in this country. They cautioned us about going out on our own, but I did one day. I walked out to the square, and it was just one great bit triangular shape.

As we approached the prison near Torgau, there was a Russian plane over the top of our column, and we started shooting at him. And he started wobbling his wings like, "I'm friendly. I'm friendly." Everybody was shooting at him anyhow. But we missed him, and he landed over in the field that day. That night, we went into the village and secured ourselves in a place to spend the night. I met a little Russian man, and he came up to me and hollered, "Amerikansky!" I'm about six foot, and he came up to my shoulder. This little Russian man had a full beard and was in his fifties or maybe even sixties, and I was about nineteen and had a young, tender face. He came up and jumped and hugged me around my neck and hollered, "Amerikansky! Amerikansky!" He wouldn't let me go at all. He followed me every step I took; he wouldn't let me stop. He wouldn't let me go anywhere; he just wanted to stay with me. Everybody was so happy, you know. That was the first night in Torgau.

The Soviets had taken this compound, and they had all kinds of people, all nationalities, I guess. They had parties and bonfires; they were burning all the furniture in the camp. The only thing left in the camp was the tables within the buildings themselves. They had gone out and raided all the whisky and wine and everything for their party. That was really quite fabulous, but they were burning the tables and chairs and bedding and everything just to make a big bonfire. They had all kinds of drinks; they were trying to entertain everybody. That was a real experience that night. The next morning, they called us and told us that we were supposed to meet the Soviets, that a patrol had been out—the one that Lieutenant Bill Robertson had been on—and we were all supposed to go up and make contact for sure.

When we got there, there were several people who came out and were dressed as the Soviet soldiers were, but they had on helmets like tank drivers wore, like a football helmet. These people came over, and we met them halfway. Everybody was hugging. The crew came over, and we noticed that four of them had full, heavy beards, and one of them didn't have any beard. All of us got talking, "Boy, he must be a young kid." And he was: he had no beard at all and no moustache, and while we were standing there talking, he took his helmet off. It was a young girl who had long, blond hair.

It was more a festive occasion than anything. There were a lot of friendships. A lot of people couldn't understand . . . how things could be so friendly at that time and turn so hostile within a couple or three years. You know, it didn't make sense. There was so much friendship and joviality. There were some incidents that weren't very nice that happened, but that's beside the point. Of course, you always have troublemakers wherever you go, on all sides. There was a lot of watch swapping and ring swapping and things like this, for remembrance—giving of our own personal little items as souvenirs and so forth.

I never heard any derogatory or hateful remarks leading up to our meeting at all. Everybody was always saying, "Well, when we meet the Russians. . . ." It was always on a joyful note. I never heard a person that I could ever recall make a hateful remark about the Russians—not one. And even after we met them and mixed with them there for about two days and then came home, I don't ever remember hearing an ugly comment made. This is why I can't figure how people arrive at their final decisions, because I never saw one of them treat any of our people out of the way at all, nowhere. I don't understand this.

I brought home an accordion that the Soviets used to play there that night, and I sold it, like a fool.

All of us studied about the Union of Soviet Socialist Republics at school; we studied their life-style, supposedly what we thought they had and all, but as far as me knowing what they were and how they were before, say, March 1945, when we were talking about going to meet the Russians, I never had any thought about them. I do recall that what I studied in school was not the Russians that we met. What I remember studying in school was that they were dancers, partiers, but I also found that they have a real gruff side and a jovial side. They were doing that Russian dance that night on the Elbe in that little village in Torgau, but this was not the common thing; they could be very solemn. They could go from joviality to solemnness in just a heartbeat. But they were mostly a solemn people, and at that time, they were more solemn because almost every one of them that we met had lost a brother, a son, or someone in the war. But when they met us, that made them happy. ○

ALEKSEY KIRILLOVICH GORLINSKIY*

After the war, Aleksey Gorlinskiy remained in the army. He retired many years later as a major general. He is a member of the Soviet Veterans' Committee and the Soviet Peace Committee of Generals for Peace. He recalled the linkup on the Elbe during the spacebridge:

> Less that two years ago, we at the Soviet Veterans' Committee received a letter from our friend Joseph Polowski, a participant of the meeting near Torgau on April 25, 1945. In that letter he bid us farewell, saying that he had cancer and didn't have long to live. He told us that in his will he had asked to be buried in the spot where he first shook hands with a Soviet soldier, at Torgau.
>
> His wish was fulfilled. Soviet and American veterans interred the body of Joseph Polowski at his final resting place on the banks of the Elbe. And we, members, participants of that meeting in 1945, repeated the vow which we had made then: to do everything to avert a new war, to safeguard the relations between our two countries. Not long ago we again went to Torgau on the Elbe and again repeated the vow—to live in peace, and to do everything to safeguard peace on earth.

In a subsequent interview, Aleksey Gorlinskiy recalled in detail his historic meeting:

○ I was then in command of the detachment at the artillery headquarters of the 5th Guards Army. The detachment was responsible for planning operations. This was especially important for artillery, for it had to be provided with info as to where to lay down its fire, when to begin shelling, what caliber shells to use, and so on. Well, I was the commander of this detachment. Our army consisted of three corps. Two were repelling a strong German counteroffensive from the south, from the direction of Bautzen; this was the German force that was trying to punch its way through to Berlin with the goal of linking up with the surrounded Berlin units. We did not allow this to happen. The third corps was the one that was to meet the U.S. forces at the Elbe.

Here is how that came about. Officers were busy fending off the German counterattack; they sent a group of junior officers, myself included, along with the corps that went to the Elbe River. We were instructed not to cross it. A short while earlier, it was decided that a predetermined line for the meeting with Americans was going to be at the Elbe. For this reason, only a small scout unit of several people were to cross to the other side.

On the 25th of April, at about 1:00 to 1:30 in the afternoon, I found

*Introduced on page 71.

myself at the observation post of one of the commander's batteries. It was six hundred meters from the Elbe. The river wasn't big, about 100–120 meters wide. I was looking at the other bank—there was the village of Torgau, until then an unknown little Saxon village. Suddenly, I noticed a flicker of light—it came from one of the towers of a small castle on the other bank. I immediately realized this could be sunlight reflected off an enemy helmet or gunsight. Germans? I began to look more carefully and discovered that there were soldiers there, not in uniforms of that mouse-gray color we hated so much but of a color unfamiliar and new to us, something quite different. We had this preliminary agreement with the Allies: for mutual recognition, in order not to shoot each other, we would fire a red flare, and they would answer, in turn, with a green one; or the other way around, they would fire a green one, and we would answer in red.

We fired the red flare—no answer. Well, you know . . . could it be that the Germans had changed uniforms? Was this a trick? Then I saw three people run from the tower toward the shore. It then became clear they were Americans. They began to shout at the top of their lungs, "Russians! Washington! Moscow! Hitler kaput!" At that point I realized I was witnessing history. There was, as I have said, six hundred meters to the shore. I was already a captain then, and I was young. I sprinted toward the river bank, followed by the rest. The bridge spanning the Elbe here had been blown up by the Germans, and only the supports could be seen sticking up out of the water. One American, not waiting for either a boat or a raft, started to cross, climbing along the supports with acrobatic dexterity. One of ours also started along the trusses. Thus did our meeting occur . . . "on the bridge," right in the middle of the river. That was our first contact. And then a boat appeared from somewhere, and the Americans started to cross over to our side.

Of course, that feeling would stay with me for my entire lifetime. We didn't know English, and the Americans didn't know Russian. But nothing could have been more eloquent than the soldiers' language: the embraces, the back-slapping, the photographs—when you knew without words that this was his wife and this was his kid. . . . We spread our waterproof capes on the grass, and we shared our simple fare. I tasted whisky then for the first time in my life, and the Americans discovered Russian vodka for the first time; in our canteens we never carried water. I have never forgotten this and never will—neither that linkup nor those men, many of whom I have seen since then.

We made an oath there. And, you know, it was because of journalists that that oath on the Elbe became famous. Years later we would be asked, where is the oath? Give us the text. But there was no official text; we never wrote anything down. We raised a toast to victory and to never having another war, and we swore that neither we nor our children nor our grandchildren would ever know war again. That was the oath. A few years later, at our meeting, we made it official in the form of a statement. But back then, it was an oral oath that we gave to each other. And that is the oath that everyone remembers. . . . you know, now when we meet with those who are still alive—and we meet every year—I always ask—we always ask each other; "Do you remember the oath on the Elbe?" And always the answer is, "I remember."

And so this meeting at Torgau went down in history as the very first one. It was later found out that about thirty kilometers to the north, at a place called Riese, our forces linked an hour before the ones at Torgau. But in the end, chronology is not that important. It was the meeting at Torgau that became history. The bridge has long since been restored, and whenever we meet there, we always meet on this bridge, which has a beautiful monument in honor of the U.S.–Soviet linkup on the Elbe River. ○

EDWARD
RUFF

1943   **1985**

*Edward Ruff lives in Riverside, New Jersey, the town in which he grew up in the
years before World War II. Nine months after he graduated from high school in
1942, he was drafted into the U.S. infantry, which sent him through a series of
engineering courses before his unit was shipped to England. From England, Ruff
went to Belgium and on through various areas of Germany, eventually arriving in
Leipzig. At Leipzig, his division had to pull back to a little town called Trepsen on
the Molda River. While there, he volunteered to be a jeep driver in a heavy-
weapons company and was assigned to the patrol of Lieutenant Kotzibue; this
patrol was to be one of the first U.S. groups to meet the Soviets at the Elbe River on
April 25, 1945. During the spacebridge, Ruff told of his participation in that
historic encounter:*

The day before, on April 24, we were on this patrol, and we had heard the
Russians were close in the area. American forces had to stop at the Molda
River, and the Russian forces were supposed to stop at the Elbe, so that
we wouldn't shoot each other. So, we went out on April 24 and were only
supposed to go about five kilometers, but after going about seven kilometers, we heard that the Russians weren't very far away. We heard this
from prisoners of war that were liberated and were on their way back.
That morning, Lieutenant Kotzibue sort of took a democratic vote, and
he decided to go on. We did go on, and at a little town called Strehla, we
met this lone Russian horseman. But before we had met him, we had seen
about five of them on horseback in the distance.

At that point, we went up to the river, and Joe Polowski, myself, and
Lieutenant Kotzibue blasted a boat loose from the river and went across
the bridge, where we saw the body of a little girl. That was a very moving
experience. We had to step over the little girl to get to the Russian
soldiers.

From that moment on, everybody was just filled with joy and back-
slapping. That evening, the Russians gave us a big dinner. General Rus-
ikov was there with Lieutenant Kotzibue. The next day, there were alot of
pictures taken. There was a young girl, a Russian army girl, with a bou-

quet of lilacs; I have a picture at home of that from a Russian newspaper that one of the soldiers gave me. It was a moving experience for all of us.

We lived, actually, with the Russian army for about seven to ten days before we went back to American lines. And after we got back, I happened to be one of the fortunate ones to whom the Russians gave, in Leipzig, the Order of Glory. I have that medal—just like it's brand new—and I have the certificate in Russian, and I honor that very much. And I will never forget the friendship shown between the two forces.

I was wondering if the young gentleman on horseback is in the audience, because I can remember very vividly his face. At that moment, we may have shared the same thoughts, because we stared at each other and were not able to say much. After about thirty seconds to a minute, I gave him a big wink, and he winked back. And I don't know if that young gentleman is there or not, but it was a very fitting moment for me.

In a subsequent interview, Ed Ruff provided further details concerning the U.S.– Soviet meeting at the Elbe as he recalled it:

○ On patrol on April 24, 1945, we had met some liberated Scottish and Canadian prisoners of war, and they told us that the Russia army wasn't too far away. This wasn't too much of a surprise because the *Stars and Stripes* radio broadcast carried everything, and we pretty much knew where the Russians were and what they were doing and how they were tearing things up. You could hear artillery in the distance, miles away; you could hear it rumble like thunder, and we often wondered whether that was Russian artillery or just Germans on another front. We were wondering whether we were going to get to hear some of this Russian artillery with the barrages they were supposed to be putting down. I mean, they tore things apart when they put them down, just like our total bombing when those B-17s went over in front of us.

A few Germans that we had captured before we met the Russians, I don't know where they got this, . . . were under the impression that the Germans and Americans were going to fight the Russians and get Berlin before the Russians got it. We could've walked into Berlin, really, before the Russians got there; we were that close. I'd say 80 percent of the German soldiers wanted to join the American army. I said, "We're not fighting the Russians." Joe Polowski explained to them that we were allies, and we had no intention of fighting the Russians.

The night of April 24th, we set up headquarters; we had thirty-three on our patrol at first. The next morning—I can remember this pretty vividly—we were talking about the Russians being near, and Lieutenant Kotzibue says, "Do you think we ought to go along?" Joe Polowski was in the group. He asked me, "Do you want to go?" I said, "I'm willing." Of course, I don't think any of us realized what significance this would have about making contact with the Russians. It's just that they were there.

The next morning we started out, and some German civilians came up and stopped us, waving their hands, and said there were some German soldiers in the houses. So, the lieutenant says, "Let's see if we can clear them out first." We stopped the jeeps and went into the houses, and sure enough, there were some young Germans there. One young boy and his mother called out in German, "Nicht schiesen." I understood a little bit of German. I said, "I don't want to shoot anybody." The boy came out of the bedroom with his hands up. There were five of them altogether who came out. I think we surprised them. We just took their weapons, told them where to go, and told them to start walking.

Eventually we came to a little town, Leckwitz, where we saw five horsemen in the distance. And I said, "They look like Russians." So the lieutenant said, "It was a Russian who went into that courtyard up there." We had seen him go in by the side gate. We pulled up to the front gate of the courtyard, and he was sitting on his horse's back. At that point we had a British flag; we didn't have an American flag. So, Joe started talking in Russian to him. That's the guy I can remember. He was very young. We just kept looking at each other.

After that it was okay. He said the Russian army was over the Elbe River, and we followed his directions. When we got to the Elbe, we saw all this carnage, all this destruction on the other side of the bridge. There was part of the bridge left, so we went down along the bank. But when we got down to the edge of the river, they started firing on either side. We jumped behind a rock because we weren't sure if they were firing at us, but the lieutenant said, "Well, let's get this boat." The boat was chained and locked, so I took a grenade, and the lieutenant put it under the lock and blasted it loose. That sort of shook the Soviets up on the other side.

The lieutenant knew that you were supposed to fire two or three green flares for recognition. "Here," he said, "Put your rocket launcher on your carbine and fire these flares." I fired the green flares, but I don't think the Russians knew what they were about. We got in the boat and went across with Polowski—the lieutenant, myself, and I think Wheeler was with us. We went upstream in the current, and when we reached the other side, we grabbed onto the bridge pilings, tied the boat, and went up on the bridge. And, oh God, there were dead civilians lying all over the place, a couple of burnt out buses with charred bodies still sitting in their seats, and dead horses. This was where we stepped over the little girl. I can practically see her today.

We made our way through to the Soviet soldiers and started shaking hands and slapping each other's backs. It was about half past eleven when we first met the Russians. I looked at my watch, and I can remember that: 11:27. . . .

After that, some of the officers came down. They must have radioed ahead. This was the 58th Guards Division, General Russikof. One general came down—he was a lower-ranking general—and the officers got together.

The officers were well dressed. They were spic-and-span compared to, well, for instance, Lieutenant Kotzibue, who had no bars on. Of course, I don't blame him. They'd pick out the bars to shoot at. The Soviet general was a little miffed that it was only the lieutenant there, Lieutenant Kotzibue. Most of the Russian soldiers were a little bit, for want of a better word, a little bit seedy; let me put it that way. I mean they were healthy enough looking, but the uniforms, their equipment, were in pretty bad shape. One guy gave me a piece of bread, black bread, that he had under his tunic. He must have got that from a German baker or something. Of course, I ate it. One guy had half a chicken stuffed inside of his shirt; of course, I ate that, too.

The next day, the Russians sent a raft back over, and we got my jeep, put it on there, and brought it over. We drove the jeep up the bank, and it started sliding down in the mud. The lieutenant got in back and was pushing with a Russian soldier; we finally got it up there.

They treated us very well, I mean excellently. A typical day we'd get up fairly early and have breakfast, and most of the day we spent sitting around talking. A couple of Russians had a German burp gun there one morning, and we were showing our carbines to them. They handed me this German burp gun, and I didn't know it at the time, but they had Russian ammo in it.

The Russian said, "Fire it." I fired it, and this stupid thing didn't go fully closed, and it got me. It gave me some little shrapnel wounds in my finger and a thumb. Then I took the bullets out and saw they weren't the right ones. I had a couple of Lugers that I had taken off two German officers, and we'd exchange and fire, do target practice, then throw a couple of grenades in the Elbe for fishing. The grenades would go off, and the fish would float to the top. We'd get the fish and cook them. It was more like a picnic, I would say.

I was surprised at the number of women there were in this Russian group. It looked like they were more at the service end of it, though. They were the KP and the cooks and the people to clean the Russian officers' uniforms, do their shoes, and all this kind of stuff. In the American army, the men got assigned to that kind of stuff.

This one Russian sergeant—I guess she was in her thirties—would have made a beautiful professional wrestler. She had two gold teeth in the front, and she must have taken a liking to me because every time I'd see her, she would pick me up and squeeze me. She had this black bread and incredibly greasy stew. But it was good. They sopped up the grease first, but we tried to skim it off. Other than that, we had good meals, and we even learned a few words of Russian.

We radioed back that we had met the Russians, but unfortunately, we sent the wrong coordinates. The U.S. army sent a patrol out, but they couldn't find us; we were about two kilometers off. In the meantime, heck, we were eating a banquet. I don't know where they got all this food. There were no trucks or tanks or visible artillery; everything they had was horse drawn.

Later, we found out that the Soviets kept all their mechanized things back about half a kilometer so we wouldn't see them. However, we eventually saw their tanks and trucks and everything, all Studebaker trucks.

We didn't know it then, but while we were eating with the one general, Lieutenant Bill Robertson's patrol up at Torgau was making contact up further from where we were. Lieutenant Kotzibue, the colonel, and the general left and, I think, went to where Robertson came across. But there we were, having a good time and drinking some of that hard stuff, oooh! This one guy with a beard—a beard that must've been three feet long—all he kept saying was, "Stalingrad," and he got the message across that he fought at Stalingrad. So we carried this six-foot man—he must have been six foot two—and we carried him just like a baby, put him in bed, drunk. But he was about the only one.

We stayed with the Russians for more than ten days. We followed no matter where they went; we were told to go with this one group. There are so many little things that stand out in my mind now from that week spent with the Russians.

What we saw of the Russian artillery were some antiquated Studebaker trucks and artillery drawn by horses and mules; their carts, their ammo carts, were drawn by mules. But soldiers, God, they had tens of thousands of soldiers. I think it upset them that every time they moved, we radioed back. I guess they got the impression that we didn't trust them. And I could see why.

Joe and I were sitting out on the steps one day, and a couple of Soviet officers came out. They made a couple of remarks that weren't very complimentary, and, of course, they didn't know Joe could speak Russian. Apparently, they didn't like us following them around. I can't say I blame them. They were young, and maybe it was just their personal opinion about the Americans.

When we finally got word to go back, the Soviets ferried us across the river, and still at that point, we didn't know that Robertson's patrol had contacted other Russians further up the Elbe. Back at our base, we were under barracks arrest for a couple of days because we weren't supposed to go out there. And everybody said, we're under arrest. I asked, "For what?" "Our patrol disobeyed orders." I asked, "What are they going to do with us? Discharge us? I could care less." So that didn't last long.

Then we heard that the Americans and Russians were getting together in Leipzig. We went to Leipzig immediately: thirty-three of us, plus some from Robertson's patrol and some Russians. We went past a Napoleonic monument and had a bit of a battle and then went to the city hall, where we had yet another battle.

Following these battles, out in the courtyard of the city hall, we gave the Russians the American Bronze Star. The Russians gave the Russian Order of Glory out, not to everybody, but I happened to be one of the group that got one of them. Why, I don't know. That surprised me. I still have that medal here on the table. After the spacebridge was over, I thought I should have worn the medal during the program. I should have done it because, as I said, I was proud of it. I didn't because it just isn't something we do in this country. It may be a funny thing to say, and I didn't know it then, but that Russian medal got me five points and got me home about three months sooner than I would have otherwise. Crazy little things like these were happening towards the end of the war to everybody.

I really think it was then, at that patrol in Leipzig, that I started to think, boy, this is the chance; it looks like we're going to get out of this thing. When they say there's no atheist in foxholes, they're damned if they're right. I don't think you came out saying Hallelujah and Our Father and Hail Mary and sign the cross sixteen hours a day. But I'm a Catholic, and I said my prayers, and I went to Communion every chance I got.

And I just want to say again that the young people are the ones that I'm concerned about. Let them do the real fighting. They're the ones that can do it. And I don't mean military fighting. Anything I have to say is all directed towards those young people. ○

**BERNARD
KOTEN**

1946   **1985**

Bernard Koten was trained at the Johns Hopkins University, Moscow University, and Columbia University. Before entering the United States army in World War II, he worked with the Russian-American Institute and the Board of Education. His father organized the veterinary system in the U.S.S.R. during the 1920s, and at nineteen, Mr. Koten accompanied his family to the U.S.S.R., where he lived for five and a half years. During World War II, Mr. Koten was with U.S. Wire and Direct Communications units on the European front. He was among those first Americans who met the Soviets at the Elbe.

Mr. Koten participated in Remembering War, *the spacebridge, although he never actually spoke during the two-hour satellite link. In remarks drawn from a post-spacebridge interview, he situates his memories of the U.S.–Soviet meeting at the Elbe within the larger context of his experiences as a U.S. soldier on the European front:*

○ I was with the U.S. forces that were the first to land directly in Normandy, on rafts, and I was sure I was going to fall over because these were open rafts, and we had to stand on them from the ship to the shore. We were in northern France for awhile until we went into Germany, Holland, and then up to the Elbe in Germany, where we met the Russians.

My job when I was in communications was to direct fire. So I'd be lying flat in a hole—there wasn't even enough room for me to get up—and I'd be directing fire against the Germans. On my communications board, I would be plugging in and telling them just where the Germans were. . . . And the fire would be directed at them from my instructions. Later on, I was placed behind our lines into the German lines, and I dug holes for myself down deep. I had a walkie-talkie and was able to follow the Germans wherever they were. I listened in; I know German also, and I listened in and got information about where they were going to strike next. They were developing a von Klausivitz division at the time, getting ready to attack us, and I got the information, passed it on to our people, and we attacked them before they could attack us. This was the Ruhr.

I just wasn't aware of fear. You see, you do things you shouldn't do, stupidly. A friend of mine, a pianist, was with us, and he knew I loved Gershwin. There we were, crossing into Germany, and there was a tremendous baby-grand piano in the middle of nowhere. He went out there and played "Rhapsody in Blue" for me, and that zeroed the Germans in on us.

We freed a lot of inmates in camps, in Ordruf and Pasau, and some of the inmates gave me their emblems, which I have on the wall there: "Jude" and "Ost-Arbeiter," which was eastern worker, and Pole, and then they had separate ones. As the Russians were getting closer, the Germans were a little bit worried. They had separate emblems for the Ukranians, the Russians, the Belorussians, and I have those in a frame.

We were the only Americans under General Montgomery, under the British. We got to the Elbe before the Russians, and we were not permitted to go across because we might have been shooting at each other. There was a big decree out at the time, and so we sat on an incline at the river; it was like being in a stadium watching the war go on.

The Germans had captured a company of our men, and I was sent across to get them back. I went alone with jeep. We had arranged for it, and I had a white arm band on. The Germans didn't pay any attention to arm bands. They were very anxious to talk with us; I spoke German. Their headquarters were in a big hospital, and they said, "If you take over all our men, we don't want them to get into Russian hands, we will give you back your company." I had been given instructions on what we could do and what we couldn't do, and I said no. I went back to our company headquarters, and before I knew it, the Germans were swimming across and coming on rafts to get away from the Soviet troops. There were women with them, doctors and their wives, who also were doctors. Our agreement with the Russians was that we would bring all the Germans back, so we took them back to the Russian side, and we marched arm in arm back and forth in front of the Germans with the Russians to show them that the Russians and the Americans were together. They said, "You're fighting the wrong people. You should turn against the Russians. Join us."

We were at the Elbe a long time before the Russians came, and so I would get in touch by radio with Soviet troops. There was a woman tank driver who was with this General Melitzen, whom we flirted with by radio. Annai, I think her name was. We talked and then met at the Elbe.

After the Russians came, they had us over for tremendous feasts and shows. We had only the food that we brought with us, whereas they used the food on the land, so it was much better food. There were these great big banquets in halls or out in the open, and we had USO performers who put on shows. It was an exciting time.

Everybody was so friendly, the Americans and the Russians. A while after we got together, there were instructions put out that we were not to

fraternize. But meanwhile, the Americans and the Russians had been running around, finding girls, and having a good time. We got into kitchens
where the workers were all Russian or Ukrainian, and they made wonderful food for us—eggs mainly, but whole, real eggs.

I think it was at Buttenberg; we got there and liberated a camp, and
the camp was full of Italian communists, men and women. The Russians
had given me their emblems and stars, and this . . . old, Italian, communist
woman was dying, and she thought the Russians had come. And they asked
me not to say anything to her, because I had the star, and she got up and
saluted me and was very excited. So I kept quiet and let her think that I was
a Russian.

At another camp, the Germans had taken American prisoners of war
and put them in a great big barn and set a fire. And as the guys were trying
to get out, they would fire at them so we lost a tremendous number of
people there. Gardelegen. Gardelegen in Hell we called it.

You know most of the medical units were Jewish—the doctors, the
nurses, men and women; they told me something very interesting. They
said, "All the tenderness we had, we gave to the Jewish boys." They were
Jewish, and they felt closer to the young Jewish soldiers. I was concerned
with what had happened to the Jews along the way because we had passed
so many areas where the Jews had been killed.

The Russian villages had been sacked by the Germans, so a lot of the
Russians, as they were passing German areas, . . . hit back. As a matter of
fact, we didn't really take prisoners; we let them kill each other. We freed
camps that were filled with German communists who had been put in
camps, and so there was a tremendous amount of ill-feeling between the
German sides. We were witness to it all. By then, I don't think anything
shocked me. Policy was to take prisoners of war, but our guys were angry,
too, and so they didn't always take prisoners. Especially after the medical
unit attached to our company had been captured; a lot of guys had been
killed, and so our soldiers were in a mood to kill back.

It was forty-eight years ago—a couple of lifetimes, and I have to
dredge it out of my memory. They gave me a Legion of Merit and a Bronze
Star. I have all my citations. ○

Opposite page: The generals link up on the Elbe River.

Victories

A German soldier, Berlin 1945 *(News Press Agency)*

Attacking the Reichstag *(I. Shagin)*

Marshal Zhukov is signing the act of the unconditional capitulation of Nazi Germany
(M. Alpert)

Wall Street celebration *(United Press International)*

Victory fireworks in Moscow on May 9, 1945 *(A. Ustinov)*

The reception ceremony for the soldiers arriving at Moscow's Belorussian railway terminal in 1945 *(G. Petrusov)*

Soldiers arrive at the Belorussian railway terminal in Moscow *(G. Petrusov)*

Sailor kisses nurse on street *(Life Picture Service)*

Soviet officer waves as Soviet crowd lifts him *(SovSoto/Eastfoto)*

U.S. army officers are enthusiastically greeted by people in Red Square on VE Day
(Y. Khalip)

Returning from Germany *(S. Alperin)*

Tokyo radio flashes news *(Press Association)*

Japanese surrender

This is all of what was left of the Melinitsa village in the Kalininsky region *(G. Grebnev)*

The American Experience:
An American Perspective

For Americans, the end of World War II was and remains an extended historical moment. U.S. history books mark not one but two occasions as signifying the end of the war: VE (Victory in Europe) Day, May 8, 1945, and VJ (Victory in Japan) Day, August 14, 1945. Neither day is a national holiday, however, and few Americans born after 1940 attach any significance to these dates. As a nation, we officially remember those Americans who died in all wars in which the United States has fought on one annual holiday, Memorial Day, May 30. And even Memorial Day, although celebrated in many communities with parades that highlight war veterans, is primarily an occasion for community and family gatherings, not for remembering war.

As the unofficial news of the end of the war in Europe spread on May 7, 1945, Americans did celebrate victory, as photographs in this section attest. They thronged to public places, like Times Square in New York City, to confirm their common pride in their country and its achievements in conquering fascism in Europe and to share their relief that the burdens and constraints of war were—almost—behind them. American correspondent Leo Gruliow, who was unfortunately cut off during the spacebridge just as he began to describe his experience of VE Day in Moscow, has particularly vivid memories of the unrestrained joy of the Soviets and of the affection they expressed toward him as their American ally in victory.

For many, however, it was both too late and too soon to celebrate. Throughout April 1945, as the Allies invaded Germany, the good news of approaching victory was accompanied by reports of the uncovering of the horrors of concentration camps. No victory could be sweet in the context of this confrontation with evil.

Americans were also still mourning for President Franklin Roosevelt, who died on April 12, 1945; his absence, when the anticipated victory in Europe finally came, was profoundly felt across the nation. Several participants in the *Remembering War* spacebridge remarked that they vividly recalled the day that President Roosevelt died, whereas they had only vague memories of VE and VJ days. Elliott Roosevelt, the president's son, of course, had a unique recollection of the death of his father, which he was generous enough to share with us:

○ I was in England. I had just returned from a mission. I had a dinner appointment in London. I went into the door of the restaurant, and I was greeted, and they told me, would I sit down, and I sat down, and they said, "Your father just died. They want you to go back to your air base immediately. General Doolittle wants to talk to you." So, I went back to my air base, and Doolittle called me and said, "Do you want to go back for your father's funeral?" and I said, "Yes, sir, I would like to if I can get there in time. I don't know that I can get there in time." He said, Well, Bernard Baruch has got Air Force Two over here, and if you fly your plane over to the airfield in the morning, we'll park it there and let someone else bring it back, and you can catch his plane. He's leaving at seven o'clock in the morning." I got on that plane and got back to Washington in time. The casket was in the East Room of the White House. My mother said, "Thank God you're here!" And I said, "Why?" And she said, "Well, the Russian ambassador's been over trying to see me, and I just saw him a few minutes ago. Stalin wanted him and some of his aides to view father in the coffin." I said, "Absolutely not. We're not having anyone see him at all." And she said, "I don't know what their reason is for it." And I said, "Well, let me talk to them." So I talked to them. They said that Stalin believed that Father had been poisoned and that they didn't think that he had had a massive brain hemorrhage. And I said, "You'll just have to take my word for it, because that's what he had. If we open this casket for you and your people to view it, we'll have to do that for the public, and we just don't want the public to see the disfigurement of the results of this massive brain hemorrhage." They said they would relay it to the generallissimo, and they came back in and said, "We've got to see the body, we've got to have it viewed." And I said, "Well, sorry." ○

While the American public did not share Stalin's paranoia about the cause of President Roosevelt's death, many were not only shocked and grief-stricken but also anxious about the change in leadership at such a crucial time. President Roosevelt had planned to open the first meeting of the United Nations on April 25, 1945 (notably, the same day that Americans unexpectedly met Soviets at the Elbe River in Germany), and Americans looked forward to this occasion with hope and confidence in Roosevelt's commitment to the United Nations.

President Roosevelt had a clear vision of the role of the United Nations and that of the United States and other nations in relation to it. According to Elliott Roosevelt, at the time of his death his father had already written three quarters of the speech he intended to deliver at the opening of the United Nations. Elliott Roosevelt attests that President Roosevelt envisioned an organization with "teeth" in it; the president intended to recommend the creation of a United Nations peace-keeping force that would automatically intervene when any powers came into dis-agreement, including the Soviet Union and the United States. "He would have put the atomic bomb," Elliott Roosevelt explained, "into this organi-zation and given the United Nations the full control of it."

We cannot know whether this vision of the United Nations would have been fulfilled had Franklin Roosevelt lived through his fourth term as president of the United States. What we do know is that the actual opening of the United Nations in San Francisco was clouded by bitter conflicts among the nations concerning criteria for membership and voting rights. Particular tension was provoked by President Truman's acquiescence to Soviet demands for separate admission to the United Nations of three republics that were arguably part of the Soviet Union. We also know that neither at the time of its founding nor subsequently was the atomic bomb turned over by the United States to the United Nations.

Weakened by these and other struggles, the United Nations had a far less glorious opening than some had imagined. Adolf Hitler's suicide on April 30, 1945, paradoxically confirmed the defeat of Germany while diminishing the symbolic significance of the final steps of Allied victory. The subsequent attempt by Hitler's successors to negotiate a separate surrender with the Western Allies that would exclude the Soviet Union delayed and tarnished the formal end to the war in Europe. The Germans signed documents of unconditional surrender to the Allies on May 7, 1945, at Rheims but then were required by the Allies to repeat the ceremony in Berlin on the next day so that General Zhukov could sign for the Soviet Union. As a result, to this day, although history records May 8, 1945, as the official date of the end of the war in Europe, VE Day is celebrated on May 7 in some nations and on May 8 in others.

For Americans, the important problem of VE Day was not the ambiguity surrounding the actual date but the incompleteness of the victory. Despite overwhelming evidence by May 1945 that the Japanese had no chance of winning the war in the Pacific, peace between Japan and the United States did not appear to be imminent. To the contrary, following the reconquest of the Philippines by U.S. forces in January 1945, the Pacific war became uglier, as Japanese kamikazes (the name means "divine wind") deliberately embraced suicide missions as an official tactic. The willingness of Japanese pilots knowingly to sacrifice their own lives by crashing into American ships and bases frightened and bewildered Americans; it also resulted in the loss of nearly ten thousand American lives in the final year of the war.

Between early May and August 1945, the United States mounted an increasingly fierce and focused assault on the Japanese home islands, destroying much of Tokyo and other industrial centers with incendiary bombs. Hundreds of thousands of Japanese were killed, with as many as eighty thousand dying in one night. U.S. Pacific-fleet submarines were relentlessly destroying Japanese merchant ships, while a new British offensive wrested Burma from Japanese control. Iwo Jima and Okinawa, taken earlier that year by American forces with great loss of American lives, were now fulfilling strategic roles as launching bases for the U.S. planes and ships attacking Japan. And the strength of the Allied forces was soon to be increased, since the Soviet Union had promised to join in the Pacific war on August 9, three months after VE Day.

An eventual Allied victory over Japan seemed assured. What remained unclear was when and at what cost. Divided in their projections as to the proximity of Japanese surrender, on July 26, 1945, U.S. President Harry Truman and British Prime Minister Winston Churchill issued an ultimatum to Japan: surrender unconditionally or be destroyed. After a long silence, the only official Japanese response was a statement by Japanese Premier Suzuki suggesting that the Potsdam declaration was absurd.

Neither the Japanese nor most of the rest of the world knew just what lay behind the Allied threat to "destroy" Japan. In the United States, only a small group of scientists, military men, and government officials knew that, over the course of the war years, the secret U.S. Manhattan Project had produced a new kind of weapon, an atomic weapon. And until the first test of this weapon at Los Alamos, New Mexico, on July 16, 1945, even the scientists and engineers who had created the atom bomb were uncertain of what they had wrought.

Once the atom bomb had been tested at Los Alamos and had been shown to be a weapon of extraordinary destructive force, the actual use of the two existing bombs on Japanese targets became an immediate issue of contention among key Americans. Several scientists involved in the creation of the bomb argued against its use, as did some government and military leaders who anticipated the imminent surrender of Japan. In contrast, some U.S. leaders not only argued for the deployment of the two atomic weapons but also urged that the first, at least, be dropped with no forewarning to the Japanese population in order, according to General Elliott Roosevelt, to create a complete surprise and create "panic among the Japanese people that would force them to surrender." Others, General Roosevelt remarked, wanted to use the bomb "to impress the Russians that we had the ultimate weapon."

In the end, a U.S. B-29 bomber called the *Enola Gay* dropped the first atomic bomb to be used as a weapon of war on the Japanese city of Hiroshima at 9:15 a.m. on August 6, 1945. Japanese citizens had, in a compromise move, been warned by leaflets of a "heavy attack," but not of the kind of terror to which they were to be subjected. Three days later, on August 9, 1945, a second atomic bomb was dropped on Nagasaki. Together, these two bombs killed at least ninety-six thousand people.

On August 14, 1945, the Japanese surrendered to the Allies, although it was not until September 2, 1945, that, on the U.S. battleship *Missouri*, documents of surrender were finally signed. World War II was over, and victory over the Axis was complete. It was not a time, however, simply to rejoice. Rather, as even American General Douglas MacArthur proclaimed to the American people, it was a moment to acknowledge that "we have had our last chance." It was the time for war to become taboo. By using atomic weapons, we had made this taboo more difficult and yet more necessary to effect. Americans may have difficulty remembering VE Day and VJ Day, but no one has forgotten the challenge and enigma of the legacies left by Hiroshima and Nagasaki.

The Soviet Experience: A Soviet Perspective

The news was announced by Radio Hamburg on May 1, 1945: the Führer was dead. This was followed by the slow movement of Bruckner's Seventh Symphony. Then Hitler's appointed successor, Admiral Dönitz, broadcast a very revealing message: "My first task is to save Germany from destruction by the advancing Bolshevik enemy. It is to serve this purpose alone that the military struggle continues." Officially, that was the motive. In fact, the truth lay elsewhere.

Insofar as destruction was concerned, it would be logical to conclude that, indeed, the "Bolshevik enemy" was out to reap vengeance for what the "master race" had perpetrated on the Soviet Union. Half of the U.S.S.R.'s twenty million dead were civilians, most of whom had been tortured and massacred by the Nazi occupation forces. Approximately seventeen hundred cities and towns and seventy thousand villages had been destroyed. There was indeed a debt to be paid. Interestingly enough, the Soviet offensive did not cause anywhere near the same kind of destruction as did the Allied air raids. No Soviet assault inflicted what the Anglo-American fire-bombing did to the nonmilitary city of Dresden. If German resistance on the Eastern Front had been less intense, there would have been even less destruction and far fewer deaths.

The German motives behind such strong resistance, however, are no secret. During the Ardennes offensive, the Germans had captured a plan of the projected Allied occupation zones for Germany. This gave Dönitz exact knowledge of proposed east-west borders while his forces continued to hold ground on either side of them. The Nazi plan was simple enough: keep the Allies in the west at bay and fight with utmost resolve in the east, thereby allowing as many Germans, both civilian and military, as possible to flee west and cross into the future western zones.

However, that plan was not feasible. While strong on paper (six million men and three hundred divisions), the Wehrmacht was, in fact, on the verge of total collapse. Military initiatives were hardly conducive to winning time. A possible alternative would be to offer the Western Powers a series of surrenders, local and partial, begin negotiations, and gain eight or ten days. This approach had proved successful in Italy. Why not try it again? Therefore, Admiral von Friedburg was instructed by Dönitz to contact Field Marshal Montgomery and offer him the surrender of all of northern Germany. At the same time, he was to "invite the field marshal's special attention to the problem of the refugees and troops in retreat on the eastern boundaries of the area occupied by the British."

When von Friedburg offered the surrender of Army Group Vistula in the east, Montgomery refused, saying it would be surrendered only to the Soviets. However, he did express a willingness to sign a surrender of those forces on his northern and western flanks, as well as to accept the surrender of all German soldiers fleeing from the east. On the following day, May 4, the instrument of surrender was signed, and von Friedburg set off for Rheims and a meeting with the Allied supreme commander, General Dwight D. Eisenhower. He offered the surrender of the German forces in the west alone. The U.S. chief of staff, Walter Bedell Smith, had been instructed by Eisenhower to demand unconditional surrender on all fronts—and that was what he did. Friedburg stated he had no authority to negotiate and relayed the terms to Dönitz who, in turn, decided on another stalling technique, enlisting chief of staff operations Jodl. His instructions were: "To try once again to explain why we wish to make this separate surrender with the Americans. If you have no more success with Eisenhower than Friedburg had, offer a simultaneous surrender on all fronts, to be implemented in two phases. In the first phase, all hostilities will have ceased but German troops will still be allowed liberty of movement. During the second phase this liberty will be withheld. Try to make the period elapsing before phase two as long as possible and, if you can, try to get them to agree that individual German soldiers will be allowed to surrender to the Americans. The greater your success in these directions, the greater will be the numbers of German soldiers and refugees who will find salvation in the West."

When Jodl arrived on May 6, he was taken to Bedell Smith's office. According to eyewitness reports, Jodl stalled. Finally, after Eisenhower had been informed of yet another request for delay, he replied: "You tell them that 48 hours from midnight tonight I will close my lines on the Western Front so that no more Germans can get through. Whether they sign or not—however much more time they take."

This was a concession, for while it did not give Germans the eight- to ten-day period they were hoping for, it did grant them some time. Jodl believed that was the maximum he could achieve and asked permission to sign the surrender terms. Permission was granted, and on May 7, the document was signed.

Meanwhile, similar events had been taking place in Berlin. The steel ring of Soviet armor relentlessly tightened around the German capital. On April 30, Adolf Hitler committed suicide—a futile gesture of defiance and a telling footnote to the history of the Third Reich, which had existed twelve years instead of the heralded one thousand. On May 1, during the early dawn hours, chief of staff General Krebbs made his way to the headquarters of Marshal Vasily Chuikov and proposed a cease-fire in Berlin. This, he explained, would be followed by peace negotiations between the Soviet Union and Germany. The Soviet answer was unequivo-

cal: unconditional surrender immediately. Krebs took the Soviet ultimatum back to propaganda chief Joseph Goebbels, who rejected the idea
of unconditional surrender and promptly committed suicide with his wife
after having killed their six children. Twenty-four hours later, the Soviet
flag was hoisted over the Reichstag. A calm descended on Berlin. The
battle had been won—the silence was shattered by a roar of joy, a rat-tat-
tat of tommy guns fired at the sky, the indescribable sounds of victory.

The battle for Berlin was over. Between April 21 and May 2, a total of
1,800,000 artillery shells had fallen on the Nazi capital, 35,000 tons of
molten steel. Nearly half a million men had been taken prisoner; 15,000
tanks, 4,500 aircraft, and 8,600 guns had been captured. But the price had
been high. Looking back on those events Marshal Gheorghi Zhukov
recalls:

○ As a participant of the Berlin operation, I must say that it was one of the
most complex operations of World War II. The foe's army group, totalling
over one million men on the Berlin line, fought furiously. In this final
operation the Soviet forces suffered heavy casualties—about 300,000
killed and wounded. ○

The Soviet chief of staff, Marshal Vasilevsky, later noted the role and
importance of the Berlin operation:

○ The battle for Berlin was the last act in the dramatic downfall of the
German Wehrmacht. The speedy destroyal of the foe's one million strong
group on the Berlin line upset all the Hitlerite plans aimed at driving a
wedge into the anti-fascist coalition and provoking armed conflict between
the Soviet army and the Anglo-American Allied Forces. ○

Such plans indeed existed, as testified to by the OKW diary:

> May 2, 1945. From this day on the guiding principle for the High Com-
> mand is to save the greatest possible number of Germans from being
> captured by the Soviet forces and to begin separate negotiations with the
> Western Allies.
>
> May 3. The decisive accomplishment of this day is the establishment
> of contacts by the German representative, Admiral von Friedburg with
> Marshal Montgomery. Thanks to this, it is at least possible that a separate
> truce will be signed with the English.
>
> May 5. Agreement has been reached with Field-Marshal Montgom-
> ery according to which a cease-fire is agreed to in Holland, the North-
> West part of Germany, and Denmark. This truce was established upon
> the orders of Grand Admiral Dönitz. However, opposition to Soviet
> forces continues. Its aim is to save Germans from being captured by the
> Bolsheviks.
>
> May 6. In accordance with an agreement reached between the com-

mand of the German forces and the command of the Anglo-American forces a truce has been established in Italy. The Grand Admiral has ordered General Jodl to fly to Eisenhower's headquarters where, depending on the situation, he must negotiate a truce on all fronts so as to win as much times as possible and save Germans fleeing from the East. On that same day the General departed for Rheims.

We already know what happened in Rheims. Unconditional surrender was what General Eisenhower demanded, and that is what he got. But there was no designated representative of the Soviet Union at the signing of this historic document—a strange fact, to say the least, considering the key role played by the Soviet armed forces in defeating Nazi Germany.

In his memoirs, Marshall Zhukov notes:

> Stalin phoned me in Berlin on May 7 and said: "The Germans signed the act of unconditional surrender today in Rheims. The Soviet people carried on their shoulders the main burden of this war, not the Allies. And therefore the surrender must be signed before the High Command of all the anti-fascist coalition, not only that of the Allied Forces." "Neither did I agree," continued Stalin, "with the surrender's not being signed in Berlin, the home of fascist aggression."
>
> "We reached agreement with the Allies to consider the Rheims document a preliminary protocol. Representatives of the German High Command and representatives of the Allied Supreme Command will arrive in Berlin tomorrow."

At 10 a.m. on May 8, 1945, in Berlin, in a building that housed the School of Military Engineers, the unconditional surrender of Germany was signed by Marshal Gheorghi Zhukov for the U.S.S.R.; Chief Air Force Marshal of Great Britain, Sir Arthur Tedder; General Carl Spaatz of the United States; and General Delâtre de Tassigny for France—for the German side by Marshal Keitl, General Stumpf, and Admiral von Friedburg.

The war in Europe was over.

Legacies of War: Some Personal Reflections

Throughout this book, we have recalled and reflected on Soviet and American experiences of World War II in a somewhat unconventional mixing, not just of different voices but of different types of voices. We have presented oral and visual stories told by Soviets and Americans who served their countries and the Allied cause from the home fronts and battlefronts of World War II, but we have also set contexts for these stories in authorial voices that have spoken less from personal memories of the war than from the histories we have read, the films, photographs, and artifacts each of us has examined, and, not unimportantly, the lessons we have learned in helping to create the television spacebridge and this book. In an authentic sense, then, the preceding pages stand alone as an apt representation of the legacies of World War II.

For both of us, however, part of the legacy of World War II is the personal, family histories and recollections that we each brought to *Remembering War*. Our own exchanges of stories, combined with the understandings we have gained as we listened to and interpreted the stories told by *Remembering War* participants, has, in turn, contributed to a dialogue between us that is at once distinctly the conversation of two particular people and, at the same time, a reflection of the national cultural perspectives each of us brings to this endeavor. Because we are also professionally responsible for representations to others of our societies and because we share a commitment to increasing mutual understanding between the United States and the Soviet Union, this dialogue suggests some of the limits and opportunities for further explorations of our histories as well as our futures.

The following conversation is thus a part of the legacy of World War II and, more specifically, is *Remembering War*'s legacy to and from the authors.

Vladimir Pozner: A legacy is usually something very personal. Often, though, it also involves millions of people, and in this case it is both. So, let me first speak about my own personal experience, which is very different than that of the overwhelming majority of Soviet people, since I lived the war outside the Soviet Union.

My first recollection of the war is a very strange one. It goes back to what I think must have been the spring or summer of 1940 in France. I was living somewhere in the country with my mother, and I remember hearing on the radio a kind of play-by-play description of a dogfight involving a French fighter pilot and a German fighter pilot. I recall this was not fiction, and the reason I say that is the way the people around me in the house reacted when the French pilot was shot down. I think that is my first recollection of war. My father had enlisted in the French army, but somehow his absence did not register in my memory. Other impressions of the war have to do with the German occupation of Paris and the French reaction to the Germans. One such memory has to do with a German sentinel. There were plenty of them around the school I attended, maybe because the older kids were giving the Germans trouble. This seemed to me to be a rather old man, although, of course, I was only six. So, who knows. Once he gave me a bag of marbles and patted me on the head. I was playing with the marbles, and mother came home, and she asked me where I had gotten the marbles. I told her that it was a German soldier who had given them to me. And my mother, who had never punished me, let alone hit me, slapped me in the face and told me that I was never to accept anything from the Germans. Just a couple of days before that, my mother had been walking down the Champs Elysées with two very handsome German SS officers and myself, each of them holding me by the hand, and my mother had seemed to be delighted. So why was that okay if I couldn't then take a gift from a German soldier? But I was quick to understand that there was a difference, that you had to do some things for a purpose—such as socializing with the Germans—but accepting a gift was a completely different situation. You'd be surprised at how quickly war makes children mature.

War for me is also when we fled from France via Spain and Portugal to the United States. As I learned later, we didn't have the money to pay off

Author-producer Helene Keyssar in TV studio, 1985

Author-TV journalist Vladimir Pozner, 1987

the Germans. My mother was French, and she could easily leave, and I was on her passport, but my father had no passport, no citizenship. He had what was called a Nansen passport, which was an international document. He needed a visa from the Germans, from the Gestapo. That was simply not possible officially because he was a pro-Soviet Russian Jew. But the Gestapo could be bought, provided you had the money and the contacts. There was a Jewish family that desperately wanted to smuggle their daughter out, and they promised they'd give us the money if we agreed to take their daughter. So my father informed me that this lady was my nurse, my nanny, and that is what I was supposed to say if the Germans or French border guards asked me on the train. Of course, I knew she was not my nanny; I also saw all the diamond rings she was wearing—more than my mother ever had in her whole life. But I never questioned what my father said, because this was war.

Later, in the summer of 1941, when we were living on Bleecker Street in New York City, I remember my father put up a map of the European parts of the Soviet Union, and every evening he would draw in with black pencil the German advances. He would explain why they would never win, even though you could see how that black margin was edging closer and closer to Moscow and gradually encircled Leningrad; when Soviet forces counterattacked, he drew that in in red. And that was my first lesson in politics, with my father explaining why the Germans couldn't beat Soviet Russia and its socialist system.

I remember all of that with utmost clarity, so they must have been very powerful impressions. I think you could say that for me, as a child, the legacy of war was not linked to any real suffering and trauma. It had to do with understanding at a very early age that war was dangerous and that fascism was something to fear. It had to do with acquiring a kind of political education from my father as he lectured me on why Hitler could not win. Those are my first images, recollections, of war.

Helene Keyssar: Some of my memories of World War II, in odd ways, are not dissimilar to yours. Paris plays a role in my early memories, although I was even younger than you. I wasn't born until 1943. So I was a "war baby," and, in a sense, my whole life is a kind of legacy of this war.

Because I was so young during the actual war years, my memories of the war are intertwined with stories told to me. I was told stories because, in my family, knowing about the war was important to understanding who we were. My actual first memory, it's really my first memory as a person, is in the apartment I lived in, an apartment with a very long hall in Jersey City, New Jersey. I lived there with my mother, her two sisters, and my grandfather. One morning, down that long hall, the door was opened, the door to the outside of the apartment, and in walked this man whom my mother told me was my father. There had been a picture of my father kept clearly on display, and this man in the picture had dark curly hair and was very handsome. But the man who walked in the door did not seem to me to have anything to do with that picture. What I saw in front of me was a gaunt man who looked yellow and was bald. I remember being frightened. Here was my father who had not seen me since I was a tiny infant because he had gone off to war—to New Guinea—and when he finally came home, I declared, "That's not my father."

It's not unimportant that this first memory is of my father. He had been released somewhat before the end of the war because he was quite sick. He had jaundice, and he had lost his hair. Many of my memories of the war have to do with stories about my father's life told to me as a young child.

The first incident I remember my father telling me about occurred in 1923 in Leipzig, Germany. My father's family, who were Russian, were involved in progressive politics and in the cultural life of Leipzig. My father's story includes remembering that at the school he went to, over time, things began to change. One day he realized that only one boy was still his friend; none of the other boys would even really speak to him. The other boys had formed a group, a group that was very anti-Semitic, and even though my father's family were not religious Jews, the German boys had cast my father aside. And my father told me that somehow, even as a child, he knew. He could feel that something bad was eventually going to happen. In 1933, when Hitler came fully into power, my grandfather committed suicide—he so despaired of what he saw as the future.

My father, his sister, and my grandmother left Germany and went to France. In Paris, my father studied medicine, became a doctor, and was working as a doctor in a small village in Normandy when the Nazis came into France. Eventually, the Nazis came close to his village, and the administrator of the village, a man who was like the mayor, warned my father that the Nazis were less than an hour a way. My father fled. He ended up in the south of France and, not unlike your story, the stories I was eventually told were of great difficulties, especially in getting a visa. My father, too, did not have a real passport. But foreseeing a Nazi invasion of France, he had gotten on a list to get a visa to the United States early on, and he was first on this list. Even with that, he could not get a visa to come to the United States until a cousin in New York put up enough money. Then he was able to get out on a Portuguese freighter. Not long after he arrived in the United States, he met my mother, who was employed as a nurse in the same hospital in which he was working.

By 1942, both of my parents were in uniform, and for a short while, they were in a slightly odd situation because my mother, who was an army nurse, was an officer; but my father, when he first enlisted, was a private. And officers weren't supposed to socialize with enlisted people. My father wrote letter after letter to Washington and kept telling people that he was a physician, but at first no one seemed to listen to or believe him. One day, suddenly, papers came through from Washington, and my father was promoted, not just promoted one rank, but from private to a second lieutenant, and there were pictures in various newspapers of this promotion.

This is the context for one of my other memories, and again it is a story told to me, although I feel as if I remember it myself. The day before I was born—this is now 1943—my father was sent out to Colorado, on his way to someplace else. My mother wanted my father to see his first child before he went overseas, and although it was difficult for her to raise the money for the trip, she managed by going through back channels to buy a train ticket to St. Louis, Missouri. So, she put me in a basket and went to the train station. In the U.S. at that time, every train was crowded, mostly with servicemen being sent from one place to another. My mother arrived in St. Louis but without an appropriate ticket for a train to Colorado. So, she was stranded in the train station there, asking the stationmaster every fifteen minutes if there was a cancellation. Eventually, a woman, a total stranger, came and sat next to her on the platform. It turned out that this woman had her own compartment because she often became sick on trains. When she saw my mother with the basket with a baby in it, the woman took my mother and me into her compartment for the rest of the trip.

My father, when he enlisted, wanted to go back to Europe, wanted to go back, very openly, to kill Nazis. That was what his mission was. So he was happy when, while he was in Colorado, he got his orders for overseas, and he was told to get winter clothes ready. He was sure that meant he was being sent to Europe. But after my mother had returned with me to New Jersey, my father called her from Oakland, California, and said that he wasn't going to be so cold after all, that he was being shipped to New Guinea, not Europe.

One other early memory I have is of my grandmother, who had been in London during the Blitz, living with my father's sister who died at the end of the war. The memory is of my grandmother coming over after the war. Somehow her body expressed the pain of this war. I felt in this woman's body all of the bombings in London. And throughout the rest of her life—and my grandmother lived a very long life, into her nineties—when there would be thunderstorms or loud noises, my grandmother's body, this frail body, would shake, would quiver, in ways that even in my childhood I understood were attached to sounds that were not thunderstorms or fireworks.

V. P.: As you talk, other events that shaped my attitude come back to me. For instance, in the Paris subway there were automatic doors that closed off the platform a few seconds before a train would pull out—this was to prevent people from dashing down the corridor and trying to board at the last moment. It's a safety precaution. Well, I recall this German officer running, pushing people out of his way, yet not quite making it past that automatic door. Everyone was winking at each other and smiling, while he glared at them. Or there was the time when my mother and I were in one of the second-class cars (the first class was reserved for the Germans), and at one point, a very pregnant French woman boarded. So, a German officer who was sitting there got up and said, "Please sit down." The French woman just looked right through him. He almost pleaded with her, saying, please, please sit down, but she wouldn't even acknowledge his presence. Finally, he just stormed out of the train. It was that kind of passive resistance that I remember very well. For example, I was living in Biarritz, where my mother had sent me to a friend of hers. I recall looking out of the window and watching some convalescing Germans on the hospital lawn playing soccer. One day, my mother's friend caught me doing that. She proceeded to draw the blinds and told me I would not get any chicken or green salad for dinner (my favorite dishes) for watching the Germans. Of course, you could look at them, but only in specific cases—such as when she woke me at five o'clock in the morning and took me down to the pier to watch the tide bring in the bodies of five dead German soldiers. There were treacherous currents out there, and people were warned. But, of course, the Germans knew better; they didn't heed the warnings. It was known that when someone drowned, the current would bring the body back in. So here I was, a six-year-old kid taken down to see those bodies brought in. And there were hundreds of people standing there just watching. So, that is another memory.

One day, in 1946 or 1947, my father was notified by the Soviet Red Cross that his father, my grandfather, had been put up against a wall and shot by the Germans in Lithuania; that also shaped my attitude toward fascism. In short, I had a good wartime education. Of course, all this was reinforced in later years by the movies and documentaries of the death camps and by stories told by Soviets who had been through it. But my initial education dates back to the war years. Nor can I forget my physical impression of the war when we left the United States and went to Poland in 1949. I saw what was left of Warsaw four years after the war was over, and to this day, the desolation and destruction are fixed in my memory.

That, as I said, is the personal dimension. Every Soviet citizen of my age or older has countless stories, certainly more powerful—especially people who lived under German occupation. But the legacy for the Soviet Union as a whole is far more complex. It has to relate to so many things: to the national trauma; to the loss of twenty million lives; to the fact that there was an overwhelming surplus of women after the war, many of whom clearly never got married, never had children, because there just were not enough men to go around; to the millions of children who grew up without parents; to the number of people who were left homeless—and that's twenty-five million—and who lived in dugouts and basements; to the peasant women who pulled plows like mules and horses because there were no mules and horses; to the maimed, the disabled, those who survived but could not really live. All of this, of course, was the legacy of the war.

What I think this adds up to, all the different things that I've spoken of and perhaps many others that I haven't touched on, is what I consider to be the main legacy of the war for the Soviet Union, and that is the absolute horror of war, the abomination of war, the fact that the word war is emotionally explosive for just about any Soviet citizen I know. That is why we still have a preoccupation with war; we keep looking back to analyze it and to try to answer the questions of why it was the way it was, why we had to suffer so much, why we lost so many people. And it's really only in recent years that those questions have begun to be answered. There are many reasons for this, but one is that we were too close to it; we had to distance ourselves. It's only as the nation has gradually moved away from the war and a new generation has grown up, one that was not as directly affected, that we're beginning to come to terms with it.

The bottom line is that war scarred the Soviet psyche, and as a result of that, we have what I would call a genetic abhorrence of war. And, of course, that's very different from the American experience.

H. K.: Indeed, very different. I think my own family history, oddly, is one that brings together a combination of the European experience and the American experience. There are the stories I tell of my father, which have been told again and again in my family and told in a ritual kind of way. It was clearly extremely important for my father that we, his children, know these stories. And I've come to learn that my father's sense of relief that finally he's in a safe place has, of course, to do with his experiences of the war.

These stories of dislocations and of refuge are one part of the American experience, but they are conjoined with stories of people prospering, of human generosity, of American pride—in other words, of the "good war." One of my memories is of after the war. Having lived with my aunts, my mother, and my grandfather, we moved to a very small, one-bedroom apartment. I remember that place because it had one of those beds—a Murphy bed—that came out of the wall, which I remember thinking was just wonderful. Then we moved to this big house where there was no bed that came out of the wall. In fact, there was little furniture. There were orange crates at first. My father tells the story of buying this house, writing to my grandmother, and her cabling back, "How could you buy a house? You haven't a penny in the world?" And he explained that he had bought a house because, as a veteran, you could buy a house without any money. You could get a 100 percent mortgage. What happened for many Americans was that the American dream—which had really been undercut in the Depression—of every American family having their own house, their own little piece of land, was renewed during and after the war. American production had surged during the war, and there was enough money for all veterans to receive Veteran's Administration benefits. Among those benefits were funds for education and home mortgages.

There was a sense in the United States after the war of a kind of ebullience that we had come out of this war in this miraculous condition, where nothing around us was harmed, no buildings destroyed. Yes, there were veterans who were maimed, who were crippled, and one saw people on the street. I have a memory of riding a bus and looking at a man who had no leg and staring at him. My mother very harshly turned me away, saying, "That man was hurt so that you could be safe, so that you could be all right." I understood that there was something about that man that was special, and he was not to be looked at as if he were grotesque. There were certainly many wounded and maimed veterans in the United States, but it was not commonplace to see a man like that. Instead, in the late forties and fifties there was this sense of people thriving, people in the United States having made it through this war in basically good shape and doing very well.

I think that the American euphoria after the war was, in a way, a hidden political lesson that jangled with other political lessons that I and others were being taught about the horrors of fascism. After the war, America's triumphs became associated for some people with a fervent anticommunism, and that, too, was a legacy. That kind of impassioned anticommunism meant that a man like Charlie Miller had no place to remember in public his positive feelings about Russians during the war. It also meant that it was difficult for Americans to acknowledge the danger of nuclear bombs and just the basic awfulness of war itself. Instead of learning from World War II—as Robert Frost said—that war was for children, too, that there could be no more wars, children growing up after the war learned about making air-raid shelters and learned the routines for air-raid drills.

From the Second World War, we don't in this country have that sense of war itself being the horror.

V. P.: I don't think you can.

H. K.: And I don't think, as I've said to you before, that that really happened to us until the Vietnam War, and that doesn't even happen for everyone; it happens for a generation, the generation that was growing up and becoming adults in the sixties. I think that for some Americans, the gradual finding out in pictures and stories about World War II was coincidental with the Vietnam War. Then war itself began to enter the consciousness of Americans, as something that one needed to be troubled about in the deepest way, that one needed to do something about.

I keep thinking about the term "legacies," and I think that among the legacies are the jobs and the high-technology factories and the plants that make military weapons that are all over so many countries. Every once in a while in the United States, someone will call attention to these, even someone like Dwight Eisenhower. I do remember that people were struck by Eisenhower's speech at the end of his presidency in which he warned Americans to beware of the industrial-military complex.

V. P.: It's an interesting sort of parallel. In the Soviet Union on Victory day, which is celebrated May 9, at 7:00 p.m. on national Channel #1, the entire nation observes one minute of silence for those who died in the war. There is a short and moving kind of narration, followed by music. All you see on your television screen is the flickering flame of the tomb of the unknown soldier in Moscow. And then the announcer says, "One minute of silence." The flame burns on, but in total silence, and it's my guess that a hush descends over the entire country. I think it's good that people are reminded of that past. The inscription on the tomb reads, "Your name is unknown, your feat is immortal." That's very important. That reflects the legacy of the war—that no one is allowed to forget. The reminders are everywhere. You travel around the country, and no matter where you go, you will find war memorials. In the villages they are very simple, just a stone bearing the names of those who never came back, topped with a red star. In the cities, they are much more elaborate. But regardless of the location, there are always fresh flowers there. Now there's a tradition—no one knows how it actually began—that newly-weds, after the ceremony, go to the tomb of the unknown soldier or the local war monument to pay homage to the soldiers who gave their lives fifty years ago so that others might live and love today. The sense of gratitude and of being indebted is thus made very clear. I believe that that is very important. And it pains me enormously when I find in many countries, not only in America but in many Western countries, that younger people, those under thirty-five, know so little about that past. A documentary film made by a Soviet director showed how Parisians walking through Stalingrad Square in their city did not know what Stalingrad was. People in the West, particularly Americans, have been induced to forget.

H. K.: I wanted to pick up on the notion of the things Americans see, or rather, don't quite see but absorb: the high-tech equipment and factories, the supercomputers, the surface signs of the defense industry that grew up during World War II and have grown and grown since. There's a consistency with World War II in that all that kind of industry is known but invisible—much as the battlefronts of World War II were distanced from us. Our defense industry is not present to us because few of us understand the technology, because various companies make separate components for military weapons, and few of us have images of family members coming home from working on nuclear weapons or on something that they can physically, empirically understand has to do with war. It's very hard to visualize.

That takes me back to something I was trying to explore earlier in our conversation about the significance of the Vietnam War. I was thinking about the serious attention given to the Vietnam memorial in this country. People go there and pay homage to those who died in Vietnam; they tell stories and touch the names written on the memorial. When you were talking about the Soviet monuments commemorating World War II that exist in every little village and how Soviets pay tribute to the veterans of World War II when they get married, I suddenly thought about the cemeteries I saw in Europe. I sometimes think that for Americans to gain access to their memories of World War II and what it was about for them, we have to go elsewhere. I found myself very moved in Normandy, seeing cemeteries with very simple white crosses "row on row," like the famous poem about Flanders Fields in World War I, but these were World War II cemeteries that I saw.

I was awestruck by the numbers. The sense of these rows and rows of crosses in Normandy, not far from the beach, made real for me an image of American soldiers coming up on that beach. I knew abstractly that we did land there with our allies, that there were lots of lives lost, but nothing ever made it as concrete to me before. And that started me thinking about how the artifacts or the ceremonies and rituals one can go through to make those legacies meaningful for Americans are scattered around the world. There are, for example, Americans who go to Hiroshima and Nagasaki, and then there was President Reagan's notorious visit to the cemetery in Bitburg, Germany, where Nazi soldiers were buried. My son was backpacking around Europe last summer and decided he had to go to Dachau. We confuse these things and aren't sure of how to deal with them. There are in this country ritual occasions or gatherings on Hiroshima day, but not to celebrate our victory.

V. P.: I understand, yes.

H. K.: . . . but people do come together. I know groups of people who come together, and there was, in fact, a gathering here in San Diego this year, and there are similar ones all over the country of people who come together to remember, to mourn, to think hard about what it meant that we dropped the first atomic bombs at what was then the end of the war. But still, even those gatherings, which may be one kind of legacy closer to something you are describing, aren't quite the same thing for us because, again, we don't have the presence on our homeland. So Americans make pilgrimages to Nagasaki or Hiroshima.

In recent years, more and more people go to Pearl Harbor, and that's obviously a different kind of thing than Hiroshima and Nagasaki, but even though Hawaii is one of our states, Pearl Harbor is still remote from most Americans. When I talked to people in France, they said that Americans come through Normandy and have something like the experience I had of a kind of shock, of a kind of presence. That means, however, that we have to go looking for it; it's not there and accessible to us at home, in a national way. It's an odd kind of endowment or legacy that we have to go find for ourselves.

As I say this, I realize that this also describes my experience working on the spacebridge and on this book. We went out searching for Americans with key experiences of the war, and similarly, we searched for photographs and film footage. There turned out to be a wealth of material, and almost every American over a certain age had stories to tell, but much of the meaning and details of the war were buried or hidden.

V. P.: You speak of a legacy not so much in the sense of what you remember as what is reflected by the artifacts. And you say the artifacts are not here, that people have to go elsewhere to look for them. At the same time, you speak of the Vietnam memorial, that is an artifact of a war that was not fought on American soil. Nevertheless, the wall is in Washington, D.C., and that makes me ask why is there no such tribute to the American fighting man who died on the battlefields of Europe in World War II? Why is it that the only monuments that I've seen pertain to World War I? Indeed, World War I is somehow considered to be a greater, if I may use that word, war, and the Vietnam War monument suggests the importance of that war. Yet, there is almost no recognition in terms of artifacts of the American fighting man who sacrificed his life in the battle against fascism.

H. K.: And there were, although it's nothing like the twenty million people who died in the Soviet Union, over four hundred thousand Americans who did give their lives in World War II.

V. P.: True, and that is far more than America lost in the Vietnam War. So, I can't help but wonder, Why is this? After all, when we speak of a legacy in terms of affecting the mind, you need no artifacts for those who actually experienced the war, which left an indelible imprint on them. But for the following generations, the absence of artifacts, the absence of things that tell them something about what that war was, must lead to their ignoring it; that's the whole point.

H. K.: Exactly.

V. P.: So that one of the legacies of World War II, vis à vis the U.S., is the absence of a legacy. And I don't think that is accidental—just as it is not accidental that in the Soviet Union the war is still very much in people's minds. There's a policy involved of reminding people of that war. Getting back to the U.S., I have sometimes thought that politics are responsible for the situation. For decades, it was not politically expedient to remind Americans about our wartime alliance, about our victory over the common foe, and that, perhaps, is one of the reasons why there are so few World War II memorials. I'm not sure of this, but sometimes I tend to have that feeling.

H. K.: I think it's tied into why there are no memorials. When I look at other kinds of things that hold in memory, one of the things we used in the spacebridge was film.

V. P.: Yes.

H. K.: . . . and I remember, I cannot tell you, how many American movies we looked at, and we wanted to, as you know, on both sides come up to the present. Well, there were all the typical movies that came out in the late forties and fifties, but they all were of a kind; they focused on a hero or group of heroes, either on a ship or in a particular isolated place; there was no historical context to these events; and these movies were almost always about the bravery of a particular soldier. By the sixties, interestingly, there seemed to be a shift to recognition of the "other," the other—being either the Germans or the Japanese—as human beings, and of course, that fit the political situation in the sixties because of the United States' relationship to Germany and Japan. (Remember John Kennedy saying, "I am a Berliner.") We had to see Germans and Japanese not as faceless people. But the larger historical context, the kinds of things I've seen in Soviet films, never did get addressed. Of course, we did finally have anti-war films. But there is something in this gap that we are talking about.

I went through newspapers, through the *New York Times*, week after week after week during the forties, and there's almost no mention, for example, of concentration camps or of the atrocities of World War II on the front pages right through 1945. Now we know that information was coming out. Then there was a little tiny bit as the concentration camps were liberated by the allies, and that disappears, too. And it's only, I think, much more recently that we've started looking at photographs, at documentaries, at books. That may have to do with one of the things you said when we last talked about this, that face-to-face we don't see the face, that we were too close. I think that's part of it for us, too, but I also think that the U.S.–Soviet relationship as it emerged in the years immediately following the war has a great deal to do with this lack of artifacts, this lack of films that represent the Soviet–U.S. alliance during the war or the larger historical situation.

V. P.: There is a major point insofar as what the legacy of the war is for the Soviet Union and for America. World War II not only gave most Americans a higher standard of living, not only improved their conditions, but was seen as an almost painless exercise, even though some four hundred thousand soldiers were killed. But as relating to the entire nation, the pain disappeared very soon for most people, and thus the war was remembered not as something horrible that sent shivers down your spine but as very gung-ho, you know, go get 'em, boys. The war became almost synonymous with a better life style, more wealth, more work, more production. I think that up until the Vietnam War that was pretty much the image, and the

Vietnam War, which was a very painful defeat for national consciousness, slightly changed the view. Clearly, the legacy of the Vietnam War is quite different from that of World War II.

Now for the Soviets, while the triumph in overcoming Hitler contributed to an enormous sense of national pride, even national identity, what war did to the people, what war did to the country was so horrendously painful that the legacy of war is one of a big, block-letter NO. NEVER AGAIN. That's something that I think has become part of what I call the national psyche, and it permeates all layers of society from the man in the street to the man in the top government office, because they all went through it, or all of their families went through it; no one escaped it. And I think that's a very basic difference in the legacies.

H. K.: That's important, because actually some of the things that leaders in the United States—not all, but certainly key figures like Franklin Roosevelt—were saying as the war was coming to an end were very much along the lines of what you are saying. President Roosevelt and others were saying that World War II taught us that we can never have war again. This is it. And certainly after the detonation of the atom bombs, there were also cries like this—that when we see this, we have to understand this to mean "never again," no more war. But I think that sense then became almost immediately confused and befuddling for Americans, because we continued to make nuclear weapons, so that we now have the many thousands that we have—and you also have. This is not to say that the Soviet Union did not do some ugly things at the end of World War II and did not also start making nuclear weapons, but we have to deal with the fact that we dropped those two atomic bombs and that we have continued to make bombs, knowing what they can do. At the time, certainly ordinary Americans knew nothing of the atomic bomb before it was used, and even those working on it or aware of the secret efforts to create it were not clear about its power. One of the legacies is the bomb and . . .

V. P.: That's absolutely true.

H. K.: . . . and that's a legacy that must trouble our national consciousness, because we come out of this war, as you've aptly said, with our land basically untouched, with things going pretty well, and feeling pretty good about what we did in the war. We can feel good because we did send troops and supplies to Europe and to the Pacific to fight for a good cause, to rid the world of fascism. We can say that this was worth fighting for, and we did well. Yet, there was this other thing we did, too; and no matter what arguments you make about the pragmatic reasons for using the bomb, we used it. And it changed the world. That may also be a reason why it's hard for us to have monuments that make us remember.

Index